D1520403

WORKING AT
WRITING

Columnists and Critics
Composing

Robert L. Root, Jr.

Southern Illinois University Press

Carbondale and Edwardsville

Library of Congress Cataloging-in-Publication Data
Root, Robert L.
Working at writing: columnists and critics composing / Robert L.
Root, Jr.
p.   cm.
Includes bibliographical references.
1. Newspapers—Sections, columns, etc.—Authorship. 2. Criticism—
Authorship. 3. Journalism—Authorship. 4. Journalists—United
States—Interviews. 5. Critics—United States—Interviews.
I. Title.
PN4784.C65R66   1991
808'.06607—dc20   90-38873
ISBN 0-8093-1686-2   CIP

For Becky, with love and pride

Contents

Contents

Preface

When, in 1981, I began reading and interviewing working writers for a study of the composing processes of "professional expository writers"—people who made their living writing nonfiction—little research had been done in this area. Over the past decade, however, a number of researchers have turned their attention to working nonfiction writers, "literary nonfiction" is a growing (if problematically labeled) field, and studies of writers in both literary and nonliterary contexts have multiplied. *Working at Writing: Columnists and Critics Composing* is an addition to the expanding literature linking literary and rhetorical approaches to nonfiction.

Prior to Janet Emig's study, *The Composing Processes of Twelfth-Graders*, most research into writing had been conducted in one of three ways: the analysis of written texts in order to determine their components and prescribe a sensible method of replicating them (the Aristotelian method); the study of the methods of creative writers through examination of their notes, journals, letters, and memoirs; and interviews of practitioners, chiefly poets and novelists, about their sources of inspiration, work habits, and personal theories of writing. Of the last, the best known and most valuable have probably been *The Paris Review* series of interviews, occasionally anthologized as *Writers at Work*. Part of the significance of Emig's study was to offer the beginnings of an answer to the question "What is involved in the act of writing?" based upon actual observation of writers composing rather than upon textual analysis or anecdotal evidence. Consequently, a number of researchers constructed projects that would allow them the opportunity to observe and analyze the composing processes of a wide variety of writers under a wide range of circumstances. These involved elementary, secondary, and college students (Beach; Emig; Graves; Perl; Pianko; Sommers; Sowers); experienced and novice writers in a variety of disciplines and under a variety of circumstances (Berkenkotter; Matsuhashi; Odell and Goswami; Roundy and Mair; Selzer); and writers composing under extraordinary circumstances (Gere). The result has been a substantial literature of composing.

These studies were particularly valuable both because they highlighted the problems such writers encountered and the strategies they used to achieve goals in writing and also because they raised doubts about the degree of reliability in textbook prescriptions drawn from textual analysis. Furthermore, they provided insight into the composing processes of writers who, unlike novelists and poets, were neither exceptionally gifted nor engaged in major creative activity; for the most part the experienced and novice writers of composing studies have been students, teachers, academicians, and workplace communicators.

One group not particularly well-investigated was composed of professional expository writers, people who, like the professional creative writers of *The Paris Review* interviews, made their living from writing and who, like students, were chiefly involved in writing informative or argumentative nonfiction prose. It seemed to me that something of value could be learned by studying a group of writers who composed short nonfiction works on a regular basis, preferably on deadline, for a specific publication or audience. Consequently, I began interviewing working writers, among whom were included the four columnists (two essayists and two political commentators) and three critics (one of drama, two of film) whose writing is the focus of this book.

The research upon which the analytical chapters of this book are based includes (1) textual analysis, the close reading of each subject's published writing in order to understand habits of structure, style, and content prior to the interview and subsequent analysis of notes, drafts, and final publication for textual evidence of composing; (2) retrospective interviews on general composing processes and specific composition of individual articles completed just prior to the interviews; and (3) comparison of textual and interview evidence for each author, between authors in generic subgroups (criticism, political analysis, and essays), and among all subjects cumulatively. Moreover, the study overall is strongly influenced by the cognitive model of composing, first as a basis for interview questions and second, after the evidence seemed to confirm the reliability of that model, as a focus for discussion.

The book has three interlocking elements: edited transcripts of interviews with writers about their composing processes and the composition of specific works, copies of the works discussed in the transcripts, and a series of chapters analyzing the interviews and articles in the context of current research into composing. In a sense there are three books here: an academic monograph on writing, a collection of interviews, and an anthology of nonfiction prose. This unusual structure invites the reader to a variety of approaches, each focused on only a portion of the book rather than on its entirety. Although I have attempted to create a unified work, I really would like to encourage such various readings.

In the course of transcribing and rereading the interviews with these writers, I came to feel that it would be a disservice to the authors and to readers to allow them to remain sequestered in my files, emerging only piecemeal as selected quotes in academic articles. I felt that the writers ought to be allowed to speak for themselves about the writing they had done and that readers ought to be able to read the finished pieces themselves in the context of their authors' comments. Concurrently, through the drafting of conference presentations and academic articles drawn from this material, I began to feel that a single article or series of articles would be insufficient to cover the data assembled here. The analytical chapters are an attempt to be more comprehensive, but I doubt that I have been as successful as I would have liked to have been. Another justification, then, for publishing the interviews and articles along with the analysis is the opportunity it provides readers to go beyond my discussion of them.

Just as I have not exhausted every insight to be gained from these interviews and texts, so I have not been comprehensive in citing prior research. In addition to the specific studies mentioned above, I direct the reader to George Hillocks' *Research on Written Composition* and Stephen North's *The Making of Knowledge in Composition*, both compendious in their syntheses and citations; I leave it to the reader to fit this book into their frameworks.

My own intentions have been modest by comparison: I have tried to discover how the composing processes of these seven writers relate to one another and to current models of composing and what might be said about these processes that would be of value to other writers. Chapter 1 discusses the context for analyzing these interviews. Chapters 2 through 4 deal with generically grouped writers by discussing, in turn, the writing of essays, political columns, and criticism. Chapter 5 summarizes the observations of the earlier chapters and discusses their implications for others, particularly student writers and, by extension, their teachers.

The models writers follow in their composing, whether self-imposed or advocated by teachers, have a significant impact on how and even whether writing is done. By listening to the reflections of practicing writers, examining the evidence of their compositions, and comparing the evidence of research with that of practical experience, other writers—and their teachers as well—have the opportunity to better understand the paradigms that govern their composing and to confirm, modify, abandon, or replace them. The result may be more perceptive, resourceful, and productive working at writing.

Acknowledgments

The composing process that resulted in *Working at Writing* as it appears in the following pages was in many ways as instructive for me as the interviews and text analyses it includes. Throughout that process I became indebted to many people for advice and encouragement.

I am particularly grateful to the participants in this study, David Denby, Jim Fitzgerald, Neal Gabler, Walter Kerr, Richard Reeves, Kathleen Stocking, and Tom Wicker, many of whom not only provided the opportunity for interviews and manuscript evidence but also reviewed and in some cases clarified the interview transcripts. I am also grateful to three additional subjects, Connie Leas, Susan Nykamp, and Noel Perrin; for various reasons their contributions do not appear in this book but their participation broadened the base of my understanding.

The initial research was supported in part by a Faculty Research Grant and a sabbatical leave from Central Michigan University, which also provided a Summer Fellowship for supplemental research. The interview with Richard Reeves is really a synthesis of a personal interview I conducted and a classroom discussion in a course taught by Ronald Primeau and David Ling.

Explorations of and expeditions with the ideas in the book took me to meetings of the National Council of Teachers of English, the Conference on College Composition and Communication, the Michigan Council of Teachers of English, and the Michigan College English Association, where conferees and fellow panelists helped focus and revise my thinking. Related articles that arose from those meetings have appeared in the *Journal of Teaching Writing, Language Arts Journal of Michigan, Minnesota English Journal,* and *Wisconsin English Journal,* almost all of them in some way discovery drafts for the book. A portion of the chapter on writing criticism appeared in "Writing in the Dark: Composing Criticism" in the *Journal of Teaching Writing.* Excerpts from the Jim Fitzgerald and David Denby interviews appeared in *Language*

Acknowledgments

Arts Journal of Michigan, and a portion of the Neal Gabler interview appeared in *The Great Lakes Review.*

In the final stages of writing the book I benefitted from the advice of Kenney Withers at Southern Illinois University Press and John Dinan at Central Michigan University, as well as that of the referees who read the typescript. In final preparation I am grateful for the editorial wisdom of Susan H. Wilson and Julie Riley Bush.

An important element of working at writing, this book argues, is immersion in context, an element that may involve a writer's family as well. Becky, Tom, and Caroline have supported the immersion. My wife, Sue, not only broadened my understanding of the study early on but also encouraged the project through all its permutations; to her I offer love and gratitude.

Working at Writing

Columnists and Critics Composing

1

Paradigms and Processes

In an interview transcribed later in this book, Richard Reeves describes his earliest attempts to be a writer thus:

> I was living in a house in New Jersey and I had all these visions
> about what writing was about, that writers had their own
> offices. And I built myself this small office in the basement with
> that little window above the ground and it was very small. I
> also had this vision, for some reason, that real writers—because
> now I was going to become a real writer as opposed to a
> newspaper reporter—that real writers wrote everything in one
> burst; it was some sort of ethic, that you sat down and began
> writing until you were finished. As I look back on these pieces,
> of course, their energy curve goes like my days. The endings
> sometimes seem to me barely comprehensible, because I was
> exhausted by that time.

As Reeves points out, the period he is describing came after a period as a working journalist. In spite of prior success at reporting, his own unexamined model of composing tended to interfere with the process of his "real writing."

The problem Reeves describes is not merely one of work habits, although that is part of the problem. Later in the interview he describes moving to a twelfth floor Fifth Avenue apartment in New York with a view of Central Park and beyond and being "unable to produce" because of the atmosphere in which he was trying to work. He says,

> I thought I was living in a painting. There was no noise, no
> nothing. So we moved to Fifty-second Street on the third floor
> because I came to realize that I needed that energy and

> interaction with people and I needed light and a room and
> noise to work and then I could work again.

Here the problem is chiefly finding the most productive environment for his individual working habits, but like the problem of writing nonstop from beginning to end, this problem too arises out of the model of composing he has in his head, the concept of the writing process under which he attempts to operate.

Similar examples abound in the literature of composing. For example, in her article "A History of Revision: Theory vs. Practice," Karen Hodges tells us that Charles Lamb was dismayed by the evidence of revision in manuscripts of Milton's "Lycidas." Lamb's reaction, she says, "reflects the nineteenth-century literary tenet that writing is inspired, not belabored; is produced as a whole, not by parts; and is immortal, hence neither 'alterable' nor 'displaceable' " (24). Hodges cites other examples of the common belief in artistic inspiration and then demonstrates that, according to the evidence of their own manuscripts, the work of such figures as Sir Walter Scott and George Eliot, far from being spontaneous and holistic acts of creation, was laborious, painstaking, and systematic (25). Yet the model of the composing process transmitted in the idealized view of the writer as a gifted creator, dependent on the inspiration of his muse or some sort of divine spark, has been long lived and, for some writers, pernicious.

Even contemporary writers sometimes feel a sense of mysticism about the act of composing. Kathleen Stocking, for example, mentions in her interview writing essays where "you feel that you're being used by the Great Unknown or whatever it is . . . where something almost seems to be generated by the karma of the planet and not really by you." Walter Kerr mentions the idea that the creative act arises from an act of self-hypnosis. Neither author actually ascribes his or her own creativity to such forces, however, and both essentially are using these examples as metaphors for occasions of comparatively unforced creation. Moreover, writers often worry that too much self-awareness may lead to an inhibiting self-consciousness. Nickie McWhirter, at the time a columnist for the *Detroit Free Press*, once explained her reluctance to discuss her composing by saying, "I guess I'm afraid that, if I come to know how I do it, I won't be able to do it anymore." She made the remark to me during a visit to Central Michigan University. Yet when incidents I and others had experienced with her on that occasion began to turn up in her column, it was fairly clear how she generated columns.

2

In order to write successfully and well, the accomplished and competent writer need not be able to explain the model of composing from which he or she actually operates. Nonetheless, some model of composing, whether fully developed or completely inchoate, lies beneath the surface of that composing. Moreover, unexamined assumptions arise not only in the composing of working writers but also in the teaching and learning of writing in every form. Recent scholarship in composition and rhetoric has produced a number of interesting attempts to identify sets of assumptions about the nature of writing and its most effective teaching. Hodges, for example, has identified the major strands of modern writing instruction as classical, neoclassical, and romantic (32); Hillocks, in a compendious review of composition research, distinguishes three modes of instruction—presentational, natural process, and environmental—each grounded in distinct premises about writing (113–132); Faigley, Cherry, Jolliffe, and Skinner have identified three current theoretical positions on composing: the literary view, the cognitive view, and the social view (13–20); Stephen North's book, *The Making of Knowledge in Composition*, discusses eight "methodological communities" (59–60); James Berlin, in his two-volume history of writing instruction in American colleges and universities, focuses on three categories: objective rhetorics, subjective rhetorics, and transactional rhetorics.

All of these systems of classification attempt to get at the underlying assumptions of models of composing and of composition pedagogy. Berlin defines these sets of assumptions as "noetic fields"; as he points out,

> the noetic field underlying a particular rhetoric determines how the composing process is conceived and taught in the classroom. What goes into the process—the way in which invention, arrangement, and style are undertaken, or not undertaken, as is sometimes the case—is determined by the assumptions made, and often unexamined, about reality, writer/speaker, audience, and language. Each rhetoric, therefore, indicates the behavior appropriate to the composing situation. (*Writing Instruction* 2)

The assumptions that underlie a rhetoric ultimately determine the approaches and experiences of both teacher and student,

> making certain kinds of activity inevitable and other kinds impossible. . . . The behavior the student is told to undertake in

3

> composing leads to his embracing the tacit noetic field
> underlying it, whether or not teacher and student are aware of
> the fact (and they often are not). (2–3)

Because the premises upon which instruction in writing is based are often naive or unexamined, the tacit model of composing by which the novice writes may be ineffective or counterproductive, or it may be productive for reasons other than those the instructor ascribes to it. By the same token, whether a writer's model of composing arises from classroom and textbook instruction, the modeling of other writers, or intuition, a "noetic field" of some kind underlies that model.

Berlin's categories of rhetoric and their "noetic fields" are, in effect, paradigms governing both theory and practice. Patricia Bizzell, in an article on Thomas Kuhn's *The Structure of Scientific Revolutions*, defines a paradigm as "a comprehensive theoretical model that governs both the view of reality accepted by an intellectual community and the practice of that community's discipline" (764). In Berlin's terms the categories of rhetoric are competing, or at least conflicting, paradigms: the view of reality that underlies instruction determines the nature of that instruction and the practices that arise from it.

Richard Reeves' example reminds us that the paradigms we operate from in writing can have an impact on the success of writing. The earlier examples of Scott and Eliot suggest that the paradigm underlying a writer's actual composing may not necessarily be the paradigm he or she formally espouses. Much of the composition research just cited arises from an attempt to discover paradigms of practice that will most effectively facilitate writing; obviously some paradigms tend rather to impede it. For example, studies of formal grammar instruction in writing have concluded that "the teaching of grammar has a negligible or, because it usually displaces some instruction and practice in actual composition, even a harmful effect on the improvement of writing" (Braddock, Lloyd-Jones, Schoer 37–38); moreover, "the same is true for emphasis on mechanics and correctness in writing. In fact, some studies indicated that when correctness is heavily emphasized in marking papers, the quality of student writing diminishes significantly" (Hillocks 225). Yet, despite an abundance of empirical evidence in support of this position,

> many elementary and secondary schools continue to make
> grammar a major component of their curricula. Many teachers
> still contend that knowledge of traditional school grammar is
> crucial to good writing. These same teachers tend to make no

distinction between grammar (a description of how a language works) and "correctness" (adherence to accepted conventions of punctuation and usage). (133)

In other words, in this instance the paradigm that many educators are still working from is one that has been rendered untenable by research and argued against by scholars in composition and rhetoric, particularly over the last twenty-five years; yet that same paradigm still governs curriculum design, classroom instruction, and student practice in writing in a majority of schools in the country. Misguided, outdated, and unexamined paradigms of writing can be detrimental not only to the individual writer but also to entire generations of composition students. Much of the research into writing since 1963, when Braddock, Lloyd-Jones, and Schoer asked the question "What is involved in the act of writing?," has been an attempt to shift the basic paradigm underlying composition instruction and to investigate the nature of composing as closely as possible in order to eliminate ineffective or counterproductive elements of the models by which we teach and by which our students write.

The interviews in this book were initially conducted in order to add to the storehouse of knowledge about the behaviors and strategies of successful, working writers with an eye to aiding the learning of inexperienced, novice writers. In effect, the following chapters will be accumulating evidence concerning the composing of working writers in order to suggest crucial elements of a model of composing that would facilitate the development and improvement of writing abilities in others. The focus of the final chapter will be the implications of these interviews and texts for an effective model of composing from which others can work.

But it should be clear from the discussion of paradigms and models above that the very questions being asked in these interviews and the context in which analysis is conducted must arise from, at the least, some sort of tentative paradigm. It should also be clear that the book assumes the validity of the process paradigm of composition. The differences between what has come to be called the current-traditional paradigm (the model of composition focused on the written product) and the process paradigm (the model focused on the composing process) have been thoroughly discussed elsewhere (Young; Bizzell; Berlin and Inkster; Hairston), but it may be useful to review some of them here, briefly.

Where the product-centered paradigm tends to view composing

as a linear series of stages and to emphasize style and language as if the text were chiefly an attempt at accurate expression of a universally recognizable reality, the process-centered paradigm of writing has tended to emphasize the simultaneity of various activities in composing, the uniqueness of each writer's interpretation of reality, and the need for the writer to use language as a means of discovering his or her interpretation both before and during the expression of it. Where the product-centered model has focused more narrowly on preparation for publication (editing of sentences, conformity of usage and format, proofreading), the process-centered model has tended to expand its focus by emphasizing prewriting activities (idea generating, information gathering, planning, exploring) as well as drafting and revising activities and by giving manuscript or typescript preparation considerably less attention. Where product-centered instruction has been concerned chiefly with initiating the composing (assigning the writing), preparing the final text (editing and proofreading), and evaluating the product (grading), process-centered instruction has been concerned chiefly (but not exclusively) with what happens in between initiating the composing and preparing the final text—the processes that make up the actual composing as the individual writer experiences them.

In the course of studying the composing process, researchers have proposed a number of models that attempt to visualize the relationship between its components (Britton et al.; Kinneavy; Lloyd-Jones; Murray; Root). In this book reference will be made most frequently to elements of the cognitive processes model of composing developed by Linda Flower and John Hayes, principally because it has proved to be a highly useful and comprehensive descriptive model (Fig. 1–1).

The model is significant in several ways. First, the section designated "Writing Processes" focuses on various subprocesses of composing and shows their interrelationships, particularly the ways that they interrupt and embed themselves in one another. Flower and Hayes have argued against a linear stage model of composing that would imply the importance of completing one stage before going on to the next; in its place they have stressed the interactiveness of their model, where planning can interrupt reviewing, editing can occur early in planning, and all subprocesses are in effect monitored simultaneously in order to allow instant shifts of attention. Nonetheless, there is room in this model to subsume alternative models, such as the Pre-Writing, Writing, Re-Writing model of Rohman and Wlecke (which has served

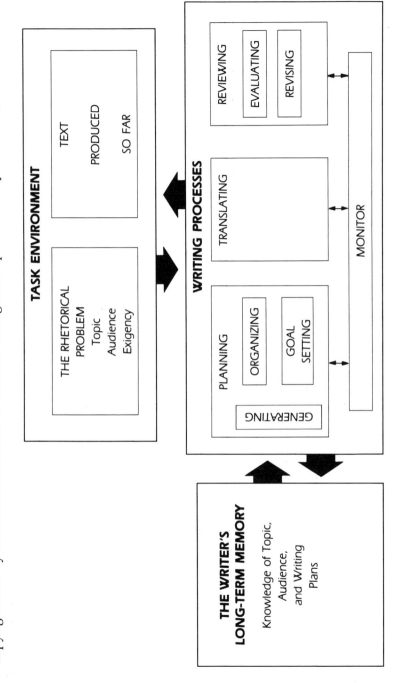

Figure 1–1. The cognitive processes model. (Figure from "A Cognitive Process Theory of Writing," by Linda Flower and John R. Hayes, *College Composition and Communication*, December 1981. Copyright 1981 by the National Council of Teachers of English. Reprinted with permission.)

as the most widely known description of the composing process) or even the invention-arrangement-style elements of classical rhetoric.

Second, the section designated "Task Environment" is far more thorough than other models in emphasizing the influence of both the rhetorical problem (the audience, topic, exigency of the writing) and the text itself, the ways in which what one has already written will affect what one will write next. The inclusion of the rhetorical problem is important because it provides for an awareness of the social context of the composition, the circumstances under which it is being composed, and the demands those circumstances make on its composition. It means that such rhetorical elements as the aims or functions of discourse, such as Kinneavy's four part model (48–68) or Britton's poetic-expressive-transactional continuum, can be considered here, as well as other insights into composition drawn from rhetorical and discourse studies. The section for the text produced so far takes cognizance of the effect of writing as a means of discovery, something that influences the writer's understanding of his subject and his attitudes toward it at the same time that it offers alternatives in the writing, for better or for worse, that planning or prewriting may not provide for.

Third, the model provides a section designated "The Writer's Long Term Memory," representing the stored knowledge of the topic, the audience, and the writing strategies available for the writer to draw upon in composition. It is the place where lessons learned from previous composing are stored, a cumulative knowledge base of both writing and subject matter from which the short term memory that operates the Writing Processes section can draw during composition. We can best understand the importance of the inclusion of long-term memory by referring to Carl Bereiter's model of skills-systems integration in writing development (Fig. 1–2).

Bereiter has argued that writing development involves the acquisition of six skills: written language production, controlled association of ideas, understanding of rules of style and mechanics, social cognition, critical (logical or aesthetic) judgment, and reflective thinking. Ideally the lower-level skills are subsumed into the higher-level skills—it is unlikely for the writer to develop critical standards by which a composition can be assessed without having first developed some means of written language production and knowledge of the usage of style and mechanics in his language community. Moreover, since it is impossible for a writer to consciously consider the constraints of each of these six skills simultaneously, some degree of automaticity has to be reached in each of them (Bereiter emphasizes the need for

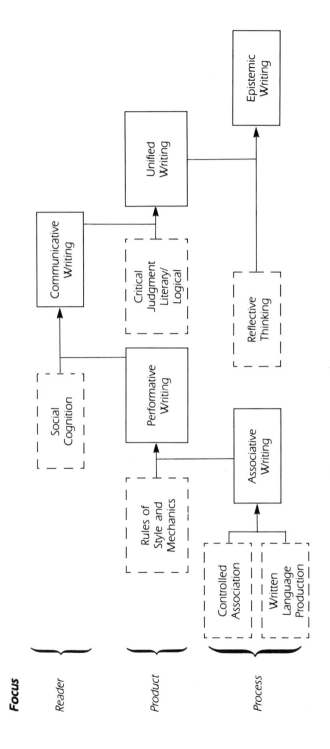

Figure 1-2. The skills integration model. (Figure from Carl Bereiter, "Development in Writing." *Cognitive Processes in Writing*, ed. Lee W. Gregg and Erwin R. Steinberg. Hillsdale, NJ: Lawrence Erlbaum, 1980. Reprinted by permission.)

Focus

Reader

Product

Process

Social Cognition

Rules of Style and Mechanics

Controlled Association

Written Language Production

Communicative Writing

Performative Writing

Associative Writing

Critical Judgment Literary/ Logical

Unified Writing

Reflective Thinking

Epistemic Writing

automaticity rather than mastery) in order to allow attention to focus on one skill at a time. Automaticity is achieved by storage in long term memory (73–90).

The element of long-term memory in the Flower-Hayes model, then, helps account for aspects of composing that understanding of the rhetoricial problem and conscious attention to writing processes do not. It also helps to account for the kinds of knowledge that a writer needs to draw upon in order to "write like an expert in his profession," which Flower has described as involving four levels of knowing: topic knowledge, discourse or genre knowledge, rhetorical problem solving, and metaknowledge ("Rhetorical Problem Solving" 13–14).

According to Flower, topic knowledge is sufficient knowledge of the subject to provide not only superficial awareness but also deeper understanding of context. High topic knowledge seems to allow writers to more readily identify significant elements of topic, to "*keep* this relevant information in short-term memory (or focal attention) while they observe, read, or" think about the topic, and to infer relationships (8). It seems to be an advantage in organizing, focusing, and thinking through ideas. However, knowledge of the topic may be more effective as a means of planning than as a means of expression; unless the writer can "restructure his knowledge" for a reader or for the circumstances of the rhetorical situation, he may be unable to share that topic knowledge with anyone except people with similar expertise. As Flower puts it, "the structure of the writer's knowledge may not approximate the structure of the reader's knowledge, or that structure which the reader needs" (9). Topic knowledge, she claims, is "a necessary but not sufficient condition for writing" (13).

By discourse or genre knowledge she means that "expert writers can draw on ready-made plans supplied by genre, conventions, or schemas for the texts they are writing" (6). As we will see in the following chapters, genre knowledge is an important part of composing because it assists writers in predicting the format of the text. A professional essayist who writes on a regular cycle develops a sense of how long his article will run, how he will pull together disparate elements, how he will satisfy the demands of his genre, because of his familiarity with it. The regularity of production and the immersion in generic context allow for a degree of automaticity that a novice in that genre would not have available. However, as Flower points out,

> for many adult texts, with their more complex goals and greater information load, these skeletal plans offer the writer only an

abstract frame and limited information about the contents of an optimal plan. Discourse conventions and schemas are valuable, but limited, guides when the writer must construct an expert plan. (7)

Genre knowledge of itself is likely to be insufficient in more demanding circumstances of composition.

Rhetorical problem solving "involves a repertory of strategies for generating ideas, for adapting to the reader, and for understanding and monitoring one's own writing process" (13). At this level the writer is capable of being selective about both topic knowledge and genre knowledge in terms of the task at hand—the goals of the writing, the audience for it, the exigencies under which the writing is done. In a sense she is able to control the uses of that knowledge rather than have it control her. Connected to this "third level of knowing" is

metaknowledge—knowing what you know. Because there are no simple rules for managing rhetorical problem-solving, expert writers often depend on meta-awareness of their own strategies and options. This knowledge is what lets writers rise above individual tasks, review their options, and consider what they *might* do in the face of a new problem. It lets writers manage their own composing process. (14)

In summary, then, a writer with only genre knowledge has nothing with which to fill in the frame of his discourse, the writer with only topic knowledge has no frame, and the writer with both may have no control over the frame he has and no selectivity about the parts of the topic upon which to focus. The writer with powers of rhetorical problem solving is better able to modify the frame and select the appropriate information for the circumstances of the composition; the writer with metaknowledge is able to recognize and select options as they are needed in a wide range of writing circumstances.

It is likely that these kinds of knowledge are built up cumulatively through experience and stored in the writer's long-term memory, available to be drawn upon when necessary during composing. All three sections of the model are intimately connected and interactive, dynamic and nonsequential. The model allows for any sequence of interaction and suggests that writing needs the potential for interacting in any sequence.

Although the preceding interpretation of Flower and Hayes' cognitive process model may be somewhat more flexible and expansive than they and, especially, their critics may have intended it, it nonetheless seems to be a comprehensive and inclusive paradigm of composing with particular value for both writer and writing teacher. Product-based models have tended to concentrate the energies of both writer and teacher on the preparation of product—the concern for appearances, correctness, conformity to academic prescriptions of standard usage. Process-based models have been valuable in forestalling those concerns until late in the process, after attention to prewriting, drafting, and revising. Product-based models have focused on the last five to ten percent of the process; process-based models, on the whole process, with subsequent downscaling of attention to product-preparation concerns. Yet as Flower and Hayes point out, the linear design of some process models invites stage restrictions in composing. For example, at least one teacher of my acquaintance who uses a process model approach regularly grades student prewriting, following an ingenious system of her own design to evaluate success with the "tagmemic heuristic" grid developed by Young, Becker, and Pike; in effect she has made the prewriting of student essays products in themselves, necessitating prewriting, drafting, and revision of the prewriting of the assignment. The problem of the linear model could also extend from the classroom to the individual writer whose search for an effective writing model leads to the adoption of one that impedes rather than facilitates his or her composing.

While Flower and Hayes have argued strenuously against a linear model of composing, the possibility of linearity exists in their model; some researchers insist that writers they have studied do in fact work from a linear process. The question of whether the composing process is linear (a position that strengthens the current-traditional model's approaches to instruction) or recursive (a position taken by proponents of a process model from the beginning) is not necessarily an either-or question. Stephen Witte has observed that

> if experienced adult writers or expert writers are given writing
> tasks that place relatively small demands on their writing
> processes generally, little recursive transcription may result,
> perhaps because all required planning occurred prior to
> transcription or perhaps because the writer's projected text or
> pre-text was appropriately altered before transcription. (261)

Witte uses the term "pre-text" to refer to the text before transcription begins. "Pre-textual revising" is his term for the changes the text undergoes before it is represented as a text. It is a "complementary process" to that of "'retrospective structuring' . . . or recursive revising of written text in light of discovery" (270–271).

As we will see, evidence for pretextual revision or "projective restructuring" will surface in the composing of the writers interviewed in this book. To some extent, for example, it will explain the relatively small amount of revision some of those writers undergo and, in particular, Neal Gabler's assertion that he does not discover as he writes because his reviews are laid out like a legal brief before he begins. The columnists whose work is regularly relatively short also have fewer demands placed on their composing—the limits of length help impose limits on complexity of thought and the "pre-text" can be generated without as much dependence on recursive revising and discovery-in-process. In a sense it is the amount of recursiveness in the pretextual stage of discovery that allows a writer to be more linear in transcribing, revising, and editing.

In my flexible reading of the cognitive process model, there is room for pretextual revision, and the value of the model itself lies in its comprehensiveness and plasticity. It directs the attention of both writer and teacher to all the factors that affect composing—the nature of the rhetorical problem imposed on the writer by circumstances, the knowledge the writer has of both subject and writing, the strategies the writer engages in while composing. It is also a useful descriptive model of composing because it emphasizes the interactiveness of its components in spontaneous shifts and embeddings that defy prescription; such activities can occur in almost any random order, interrupting and facilitating one another.

However, as I intimated earlier, my intention in discussing these matters has been to provide a context in which the analysis of the composing of working writers will be made throughout the following chapters. Although, by and large, the evidence of these interviews will confirm the validity of the descriptions of the writing process just reviewed, it will not invite doctrinaire acceptance of them. More important, once we have examined the composing processes of the individual writers, will be the implications of those processes for other writers. In that discussion, the business of the final chapter, we will be searching for the paradigm that emerges from the experience of working writers and exploring their implications for other writers, within and without the classroom. Such a discussion will surely demand even greater flexibility of the paradigm sketched in this chapter.

2

Writing Essays

The essay, one of our most flexible, enduring, and Protean forms of literature, is currently undergoing something of a revival with the publication of an annual anthology of "best essays," increased attention in literary and little magazines, and inclusion in generic anthologies for college introductory literature classes. Particularly (but not exclusively) among essayists specializing in nature, science, and travel, essay collections are continually available. Many of these are culled from newspapers and magazines that have continued uninterrupted the tradition of the popular periodical essay begun by Addison and Steele in the early eighteenth century. Ellen Goodman, Russell Baker, Bob Greene, Mike Royko, and Andrew Rooney, for example, regularly collect their columns, and regional columnists around the country often do the same.

Writers of the popular periodical essay have in common both brevity and regularity; their essays are generally intended to fill a specific space in their publications, be it so many column inches on a feature or op-ed page or a page or two in a predictable location in a magazine. Unlike freelance essayists who can shape the article to serve the subject matter, the columnist more often shapes the subject matter to fit the restrictions of the column. In some ways this is inhibiting, because it forces the writer to limit and omit material; in other ways it is liberating, because it frees the writer from the need to worry about finding a form and lets him or her concentrate on the development of ideas.

Some sense of the similarities and differences between the literary essayist and the columnist can be had by briefly examining the composing processes of two essayists, John McPhee and Richard Selzer, before turning to an extensive examination of the work of the two columnists interviewed for this book. Charles Schuster has worked extensively with both McPhee and Selzer; his study of McPhee confirms and extends the earlier description of McPhee's writing by William Howarth.

McPhee begins a writing project with a sense of a topic he wants to explore and a lengthy period of interviewing, observing, and exploring. When he feels fully steeped in his subject he types up his notes, duplicates them, and places them in a binder, reading and rereading them to discover the structure within the material. He eventually annotates the notes, coding them according to subject matter, and then arranges coded notecards in an order he intends to follow. For each notecard he labels a file folder, cuts up one set of notes and categorizes them in the folders, and writes the article by working on one folder at a time, in order, carefully drafting each section, and then revising the whole. As Schuster observes, "You can hear always in McPhee, 'Structure, structure,' but structure is not something imposed from without, it comes from within the material that emerges from that story." Once McPhee knows how he will end and how he will get to that ending, he feels ready to begin. "I don't just take off from some point and go along and see where I'm going to," he says. "This is a time-honored writing method that just doesn't happen to be mine."

Selzer, on the other hand, writes spontaneously, trying to create a first draft and allowing himself to discover content and meaning as he writes. His approach is intuitive and unpredictable rather than systematic and controlled. As Schuster reports, "Richard Selzer is much more inclined to use that time-honored writing method to follow his intuitions, to discover a piece of writing as he writes it, to work from a feeling, from 'the idea that first began it' . . . After his often hasty initial draft, he begins a second handwritten draft in which he struggles toward an original expression of that idea or feeling." Most of his energy on a given piece is expended in revision.

McPhee and Selzer are apparently polar opposites as essayists, and their painstaking and laborious composing may seem remote from the regular and often hasty composing of columnists facing constant deadlines, but in fact the differences between them help identify the elements that distinguish essayistic writers from one another. Those elements are the relationship that the writer has to his topic and the role the writer defines for himself in the essay. The range of the essay is such that at one end is the exploration of personal feelings and experience and at the other end the exposition of impersonal events and observations.

Chris Anderson, in *Literary Nonfiction,* makes the distinction that Selzer is an essayist, McPhee a "journalist or informative writer" (x). Beyond the personal pole is the private writing of the diary or journal; beyond the impersonal pole the public writing of reportage. In the attitudes recorded in the interviews that follow and in the evidence of their written work, Jim Fitzgerald and Kathleen Stocking place themselves at different ends of the line between those poles.

Jim Fitzgerald began writing essays in St. Stephen's Catholic High School in Port Huron, Michigan, then attended Port Huron Junior College and majored in journalism at Michigan State University, graduating in 1951. He was hired by the *Lapeer County Press* to sell advertising and write a weekly column, "Along the Main Stem," that would help sell the advertising. Eventually he became editor of the *County Press* and continued writing a weekly column, syndicating it around the state. In 1976 Kurt Luedtke, then an editor at the *Detroit Free Press,* hired Fitzgerald as a full-time columnist.

His column appears four times a week, Sunday, Monday, Wednesday, and Friday, forty-eight weeks a year. In the past twelve years he has written twenty-three hundred columns (each seven hundred to a thousand words long). To be that productive he has a set routine for his writing. Every day he reads the two Detroit morning papers, watches television, and goes about his life. As he says in his interview, "I'm making notes, sitting over there with a pad, all the time, and I'm clipping newspapers, and living my life the way I want to live it . . . Those are my three sources—how I live, what I read, and what I see on television or hear on the radio." He keeps a folder in which he places clippings from the newspaper or from magazines, notes to himself about something he saw on television or noticed in conversation, and random ideas for potential columns. Periodically he lists the items in the folder and comments on them, often making connections between disparate items. For example, referring to items in his folder, Fitzgerald said:

> I made a note there because my wife gets so mad at me for
> bringing fudge home from work (she can't eat it and I can), and
> I wrote down here: "She was criticizing me about losing my
> temper watching a Tiger game and they lost." I got down here
> and I thought, Those two might make a column together, and
> they did. They did, believe it or not.

He writes the column at the offices of *The Detroit Free Press.* On Monday he writes Wednesday's column, on Tuesday Friday's column, on Wednesday Saturday's column, and on Friday Monday's column. The schedule gives him some flexibility in that he can change a column in order to respond to current events, as he did when he substituted a column on the explosion of the Challenger for a lighter piece he had already written. More important to him, it sets up a schedule in which he has some predictability and expectations: each day at the office must produce a column, and Fitzgerald takes anywhere from three to six hours to write one.

Column ideas are generated by Fitzgerald's ability to make connections between disparate subjects. As Elmore Leonard has observed in *If It Fitz,*

> The thing that amazes me about Jim Fitzgerald's columns is they can veer off in unexpected directions, appear to be topic-hopping, observe llamas and Lee Iacocca in the same piece, but always manage to get back in time to arrive at a perfectly logical conclusion. Within this sometimes astonishing structure is an essay composed of clear, expository sentences. (Introduction)

The folder stores current items that Fitzgerald can draw upon to make the kinds of connections that make his column, but he supposes that

> ninety-nine percent of what goes into this folder never goes into a column . . . No matter how many things you have in a folder you're more likely to write about what's on the top of your mind . . . Most days I think about it while I'm walking to work and generally I'll have a pretty good idea of what I want to write about. Lots of times I'll have that one topic.

For example, on one occasion he walked to work thinking about a recent comment by Richard Chrysler, then a candidate for the Michigan Republican gubernatorial nomination. The incumbent governor, James Blanchard, a Democrat, had offered amnesty to tax delinquents if they paid their taxes instead of forcing the government to track them and prosecute them. Chrysler, a Michigan businessman and self-made millionaire, announced his political opposition to the tax amnesty program but simultaneously revealed that his business was itself delinquent and he intended to take full advantage of the amnesty. (It later turned out to be the remark that ended his credibility as a candidate.) In the office Fitzgerald had on his desk a Puffalump doll, sent to him by a manufacturer hoping for free publicity by promoting a contest nominating local celebrities, including Fitzgerald, as potential Puffalump dolls. Fitzgerald had no intention of publicizing the contest but, as he mused about Chrysler's remarks, he made a connection. Fitzgerald recalls,

> I'm sitting there and there's this Puffalump doll on my desk and I said, "Well, I was nominated to be a Puffalump and this clown wasn't. That's probably why." A crazy idea but that's my style . . . So I tie in there with the Puffalumps, get a few laughs, at the same time make a point.
> . . . how I knotted that together was, "I'm against the Puffalump contest, but if I win it I'll take whatever comes with it in the spirit of Richard Chrysler who did the same thing." That's reaching pretty far, but that's what I do.

The resulting article is one fairly typical of the kind of associations upon which Fitzgerald's columns turn. As he observes,

> I'm always looking for ironies . . . But I am conscious when I get to the end that I've got to button it up . . . with the top so it's logical, so people . . . can see why these disparate subjects all got in the same column. It's a technique that comes naturally to me after all these years.

In his composing, Fitzgerald relies upon knowledge of writing plans stored by successful repetition and also upon continual engagement with subject matter; he continually stores new information and reviews his information for connections. Both storage and review of information are guided by selection for potential as column topics. Both self-selection of topic and the immediacy of his interest help generate ideas. Finally, the regularity of the writing, the continuity in the rhetorical situation of the column, and the task environment itself also facilitate composition.

In Fitzgerald's composing, one aspect of the task environment, the "text produced so far," seems to play a particularly important role. This is the way he describes the actual drafting of an individual column:

> The start and the end are always the toughest part of the column. The first couple paragraphs I try to get going. As a much better writer, Sydney Harris, put it in one of his columns once, "One paragraph gives birth to the next paragraph." It does to me very well.
> . . . I often won't know where I'm going to go; often one

paragraph gives me the idea for the next paragraph and so on. That's why these notes are written. One paragraph will give me an idea for a paragraph six paragraphs later and I don't want to forget it, so I reach over and make that note on a pad. I'll start columns and I'll end up going where I had no idea I was going to go.

. . . I don't have writer's block. If [some people] can't get their original idea of what they're going to write, the whole idea, or outline it in their mind or on a pad, they don't even start. I never do that. I say, "Well, I don't have much of an idea here, so let's write this first paragraph; maybe that'll give me an idea for the second."

Fitzgerald relies on the text he produces to help generate the rest of the text. For novice writers the text often controls the drafting; starting too far back in a story, for example, tends to make them overdevelop the preliminary background and underdevelop the event or incident or idea that was originally intended to be the focus of the paper. Fitzgerald, on the other hand, draws upon the generative power of the text and harnesses it through planning *while* he composes the first draft. Often the column will have already been rehearsed mentally while he walks to work, but not always, and even when it has been, the rehearsal isn't always thorough.

For example, one morning a taped remark on radio by the mayor of Detroit, Coleman Young, about a memo circulated at city newspapers, triggered Fitzgerald's memory: the memo had been the subject of a column of his that had been denied publication ten years earlier by Kurt Luedtke, then a *Free Press* editor, but recently better known as an Academy Award-winning screenwriter for *Out of Africa*. Fitzgerald immediately felt sure he had a column; as he says in his interview, he "just went to work and wrote it," beginning with references to the Young remark and to having had two columns killed in ten years, one of them by Luedtke.

This is what I mean about paragraphs spawning paragraphs: the minute I'm into him I'm into the fact that currently he's fighting the JOA [Joint Operating Agreement between the *Detroit News* and *Detroit Free Press*] and I know I can make a little crack about that so I did this obvious piece of satire . . . "I understand Luedtke's writing an expose-type screenplay about two boys, born in different hospitals, who grow up to be Siamese twins and endanger the free enterprise system by

jointly agreeing to operate the same waterfront joint (WJJOA)."
It's quick satire and I know he'll get a kick out of that and it
gives me a chance to make *that* point. And by then the column
is about written and I've made all these points and hopefully
twitted your curiosity, and then I've got to explain why Luedtke
pulled the column . . . and then once I've got that explained, I
got to say what's in the memo and that Mayor Young is saying
the very same things he said ten years ago and my response,
which I took almost word for word from the ten-year-old
column that never got printed . . . By then the column's over
and I get to the end and what I did up here I knew was going
to happen; if I said there were two killed and I'm only going to
talk about one, somebody's going to wonder what that second
one was, so I use that to close the column . . . I didn't know all
these things when I started. It just came to me.

Fitzgerald relies upon the text he has produced to help generate the
text he has yet to produce. Part of the power of that text to generate
further text lies in the ways the writer creates a lead or a beginning
portion that does not so much predict text for a future reader (although
it probably will) as predict text for the writer himself.

For this interview, Fitzgerald brought home his folder filled with
clippings and notes and displayed some examples of the kind of work
he does. For the article titled, "Yeah, but Could Roger Help Ann with
Banking?," Fitzgerald had the following items:

1. two small clippings from the *Detroit Free Press* introducing
   and excerpting a portion of *The Big Boys* by Ralph Nader and
   William Taylor in which Roger Smith, chairman of General
   Motors, and advice columnist Ann Landers are discussed; at
   the bottom of the introductory clipping, in black ink, is a
   note in Fitzgerald's handwriting: "Did she phone on Saturday?"; at the top of the excerpt the comment, "How to buy a
   car—even on Saturday," is linked by an arrow to a
   paragraph in which Landers describes calling Smith to find a
   1980 baby blue Cadillac with everything on it;

2. a 3 × 5 sheet of paper with the note, "What's all the fuss
   about not being able to buy a car on Saturday. Just do what
   Ann Landers did";

3. another 3 × 5 sheet of paper with one note in black: "Communities—including states—should do what baseball teams
   did to free agents—quiet collusion—and quit giving tax

breaks," and another, later note in blue reading: "—'get together and agree'—mentally—extra sensory perception";
4. two sheets from an 8 1/2 X 11 yellow legal pad with phrases interspersed down the pages:

But so what?

Kirk Gibson   colluded

  -while you're talking about to
  Roger Smith—

  Speaking of getting together !

   Banks!
   9:30 to 4

  get even—stop tax breaks

ask Roger
to ask
his dealers

  Ann Landers   automatic tellers
           slightest idea
           make a deposit—

           [illegible]
           mistake—can
        lose all my money.

Do you suppose she
  called Roger on a Saturday.

 Would Roger Smith write Ann Landers

  no elitist—   production lines
 Roger wouldn't do anything w/
  Ann Landers that he wouldn't
  do for you

 You can surely do the same.
  Financing?—payment book?
  While I have him on the line—

5. a printout of the untitled final draft.

The items on the legal pad sheet correspond roughly to the position of complete sentences and paragraphs on these subjects with the word processor printout of the final draft of that particular column; they are both a means of reminding himself about comments he intends to include and also a way of indicating relative placement of comments in the article. Together the notes and printout demonstrate the ways Fitzgerald is able to concurrently plan, draft, and revise his columns, since many of the notes and comments are written during the period he is composing rather than prior to it. A comparison of the notes with the published article will make that relationship clearer, as will Fitzgerald's own remarks in the interview.

Like Jim Fitzgerald, Kathleen Stocking was born and educated in Michigan, a generation later and at the opposite edge of the state, in Glen Arbor, on the Leelanau Peninsula, the little finger of Michigan's mitten. After attending the University of Michigan and living for a time in the East, she returned to the Leelanau Peninsula and, at the time of the interview, lived on the outskirts of Lake Leelanau, about twenty miles from where she grew up. In March of 1984 she began a monthly column called "Up North" for *Metropolitan Detroit* Magazine; revised versions of the columns also ran in *Traverse the Magazine.* From March 1986 to January 1989 she wrote the "Up North" column on a bimonthly basis for *Detroit Monthly.*

Stocking's column is nominally focused on the Northern Lower Peninsula, particularly the Leelanau Peninsula between Lake Michigan and Traverse Bay, almost three hundred miles northwest of Detroit. The sense of place is sufficiently important that a collection of her essays, each of which runs about six and a half to seven and a half pages (fifteen hundred words on average), is titled *Letters From the Leelanau.*

Like Fitzgerald, she has a definite sense of what she is trying to accomplish in the column. She says, "My columns deal with ethics and morality and basic philosophy of life and what we would call basic truths," and she thinks of her persona in the column "as the alter ego part of the reader . . . I try to be Everyperson to the extent that I can be, just an impression absorber."

She says that "a typical column has its genesis months and even years before I actually write it," and she tends to decide on a topic by making connections. She describes the process this way: "Generally I get the idea for a column and then I do the research and then I do the writing and then I let it sit and then I refine it." For example, the column "Dreaming Detroit" began out of a random observation in a bleak period of winter, a thought about how nice it would be to be enjoying the cultural life of Detroit rather than the isolation of snowbound Leelanau. "I kind of thought that and that's when I wrote the first sentence: 'Detroit looms in the dead of winter up north like an oasis of civilization somewhere to the south of us.' I had that line and I just scrawled it down." Later she read a piece in the *Michigan Quarterly* about Ovid's complaints about his exile from Rome and taped some of it near her typewriter. It was the connection between these two items that inspired the topic. Not unlike Jim Fitzgerald, she believes

> an essay always has to have a counterpoint, a contrapuntal
> rhythm. You have to take two opposite perspectives and mirror
> them or mesh them or twist them in some way. So in
> "Dreaming Detroit" I took the Detroiters' feelings about them-
> selves, their inferiority complex, my feelings about longing for
> contact, and mirrored them in myself for awhile.

As she says, "there was a basic connivance in this," an attempt to satisfy a reading audience downstate at the same time that she talks about what interests her. Her topic decided, she drew upon a few memories of having traveled to Detroit but deliberately set out to get information from others, already having a rough idea of how she intended to conclude the piece.

> I wrote it and I didn't have an ending. I knew roughly what the
> ending had to be, and I tinkered with it, and I let it sit around
> and I thought, How am I going to end it in such a way that
> there's a feeling of resolution and completion, and the reader
> feels that it's come full circle? . . . So the endline sort of came to
> me.

For her actual composing, Stocking uses "a long legal pad for the notes and ideas" and then types her drafts on "cheap newspaper-print typing paper—reams of it." It takes her multiple drafts of each individual page to arrive at a final draft, because she will often write one page and then retype the entire page to change a single sentence. Almost none of the writing is done before that kind of drafting starts, although, like Fitzgerald, she may have rehearsed the article in some fashion before composing.

In another article, "Piecing the Ribbon Together," an invitation from a friend to work on the peace ribbon came three months before the event, prompting Stocking to agree to participate in hopes of generating a column. In this case, as she observes, "I began working on the column before we actually ended up putting those pieces together." In the intervening period she began to notice other elements of the column—visits by Jehovah's Witnesses, a dream about the ribbon, a cat attacking a rabbit—and essentially began putting the column together mentally even before the event it was supposed to record. When the actual writing took place it went quickly.

Stocking has described the experience in almost mystical terms: "When a piece is being born through you, not only will the pieces come in spite of you but it's almost like incidents will happen that will feed into it." She makes a distinction between "pieces where you say, '*This* I did' " and "other pieces where all you are is a conduit: the piece writes itself." It is probable, however, that the "conduit" pieces are easier because they are more substantially prewritten or rehearsed than the other pieces; the drafting taps into a reservoir of subconscious preliminary drafts, thoroughly incubated both in ideas and language. The more difficult pieces often are those where the material depends on external sources—the decision is made to write about a topic but the research doesn't pan out as expected and the draft is harder to produce in part because the material is not only undigested and unrehearsed but also unpredictable. A piece on casino gambling doesn't go as expected because upon actually visiting the casino she discovers little to describe and finds the operators uncommunicative; she is forced in the piece to fall back on internal reflection and weaker connections to other material. A column on a local coffee club doesn't lead to the quaint, folksy atmosphere she had told her editor she would find but to a sour, narrow meanness that alienates her and leaves her struggling to walk the line between approval of the reprehensible and condemnation of the petty.

Moreover, the manuscript evidence suggests that, at least for some columns, the early drafts are far more inclusive and data-laden than the final draft proves to be. During the interview at her Lake Leelanau home, she produced a pile of newsprint that proved to be draft pages of a recently completed column, "Mozart and Ace on Omena Bay," about two elderly black musicians who had been performing at a bar in a nearby town. Of fifty-four sheets, seventeen were carbons of other sheets that bore evidence of not only typewritten revisions done in the course of composing but also handwritten revisions as well. Of the remaining thirty-seven sheets, most were part of four discrete drafts of either seven or eight pages in length and the others pages of variations or trial runs of openings and particular passages. The final draft, when she eventually typed it up on bond paper to send to her editor at *Monthly Detroit,* was seven pages long. Even then changes to accommodate length might still be made by her editor.

The revisions revealed by the multiple drafts accomplish a variety of changes. Some are merely stylistic, such as deciding whether a phrase should read "church or work" or "work or church." Others not only struggle with the sound of the sentence but also with the strategies for introducing characters and ideas. On a single page is a series of trial leads. (Brackets indicate deleted or marked out material.) The first lead reads:

> The image that comes to mind when I think of Mozart and Ace playing sweet 20's and 30's and 40's jazz last summer at the Omena Harbor Bar, is of [them and their instruments floating] Mozart at the piano and Ace on the bass, floating in the moonlit sky over Omena Bay, light-filled holograms. Something happened when those two old men brought their music to this remote northern county and the place might never be the same again.

The second reads:

> This is the story of how two old black jazz players came to a remote northern Michigan county and won the hearts and minds of the people there with their music. It is the story of the triumph of people over prejudice and the triumph of music over both of them. It starts at the Omena Harbor Bar, a plain kind of bar with a stunning view of the bay, a bar caught in a tuck between the bay and the highway.

The third reads:

> The Harbor Bar at Omena sits in a little tuck of the bay—a place where the bay curves in and the highway curves out so the two almost touch, except that in between is the Omena Harbor Bar. It's always been known in the county as the Indian bar, a place of few patrons and occasional brawls and a primarily Indian clientele. Sometimes tourists would come by in the summer to cast sidelong glances at the Indians; sometimes local people who were friends of the barowner or who lived near would come in there, sometimes a band would draw a few of those who weren't "regulars."

Each of these openings suggests a range of approaches and interests that Stocking is bringing to the material. The first paragraph will eventually find itself revised and transported to the conclusion of the article as the closing image rather than the opening one. The second paragraph introduces themes that will be elaborated on in early drafts: in various places Stocking expands upon the reputation of the Harbor Bar as an Indian hangout, the tension between whites and Indians on the Leelanau Peninsula, the character of the owner, Keith Brown, and his attitude toward racial matters. In connection with the racial theme she mentions in one draft, "Even our family which is a mixed-race family, half-Indian and half-white, learned to avoid the bar when we had our children with us because of the occasional fights that would break out there." In another draft she writes of the people on the Leelanau Peninsula,

> We do not have live music in our bars and we do not see black people. When my [daughter who is five] five year old daughter saw two young black [girls] women on the streets of Traverse City, she said, "There's some people from *The Color Purple.*"
> You have to know this, because otherwise you wouldn't [have] know what an anomalous [experience] event it was for Leelanau County people to experience the music of John "Ace" Davis and Mozart Perry.

In addition to the racial emphasis in early drafts there was also a variety of detail about the musicians themselves, the scene at the bar on the occasion she watched them perform, and the additional work they did during the summer. In her portion on the history and attitudes of the two men, there was considerably more dialogue.

As we can tell from the second lead mentioned above and the subsequent references to race relations throughout the earlier drafts, Stocking's original feelings about the significance of Mozart's and Ace's popularity were more intimately tied to her sense of racial attitudes and behavior on the Peninsula. At the same time the earlier drafts attempt to tell the story of the musicians and their performance almost equally fully. Throughout the process of tightening the language and restructuring the article, Stocking eliminates virtually all the racial references. Some of the eliminations are related to her reluctance to focus on herself in the article—during the interview she specifically mentions her daughter's remark and her excising it—but others have more to do with defining the tone and focus of the article: the racial material shifts attention away from the musicians who are equally interesting from an aesthetic perspective. In early drafts most of the comments made by members of the audience are included as well as the reference to Basho in the quote from Berrien Thorn, giving the article a dual focus, aesthetics and race. Ultimately, Stocking opts to center on aesthetic considerations, how people react to the musicians, and to reduce the racial material to the single sentence, "We do not, as a rule, have live music in our bars, nor do we ever see many black people."

The manuscript evidence, then, of a fairly typical composition suggests that Stocking's laborious process of multiple drafts of individual pages and the entire article helps her first spread out her material in front of her—in this case, the various attitudes and resonances provoked by the circumstances as well as the specific details and associations of character and place—and then select, organize, and refine the material as she works with it. Many of the writers in this book, Stocking among them, profess confusion about the difference between style and content. In Stocking's manuscript, revisions are made for reasons of sentence rhythm, word choice, balance, structure, and focus, affecting not only the language but the context of the language and the overall organization and general thesis of the article. At least in the example of "Mozart and Ace on Omena Bay," Stocking is clearly discovering through revision; in other articles she is much more certain about what she wants to achieve and selects material for inclusion more deliberately before composing, as her comments in the interview on "Dreaming Detroit" and "Piecing the Ribbon Together" will make clear.

Essentially, then, the difference between the composing process of Jim Fitzgerald and that of Kathleen Stocking is based on the task environment, particularly the circumstances under which they write their columns and the way they see their own roles in the columns. Fitzgerald writes four times a week, sixteen to eighteen times a month; Stocking writes once a month or even less, now that she has switched magazines. The spaces in between her writing on the column impede the development of regular strategies for writing the column, and forestall planning by making her feel she has plenty of time to develop that one column. Regular composition may make regular composition easier.

Fitzgerald sees himself and his reactions to the world around him as central to the column; Stocking tries to keep her distance, to make the column about other people than herself. In a sense, although both writers are columnists producing what would be described as essays,

Fitzgerald operates in the reflexive mode almost entirely, and Stocking tends to operate closer to the borderline between the reflexive and extensive modes; that is, Fitzgerald writes more about his personal thoughts and experiences and virtually writes for himself while Stocking observes and analyzes but always remains aware of her distant audience and feels obliged to maintain a certain objectivity. For example, in "Mozart and Ace," she excised the anecdote about her young daughter seeing blacks and identifying them as people from *The Color Purple* because she found her own presence in the piece diverting; Fitzgerald, on the other hand, regularly hears from readers who enjoy his stories about his granddaughters.

Both writers also rely on the task environment in the sense that the text produced so far is a regular resource in producing further drafts, Fitzgerald expecting paragraphs spawning paragraphs to lead him through a piece, Stocking using multiple drafts of individual pages to think through the balance and content of an article. But Fitzgerald's pieces have a great deal more gestation preceding them, and the typical approach to the column—the intention to join disparate topics—invites the explorations inherent in relying on the text. Stocking, on the other hand, may have to juggle outside information whose disparity is harder to reconcile—Fitzgerald, after all, begins by making connections among the disparate topics while Stocking is uncovering disparate topics and hoping to find the relationship between them. It may well be that the regularity of Fitzgerald's production makes it easier for him to write, while Stocking's frequent change of subject, limited production, and considerably fewer articles yearly tend to make each article a separate piece, drawing far less on predictable strategies.

Unlike other writers, an essayist is likely to feel, with Montaigne, that he is himself the matter of his book. That means his immersion in context is likely to be of a different order than that of, for instance, a critic or political columnist, one in which the exploration of his own reactions is not only the subject of his writing but an influence on the means by which he writes. That is, the essayist may have to turn earlier to the draft because the text helps produce itself more than in transactional writing; the ideas are within the writer, not external to him or her, and therefore the means of organizing and discovering are less able to be performed in an external way.

Interview with Jim Fitzgerald

Root. What is the charge from the *Detroit Free Press* about the column? What are your requirements in regard to length or subject?

Fitzgerald. Just about the only constant positive restriction is the length. Usually now we compose on the computer and just press a button and it gives your length. People ask me when I stop and I say, "When I press the button and it says fifteen inches, I quit."

Root. The word processing program tells you the length in column inches?

Fitzgerald. Or the number of lines, either way. When it's between fifty-five and sixty lines, or fourteen to fifteen inches, I quit. As I go on I press the button to find out how near I am to the end and what I have to do.

Root. How many words is that?

Fitzgerald. I haven't the faintest idea. Seven hundred to a thousand words, I guess.

Root. Is there a set number you have to produce?

Fitzgerald. Four a week. I get four weeks vacation a year.

Root. What about subject? Is there anything that they tell you you can't write about simply because it's not what they want of that kind of column?

Fitzgerald. No. Did you read today's column? There you are. They killed two out of two thousand. I was hired by Kurt Luedtke, as I said in the column. Before, I had been in a weekly, but I had syndicated all around to a lot of the dailies in Michigan and a couple of editors had read it and they liked the style so they bought it for that. It was kind of light, humorous, even when it got serious. So they just said, "Continue with what you've been doing," and I did. As far as subjects I don't think I've gotten as many as five suggestions in ten years from anybody at the *Free Press*. They've never said, "Don't write about anything." They've just given me a free hand.

Root. Do you feel any restrictions, that there's something else you'd like to do but can't because it's not that kind of column?

Fitzgerald. I hate to get serious but I do once in a while. It's kind of funny how I'll do it. If it's a real deadly serious subject I'll hope that somebody else in the *Free Press* or at least the *Detroit News* will do it in an editorial or a column. If they don't it will sometimes bug me so long I think, "I'll do it myself." The really dead-straight serious stuff is not my style, but I used to write editorials—I was an editor for a long time before I came here—I can do it. But the only time I'll do it now is if nobody else does it.

I know it sounds kind of silly to say that. A good example is what happened yesterday with Gilbert DiNello, the state senator who made that terrible remark. He voted against an appropriation for the Holocaust display in one of the synagogues here in town—the state was going to give them a few thousand dollars. It would be all right if he wanted to vote against it, but he said he voted against because he never knew a Jew that needed money. That's the old stereotype, and I sat around making notes right away, saying he probably never knew an Italian who didn't belong to the Mafia or a black person who couldn't tap dance. That's pretty serious stuff and I'm not going to write another column until Monday, so I hope that between now and Monday somebody will get onto that, either at the *News* or the *Free Press*. I'll be glad they did so I won't get that serious. If they don't I'll probably get into it.

Root. What is your intention in the column? What are you trying to accomplish?

Fitzgerald. Number one, I'm trying to be interesting. I'm trying to catch 'em with the first paragraph and keep 'em to the end, if I can. It's a technique. Today's column is a good example. In the top paragraph I said the *Free Press* refused to run a column I wrote. Supposedly that's going to interest somebody; they're going to want to keep reading to find out why they rejected it. I want it to be interesting and I'd like to touch them, either make them laugh or make them cry. The best column you can write is where you can make them both laugh and cry at the same column. Be interesting. Touch their emotions. Make some points.

Often I think that I write on two levels: on one level just for amusement, spoofing something, but on the second level I'm making the point that this is ridiculous and we should realize it. If I had to put it in one word, I'd say "Interest them; make it something they'd want to read."

Root. When are your deadlines?

Fitzgerald. I keep it comfortable. We did it at the suggestion of Luedt-ke all those years ago and it stayed that way. I'm twenty-four hours ahead of everybody else's deadline. In other words, on Monday, say by four o'clock, I'll hand in the one that runs Wednesday, so I'm a day ahead of everyone else. There's no pressure on me. I love it that way. It gives the editors something they can do ahead of time and get out of the way, although they always forget and at the last minute they're scurrying around. But that's flexible; if you wrote one for Wednesday on Monday, something might happen on Tuesday and you could still write a new one. An example is the explosion of the Challenger. I had already written a column for Wednesday and it blew up on Tuesday while I was at the office. All of a sudden you couldn't think of anything else, so I pulled what I had written and wrote a new one. So I really have up until four o'clock of the afternoon before its appearance and generally it's twenty-four hours ahead of that.

Root. Do you give yourself a schedule for writing?

Fitzgerald. Generally with four a week I'll write one on Monday, Tuesday, Wednesday, Thursday. I get them out of the way and I'm done now. I never work on Fridays and I've already written the one for Monday—I wrote that yesterday, so I take these long three day weekends and I love 'em. For me at least it's an incredibly easy job by hours because when I had to edit a newspaper for all those years if I didn't work sixty to seventy hours a week I was cheating. It was every day including Sundays. But here, if you're a full-time columnist, technically you're working all the time—you're always thinking and watching—but as far as office hours I probably work about twenty-four hours a week. That's about it. I get up, walk down to the office from here—I could stay here but I like the machinery down there—get there around ten, and if I want I can be back home about one or two. But if I lolligag around, I won't get home until four o'clock.

Root. When you go in to do a column, what have you prepared before you sit down at the terminal?

Fitzgerald. I keep a folder. I'm making notes, sitting over there with a pad, all the time, and I'm clipping newspapers, and living my life the way I want to live it, going out to nightclubs and plays and anything. Those are my three sources—how I live, what I read, and what I see on television or hear on the radio. Notes and clippings all go into this folder, and after about two months it gets so fat I throw it out and start a new one, and I've never figured it out but I suppose ninety-nine percent of what goes into this folder never goes into a column. It's just things that I think might make a column so I write about them.

Let's see. Here's a note: "What's all the fuss about not being able to buy a car on Saturdays in the Detroit area? Just do what Ann Landers did." This clipping last week was from an excerpt from Ralph Nader's book where Ann Landers described how she bought a limousine by picking up the phone and calling Roger Smith, the president of General Motors, and he delivered it to her door next day. I said, "What the hell, Roger's not an elitist. He'd probably do the same thing for me if I wanted." I thought there'd be a column in that so I made the note, and I've got the clipping. I made another note here, which occurred to me one day as I was sitting there. "Why don't the states do what the baseball teams did to the free agents?" My thought was that in baseball the owners all sign free agents—Kirk Gibson couldn't get a better deal. Obviously they met somewhere on a dark night and said, "Let's do this," but you're not supposed to know that. Why don't the cities and states do that and quit giving tax breaks to GM and the rest of these guys looking for the cheapest place to build a factory?

There are three ideas there. So I ended up writing a column and while I was writing on the keyboard I got another idea: "Why do they pick on the auto dealers' hours when I think the bankers' hours are more outrageous than that?"

Root. Are you trying to create an outline that you might follow?

Fitzgerald. Not really, it's not that formal. I'm just thinking about something I might do later on the keyboard so I wrote "Roger Smith" there, "automatic tellers," and so on. I usually make about that many notes while I'm writing the column on the keyboard and then throw them away. And I ended up with Monday's column: "A lot of people, not to mention the federal government, are apparently unhappy because practically all car dealerships in the Detroit area are closed⁻ Saturdays. They should write to Ann Landers." It all grew into that and a little bit later in there I got to say something about the bank hours. There're two things I want to say so I build a column to give me a chance to say them. In the last paragraph—I never even did use the baseball agent thing, but the thought was there about the collusion on dark nights—I said, "While I've got Roger Smith on the line, I'll ask him what he would do if all cities and states got together one dark night and conspired to help ordinary tax payers by no longer giving tax breaks and free lollipops to auto manufacturers looking for the cheapest place to build a factory. If that happened, would Roger Smith write to Ann Landers?"

That's how those disparate thoughts got woven together. That's how I work. When this pile of notes and clippings get so big maybe halfway through a two-month period, then I'll get my pad out and go through and write down on here the most promising stuff in there. For example, I wrote: "Robbery of nun at FOCUS." If it's crossed out that means it eventually got to be a column. I did write about her place getting robbed. There's a note I got about Amway bumps and grinds. Amway's a religious business. I've picked on them so much I never did write that one, but they did have a bump and grind show in New York to introduce some of their products. It's so unlike the face they've put on themselves for all these years. The main reason I didn't go into was that a few months ago they used Zsa Zsa Gabor to introduce one of their things over in Canada and I did write about that. Things like that strike me.

I was going to write something about how ridiculous it was for the TV to have a show on the NBA draft when all they did was draw names out of a bowl. I thought it was kind of dumb but I never wrote on it. I was going to do something on capital punishment; I didn't. I brought home a loaf of Wonder Bread in a big bag one day and forgot it was there and a lot of other stuff got on it and it got so stuck together my wife could never use it. Things like that strike me that I might write about but I never did.

Here's some that I did, that I crossed out because I did them. Something Al Ackerman said on TV I wrote about and so on and so forth. Every once in a while I'll think I've got one there and I've got one down there and I can tie those together, because that's what I do, tie things together. So I draw one arrow going to another. I made a note there because my wife gets so mad at me for bringing fudge home from work (she can't eat it and I can), and I wrote down here: "She was criticizing me about losing my temper watching a Tiger game and they lost." I got down here and I thought, Those two might make a column together, and they did. They did, believe it or not.

And this is the same thing, but you can see how many never did turn into columns and some that do. But it's usually a matter of the day that I make the note or make the clipping; it won't immediately come into a column. Maybe a week later something else along the same subject will occur to me and I'll tie them together. It gives you one thing to play off the other. I've been doing it so long I do it unconsciously and I never thought about it until you called. That's the way it happens.

Root. I noticed that about your structure. Elmore Leonard says, in the introduction to your book, *If It Fitz:* "The thing that amazes me about Jim Fitzgerald's columns is they can veer off in unexpected directions, appear to be topic-hopping, observe llamas and Lee Iacocca in the same piece, but always manage to get back in time to arrive at a perfectly logical conclusion. Within this sometimes astonishing structure is an essay composed of clear, expository sentences."

Fitzgerald. Bless him for that.

Root. One of the things I notice going through is that very often there are two things that don't appear to be connected and by the end of the piece they are. Is there some reason for your choosing that approach as much as you do?

Fitzgerald. I've never gone into it. I'm never conscious of choosing that way. But as the years have gone by that's what I do and I've always explained it to myself that you take a single subject—I'm too dumb, I don't know enough just to stick to that, I've got to get a second and maybe even a third and tie these things together, see the similarity in them, and use them to play off one another, their ironies. I'm always looking for ironies. It just evolves that way. But I am conscious when I get to the end that I've got to button it up, as they say, button it up with the top so it's logical, so people, when I finally get to the end, can see why these disparate subjects all got in the same column. It's a technique and it comes naturally to me after all these years.

Dutch Leonard said that one night when we were out, so when the book came up, I asked if he would say that in print. He did a good job of describing what I do. The start and the end are always the toughest part of the column. The first couple paragraphs I try to get going. As a much better writer, Sydney Harris, put it in one of his columns once, "One paragraph gives birth to the next paragraph." It does to me very well.

I've talked to some writers who don't believe that I don't know where I'm going once I start. I often won't know where I'm going to go; often one paragraph gives me the idea for the next paragraph and so on. That's why these notes are written. One paragraph will give me an idea for a paragraph six paragraphs later and I don't want to forget it, so I reach over and make that note on a pad. I'll start columns and I'll end up going where I had no idea I was going to go. I'll just get a crazy idea and go with it.

So that's my idea. I don't have writer's block. Some people if they can't get their original idea of what they're going to write, the whole idea, or outline it in their mind or on a pad, they don't even start. I never do that. I say, "Well, I don't have much of an idea here, so let's write this first paragraph; maybe that'll give me an idea for the second."

Root. How did things come together on this one? How much work was it to get that—any false starts, any place where you changed direction?

Fitzgerald. No. A lot depends on what I've got going on that day. I might go in at ten with no pressure and not come home till four. But if the grandchildren are coming or if I have an appointment in the afternoon, I'll get right to it at ten to get this out of the way, because I don't want to go back in the office. With this one I was done at twelve-thirty. It took two and a half hours, the whole thing. I've had days where I was done in an hour. Other days it's harder. I think the longest I've taken is five hours.

Root. Have you ever given up and came back the next day?

Fitzgerald. Never. I never started anything I didn't finish. Some new people in the business will ask, "Isn't there some day that you just can't do it? just want to say, 'Oh, the hell with it,' and come back later?" It just kills me. I just hate to waste it. Even if I know its lousy I'll go back and edit it, make it a little better, but I'm damned if when I've spent a few hours on it, I'll *throw* it away.

If there's a rush I can get them done much quicker, but most days there isn't. After all that's all I do. Based on the fact that I'm back here in the afternoon, people think I don't work at all.

Root. Out of that list how soon in the process do you know you have a topic? You don't sit down to write unless you know pretty much what's going to come out, right?

Fitzgerald. The big decision made every day—and it probably determines if it's worth a column—is what to write about. No matter how many things you have in a folder, you're more likely to write about what's on the top of your mind. Something's happened, something's in the daily paper, the Challenger has blown up, you want to comment. Most days I think about it while I'm walking to work and generally I'll have a pretty good idea of what I want to write about. Lots of times I'll have that one topic.

What was that stupid column about the Puffalumps? That thing, a release about a promotional contest nominating local celebrities to be Puffalump dolls, arrived on my desk a few days ago, and I thought it was stupid. I had no intention of writing about it. What was on top of my mind that day coming to work was what I thought was a dumb move by Richard Chrysler. The point was he was against tax amnesty but he'll take advantage of it because it's legal. And he spent a lot more money than that on advertising. What a stupid thing. I'm sitting there and there's this Puffalump doll on my desk and I said, "Well, I was nominated to be a Puffalump and this clown wasn't. That's probably why." A crazy idea but that's my style and if I don't do it a little different, if I write a straight column, it would be an editorial saying, "Chrysler's a jerk because he did this." That wouldn't have any originality or anything innovative in it, which is what I try to do. If I wanted to write editorials, I'd write editorials. So I tie in there with the Puffalumps, get a few laughs, at the same time make a point.

Incidentally, there were ten nominees for the Puffalump contest and I came in ninth. The only guy I beat was the guy from the *News*.

That's an example where one thing was on the top of my mind, this Chrysler deal, and this other crazy thing ninety-nine times out of a hundred I never would have written anything about, but this one time I tied the two together. It's a pretty strenuous tie. What Leonard is referring to at the very end is that you knot it together so how I knotted that together was, "I'm against the Puffalump contest, but if I win it I'll take whatever comes with it in the spirit of Richard Chrysler who did the same thing." That's reaching pretty far, but that's what I do.

Root. Can you think of a topic you've rejected? On that list are there things where you say, "There's just no way I'm ever going to do that"?

Fitzgerald. I don't know if rejection is the word or not, but it's just that I can't make it work. I can't come up with an idea. What happens is I'll end up with all these things that were never developed into an entire column and I'll write a potpourri column. That's what I did Saturday. I hate to do that because I always figure there is a whole column there; if I use seven items in a potpourri column that might have been seven separate columns.

Some of these things I just could never work into a whole column. I'll do something like: "According to the newspapers Brooke Shields just celebrated her twenty-first birthday. That has to be nonsense. I'll swear I've been sick of Brooke Shields for at least forty years." That's just one thing. I might have been able to develop that into a whole column. I think I could've but I didn't because it reminded me of the next item. At a banquet a few weeks ago a guy said, "Fitzgerald's got to be a phony. He says his granddaughter Emily is four years old, but I've been reading about that kid for at least eight years." Same deal.

Anyway, sometimes all of these items don't develop into a whole column. A lot just don't get used at all. They get old. I usually save up to two months, then take the folder and throw it away and start a new one. People can't believe that either: "There might have been some good ideas." I'm sure there were, but if I kept them all I wouldn't have enough storage room. They do get old. So it doesn't bother me at all. Once in a while I'll get an idea and I'll think, "Geez, I wish I had that thing but I threw it away last week. That's too bad."

Root. So you never have to do any research, except as it's coming along.

Fitzgerald. We have a great library system at the *Free Press*, which is another reason I like to go to the office. Now, especially since it's on computer, you call up and if you have something you want them to run, they can get it just like that. I use the library probably less than anybody there. I interview very few people. If I can just get it from my head and out of my notes, that's the way I like it. Occasionally I have to call somebody up but it isn't that type of column, you know.

I do get material from readers through the mail or on the phone; quite often they'll give me good ideas or they'll have an experience that'll make a column. Generally it just comes out of this folder.

Root. Is there any way you can figure out what makes you save a particular piece out of the paper? You read the *Free Press*, the *News*, and the *New York Times?*

Fitzgerald. Just the two Detroit papers. I read *Newsweek, Playboy.* That's about it. I read the paper real closely, I read everything, and if you do two a day that takes a lot of time. I never go to bed before two o'clock, and I don't think I'd read them that closely if I wasn't writing. Very often the nugget that will strike me will be the bottom of the story. Sometimes reporters don't realize that they've got something there. For somebody, its a throwaway line in an interview, but that strikes me. It's usually ironical, like that Ann Landers thing, something that will be grist for my mill, to use a cliché.

Root. Does doing this column make you always look for topics for the column? Are you constantly aware of deadlines?

Fitzgerald. Yeah, but it's unconscious. As I've often said, I lead the same life I'd lead if I were a milkman. I just lead the life I like to lead. So unconsciously I'm picking up on all these things. Things I reject doing often became topics for a column not because I did them but because I didn't do them and why I didn't do them. I think I have a great job because I go where I want to go and do what I want to do. Sometimes a column comes out of it—if it does I can put it on my expense account; if a column doesn't come out of it, okay. I had a good time anyway.

Root. What do you see as your relationship to the material? The role that you play in the articles? What kind of persona are you trying to convey, about yourself?

Fitzgerald. Every so often some readers will write to Bob Talbert of the *Free Press,* who publishes what readers write, and someone wrote the other day, "How did Fitzgerald ever keep out of the seminary?" Well, obviously whoever wrote that has the impression that I come off like a saint sometimes. That's not the image I try to project but I can understand people reacting that way because the most popular subject I write about, according to my readers, is my grandchildren, particularly Emily. People *beg* for more stuff about her, and I hate taking credit for that because you're supposed to love your grandchildren. That's obvious.

But other images I give aren't that popular. I'm a peacenik. I always have been. I marched and all that stuff since I was a kid, Vietnam War and all that kind of thing. I've got a great following because of that kind of thing from people who agree with me and when we go to those kind of banquets my wife and kids almost throw up from all the adulation I get. On the other hand the people who disagree with me have the image of a wimp or whatever. They hate my guts and I get nasty mail from them. I try to mix 'em up. I love to hear from people who say, "I hated that one but I liked this one." At least you've got them coming back every day and seeing what you're writing about.

Root. Does that have any impact on what you do? Do you feel that if you did an Emily column on Monday that you can't do a Michelle column on Wednesday? That it has to be something else? In the course of the week are there different things you're trying to do?

Fitzgerald. Definitely. I try to mix 'em up. Generally the columns about Emily would come from when she's around, and I don't see her that often, but when she comes she stays a few days and there might be material there for three or four columns. But I only write the one and leave in the file the notes on another and it might get in a month later or might not. You're right. If I wrote about a particular subject yesterday, any subject, I'm not going to write about it today. I mix 'em up, I always have.

Root. Do you ever worry about repetition?

Fitzgerald. Yeah, and I feel guilty of repetition even if I don't treat the same subject—actually I probably don't write about Emily twelve times a year, maybe a little more. That isn't a lot out of 192 columns a year.

But if you've been writing about the same subject since 1951—I used to write about my kids in the same way I write about my grandkids now. I've been anti-hunting, anti-war, anti-this and that. So I feel repetitious and I've got to remind myself that people don't remember as well as I remember. Not only that but I keep a file in the office—I probably should have mentioned that—I keep clips of every column I've written since '51 and they're categorized roughly, for instance, sports, hunting. I get on a subject and I'll reach down and use maybe word for word something I wrote fifteen years ago. I'll consciously try to change it because I feel that's repetitive.

If you've been doing it as long as I've been doing it, there are only so many subjects and I don't think I've ever changed my mind on anything; you're bound to repeat yourself.

Root. Do you know what you're going to do on Monday?

Fitzgerald. No. I almost consciously don't even think about it. I'm just relaxing and I know it might be something out of the folder but more likely it'll be something I'll read in the paper on Sunday or Monday morning. The first thing I do every morning is read the paper. I take a commentary role. Sometimes I feel like a scavenger. Sometimes I thank the reporters. They did all the work and I have all the fun.

Root. This one that came in today, "Crime Coverage." Do you recall anything about when you decided to do that?

Fitzgerald. Yeah. That appeared on Friday so I wrote that on Wednesday. That's when that story came out. I listen to WJR, it wakes me up in the morning, and the news program played a tape of Mayor Young complaining about the crime coverage and in a very quick phrase he said something about "'writing only sensational stories' to quote from a *Detroit News* memo." Well, he was referring back ten years. The *Free Press* didn't pick up on it at all. The *News* ran a transcript. Nobody caught what he was talking about with that reference to a memo, but it struck me right away. I said, "Hell, that's that same memo that I had all the trouble with and they wouldn't run the column ten years ago and I still have it in my file." I knew right then I had a column.

I just went to work and wrote it. The minute I heard that I knew I had it. It gave me a chance to take a crack at Luedtke who's leading the fight against the Joint Operating Agreement between the *Free Press* and the *News*—it gave me a chance to have a little fun with him and how I ruined his career because he cancelled the column. He's a good friend and he'll get a kick out of all that; he could introduce me to Meryl Streep. You get that idea and you've got to fill it out so you get a chance to take a little jab at him, take a little jab at JOA, take a jab at the editor who killed the last column. He's still here and he probably read that; I don't know how funny he thought it was.

Root. There's a line in there about Luedtke "out on the street scrabbling to make a living writing Academy Award-winning screenplays"; you're trying to twit him but there's also a compliment in there so that he may feel a poke but may say you're actually not treating him very harshly—you're identifying him as a very important person. Did you want to do that, temper that that way?

Fitzgerald. Yeah, that's exactly what I wanted to do. I do that all the time. I just call it satire. It's a bit of exaggeration. It's what I call disagreeing without being disagreeable. But he knows and most readers know what I'm saying. It's ridiculous for me to suggest that his leaving the *Free Press* would have anything to do with the fact that he killed my column. It's ridiculous for me to suggest that, but I'm going to suggest it anyway. I make it clear that I'm not very serious about that by saying, "Yeah, the poor guy had to go out and become famous and win an Academy Award."

Root. In a sense it gives you a character that I think the reader sees through, as one who has misunderstood the situation.

Fitzgerald. They know I really haven't and it's really self-deprecatory. It's a little jab at myself for even suggesting such a thing. It's a technique. I do it all the time. Readers see through that, they see through it all. I'll write about my big sister as "Terrible Jean." Terrible, hell. And they all know I love her and they tell me that. I know they see through it when I do it. It's just humor, satire. It's all based on exaggeration, I think.

Root. How long did it take you to write the Luedtke piece?

Fitzgerald. Let's see, I wrote that Wednesday. That didn't take long at all, because I had the idea when I sat down, before I started, and that's one I saved notes on. I know I was making notes while I was doing it. The minute I got into the fact that I was going to write about that old memo, immediately I'm into the fact that the guy who cut it was Luedtke and I knew I could have some fun with him.

This is what I mean about paragraphs spawning paragraphs: the minute I'm into him I'm into the fact that currently he's fighting the JOA and I know I can make a little crack about that so I did this obvious piece of satire—what the hell was it? Oh yeah—"I understand Luedtke's writing an expose-type screenplay about two boys, born in different hospitals, who grow up to be Siamese twins and endanger the free enterprise system by jointly agreeing to operate the same waterfront joint (WJJOA)." It's quick satire and I know he'll get a kick out of that and it gives me a chance to make *that* point. And by then the column is about written and I've made all these points and hopefully twitted your curiosity, and then I've got to explain it, why Luedtke pulled the column—and he had a good point—and then once I've got that explained, I got to say what's in the memo and that Mayor Young is saying the very same things he said ten years ago and my response, which I took almost word for word from the ten-year-old column that never got printed, so I finally got some use out of that. I don't feel so bad about wasting the time. By then the column's over and I get to the end and what I did up here I knew was going to happen; if I said there were two killed and I'm only going to talk about one, somebody's going to wonder what that second one was, so I use that to close the column.

Root. How quickly did you know you were going to use that ending?

Fitzgerald. It was another example of one paragraph spawning another. Going in all I knew was I was going to write about that ten-year-old memo. Then that brought up Luedtke and then it occurred to me what he was doing about the JOA. I didn't know all these things when I started. It just came to me. The minute I'm going to say, "Well, I've only had one killed in two thousand," that's not right, I've had two killed—the other was just a couple months ago—so I mention having two killed and the moment I mention that, I know that later on I've got to say something about that second column.

My motto as an editor and later as a columnist—and I have a son who writes and he gets tired of me telling him this—"Never raise any questions that you don't answer." If you haven't got the answer, don't raise the question. If I wasn't going to say something about that second column that was killed, I never would have mentioned it. I could have lied and said they only killed one. Nobody would have known the difference.

Root. Can you think of a piece you've published that you're not satisfied with?

Fitzgerald. In particular? That's always a problem. I'm asked that quite a bit. I don't think I've ever reread one, maybe after a month's time or upward of two years, where I haven't seen where I could have made it better—maybe just one paragraph, one word—"God, why didn't I say that?" I don't disagree that I should have written it—I just didn't do as well as I could have. Maybe I should have worked a little harder on it, because I do spend a lot of time going for the right word or the right sentence. So I could read over these right here and think of a better way to do them.

Root. In the Dick Chrysler-Puffalump piece you said something about the way in which you drew that together, that it was a more tenuous connection.

Fitzgerald. You always think, "I could've done better, I could've done better." I think that's kind of tenuous and silly.

Root. Is there a point at which you say, "This is good enough to print but it's not good enough for the Pulitzer Prize?"

Fitzgerald. Nothing I ever wrote was good enough for that. Yeah. Definitely. I'll tell you what I think; probably all columnists do it. I think back to the weekly. Running your own paper—of course you're the editor too—you put in what you want to. Coming to the big time, in the *Free Press* and syndicated in a few other papers, if you read other columnists and they're in the big time, you think, "Hell, I can do better than that." It's the same line of thought as, "This is good enough to go in because there's things in the papers around here that aren't as good as this." It's still not very good, but it's good enough. You can't hit a home run every time you're up to bat. So you do have favorites. You find that out at the end of every year when they ask you—I have to do it—to pick out your ten best of the year for contests and you have to prove it and there always is. When I get done with one I think is really good I'm conscious of it.

Root. Tom Wicker, when he wrote three columns a week, said in *On Press* that about a third of his columns were first-rate. The rest were professional. What do you think would be your percentage?

Fitzgerald. Not that good. I like to think they're professional—that's a good word—and I strive for consistency. I'm prouder of that than anything else. I like to keep the level consistently high and I think I do for the type of thing I do. I mean, I'm no big brain on any particular subject so you got to write on general interest. I go for laughs more than anything else. When they get to end of the year and it comes time for the contest, I have a hell of a time picking out ten first-rate ones, whatever percentage that is. You always start out to say something, no matter what your approach is—if it's silly you write on silly stuff—there's always a point, you want to say something. Maybe the next day I read it and say, "Did I say what I wanted to say?" And then, "How well did I say it?" And then every once in a while, like the thing I wrote on Ann Landers for Monday, I think I said what I wanted to say.

Root. When you put together the book, *If It Fitz,* after writing two thousand columns, how difficult was it to find the stuff?

Fitzgerald. I had to pick approximately 140. At the time I thought an editor was going to weed that down to a little less, but they only weeded one out. Getting 140 out of approximately 1800, I sat there several nights in a row just thumbing through them and picking out the ones I thought might be worth putting in a book. Well, when I went through the first time I had less than a hundred. In other words, I couldn't find enough good ones either. So I had to go back and dig a little deeper to come up with 140, and some of them shouldn't be in there. But, yeah, it was hard to find ones. I always try to put on a humble image anyway. I'm proud of being humble. That's a contradiction right there. But I finally got them, categorized them.

Root. What were your criteria for putting the book together?

Fitzgerald. It was all the *Free Press*'s idea and I'll do anything for money. My criteria was getting 140. They didn't want to go back beyond anything I'd written for the *Free Press,* because I've got a million of those, so I started in 1976 and went through '83 or '84. My criteria were always what I liked the best. I write to satisfy myself. I don't know how else to do it. I knew I'd written some stuff about my mother dying that I liked; come right off the top of my head and I knew that I liked it. So I picked them and then I had to get the balance.

Root. There aren't any potpourri columns in there. Did you say, "It's got to be a solid piece and it's got to be in one of these categories: Just for Laughs; etcetera"?

Fitzgerald. There is another criteria that I should have mentioned. They've got to be timeless. So many, particularly the way they're written, are based on a big news item the day before. You don't have to explain the news item because people know what you're talking about *then,* but not five years later. So I would say that easily eliminated half the columns. Like this thing here, taking cracks at Richard Chrysler because there's a campaign going on. No one's going to want to read that five years from now.

Root. Are there any topics where you've gotten halfway through a draft and then quit on it?

Fitzgerald. No, I'm too lazy. If I get halfway through I'll feel like I wasted whatever time I spent on it and I can't stand to waste it. I'll finish it if it kills me. I don't think I've ever started a column I didn't finish.

Root. What kinds of revision do you do?

Fitzgerald. It's generally paring down. When you start out you might think, Boy, can I say enough about this subject and get my fourteen inches?, but generally they're too long. You have to go back and take something out probably nine times out of ten. I was an editor for so many years and with the new technology you edit as you go along. It is conscious. When I'm writing, up early in the column, and getting a little too silly or a little too smart in the back of my mind I usually say to myself, "Well, I'll probably take this out later," and I usually do. Because if it gets too long, you leave the best stuff in and take out the crap.

Root. Is that preferable to having to add?

Fitzgerald. Yeah. I prefer a short column. I never have padded. It's always trimming down. Sometimes you trim as you do it. I'll say, "I could put this in," but it would make it too long so I wouldn't put it in. Or I'll put it in knowing I'll probably take it out. That's the beautiful part of writing on the word processor—it's so easy to edit and take it out. Back when I was doing it on a typewriter it got so hen-scratched you had to start all over again to get a clean copy. I probably threw away six or seven or eight false starts. That's why I love this machine. It probably takes an hour off the working time on the column.

Root. You said you do a lot of worrying about sentences and the right word. In the Ann Landers thing, for example, can you think of any changes that you made there where you altered sentences?

Fitzgerald. The start is usually the big struggle, to get that lead and then the next couple of paragraphs. I think I had some false starts on that. Some things I put in there just for effect, like the thing about the dealers getting together one dark night. That wasn't in there at first. I put that in later.

I avoid clichés like death, and when I do use them, I make fun of myself for using them. I just try to say it differently. I think Elmore Leonard said something about that in his introduction, about my avoiding clichés. I want to sound a little different so I will sit there for a while thinking, What's the way to say this? I think when I said something about Roger Smith delivering a car to my front door I could have left it at that, but I added, "along with a payment book." I think that's a little funnier and more honest too. Makes more of a difference between me and Ann Landers.

Generally, as I say, one paragraph spawns another and I'm making notes with my right hand. I couldn't get into banks without pointing out why half the teller windows are always closed. Certain things

I harp on all the time. When I use a certain word sometimes I'll think there's some humor attached to it. Maybe it's unusual or just automatically funny, like New Jersey. I can't find anything in here but I'll do that frequently and I won't know I'm going to do it. I'll just use the word because it's the right word but it's a real strange word. I have a phrase I used a few years ago, "harking back." I'll get further down the column then I'll "hark back" to that funny word. It's all technique, I guess. You do it automatically after you've been doing it so many years. It just happens. It's hard for me to talk about it or explain it because it just happens.

Root. Is there a Jim Fitzgerald kind of sentence?

Fitzgerald. I don't think so. I try and pride myself on being understood. I want to be clear. On the average I've always come up with short paragraphs and short sentences. I'll throw in an occasional long sentence, maybe real long, just for the effect. It doesn't matter how long the sentence is, just as long as it progresses logically and doesn't have dependent clauses that you don't understand. I want to be clear and to be understood.

Crime Coverage Has Been Touchy Topic for Ten Years

Jim Fitzgerald

On Monday, while criticizing the crime reporting by local media, Mayor Young mentioned an old *Detroit News* memo that asked employees to produce sensational front-page stories that would be talked about at suburban cocktail parties. I remember that memo. It inspired me to write a column that the *Free Press* refused to publish.

That was about ten years ago, when Kurt Luedtke was our executive editor. Killing something I wrote was obviously the beginning of the end of Luedtke's newspaper career. Only a few years later he was out in the street, struggling to make a living by writing Academy Award-winning screenplays.

Luedtke is now living in obscurity, a suburb of Birmingham, still trying to deal with the guilt of having kept my art from the reading public, not to mention countless canary cages. Also, I understand Luedtke is writing an expose-type screenplay about two boys, born in different hospitals, who grow up to become Siamese twins and endanger the free enterprise system by jointly agreeing to operate the same waterfront joint (WJJOA).

I still have that rejected column. During the past ten years, I've written two thousand columns and the *Free Press* nixed only two of them. I keep them in my desk as a constant reminder that 1,998 times out of 2,000, it's less trouble to write about my grandchildren.

As I recall, Luedtke rejected that column not because of what it said, but because of its source, which was the aforementioned memo. A *Detroit News* employee swiped the memo from the *News* city room and leaked it all over the Anchor Bar, reaching my stool. Memos are also written at the *Free Press*, and Luedtke didn't want to encourage

---

such incestuous journalistic thievery by publishing the loot in my column.

However, the memo eventually leaked into Mayor Young's office, and he read it very aloud at a news conference, resulting in widespread publicity and tch-tch-tiching about the news policy of the *News*. So, ten years later, and in the context of Mayor Young's remarks Monday, I guess I can revive that rejected column without defying or offending a former editor who was unquestionably correct, not to mention he could introduce me to Meryl Streep.

The memo, written by the front-page editor, suggested the ideal front-page story "won't have a damn thing to do with Detroit and its internal problems" but should instead be "the horrors that are discussed at suburban cocktail parties." A recent report about a rape and mugging in downtown Detroit was cited as "a fine example" of the type of news desired.

That was ten years ago, remember. But Mayor Young believes at least some local media still trash the city for the entertainment of the suburbs. My comment today is the same as in 1976:

The mayor is nuts if he thinks only suburban cocktailers discuss rape, mugging and break-in horrors. Those are hot topics at city parties, too. And the dismayed talkers come in all colors.

But that doesn't justify a constant run of such horror stories on the front page or the top of TV news shows. When an article makes the front page, it is supposed to be more important or more interesting to more people than the articles on ninety-one inside pages. And, due to TV's built-in constrictions, if the news isn't page one or two material, it probably shouldn't be on television at all.

Most days, I'll strongly defend the *Free Press* against Mayor Young's charges that some other criteria—such as race or geography—are used in reporting crime news. The rest of the media can take care of themselves.

Finally, I mentioned earlier that the *Free Press* has rejected two of my columns in ten years, and you probably want to know what I wrote in the second one. Interestingly, it also concerned the *Detroit News* and racism. But I'm running out of space.

Besides, the editor who killed that gem of art hasn't yet been forced out into the street to scrape for a living by winning Academy Awards.

When It Comes to Taxes, This Chrysler Uses a Dodge

Jim Fitzgerald

Republican gubernatorial candidate Richard Chrysler was not nominated for most puffalumpable personality. I was. It's not surprising.

Chrysler says he's against Michigan's tax amnesty program. But he also says he'll use the program to avoid paying about $147,500 in penalties his company owes the state for not paying taxes on time.

If the state "wants to allow that, then it's a prudent business decision to take advantage of it," Chrysler said.

Chrysler is also against abortion. But if he were the pregnant mother of eight children, and couldn't afford to feed one more, would he take advantage of what the state allows—legal abortion? It would be a prudent business decision.

Here's a guy who will spend uncounted hundreds of thousands of his own dollars on campaign advertising, but he won't pass up the chance to stick the state—the taxpayers—for $147,500, even though he thinks the amnesty program gives tax laggards—like himself—an undeserved break at the expense of people honest enough to pay their taxes on time.

Whatever happened to principles? Chrysler had a splendid opportunity and blew it. He could have refused to make money off an unfair program supported by the Democratic governor he wants to replace. He could have been a hero—a man of principle—to a lot of voters.

If he'd said to hell with the money, Chrysler would have gotten more favorable publicity for $147,500 than he could buy with a billion dollars worth of boring TV commercials.

I understand why Chrysler was late paying some taxes—it was another "prudent business decision." I don't understand why he can't see what a mistake it is to grab that $147,500. Anyone that dumb shouldn't be governor.

So it's not surprising that Chrysler wasn't even nominated for the local puffalumpable title. Lee Iacocca was. So were Kirk Gibson and Isaiah Thomas. Also seven representatives of the media—J.P. McCarthy of WJR, Chuck Gaidica of WJBK-TV (Channel 2), Steve Gannon on WNIC, Steve Garagiola of WXYZ-TV (Channel 7), Tom Greenwood of the Detroit News, Dwayne X. Riley of WDIV-TV (Channel 4) and me.

The nominations were made by Fisher-Price, makers of a new line of plush dolls called Puffalumps. They are described as "high-touch" toys, as opposed to the "high-tech" variety that encourages children to blow away the world in the spirit of Rambo and G.I. Joe.

To hype the sale of Puffalumps, a "Mother's Opinion Poll" will be held at Northland Center on Thursday. Participants will be asked to rate the "Puffalump Quotient" of the 10 "Puffalumpable Personalities" nominated for the honor.

Can you hardly stand it?

Puffalumps are described by Fisher-Price as "an irresistibly soft feather light soft toy that asks to be hugged and squeezed."

I'm betting that Dwayne X. Riley will finish first in the Puffalump Personality Poll. He is the only one of the nominees who looks like a Puffalump.

I certainly hope I don't win, because I'm against such phony contests. The world is full of people whose personalities are more puffalumpable than Lee Iacocca's, but he was nominated simply because he's famous. And I was nominated simply because Fisher-Price thought I'd be so flattered I'd give their toy free publicity.

I deeply resent anyone thinking I could be that easily swayed by puffalumpable glory.

However, the puffalumpable poll is allowed under Michigan law, so if I win it, I will prudently accept whatever cash goes with the dishonor. I will do this in the spirit of Richard Chrysler.

Yeah, but Could Roger Help Ann with Banking?

Jim Fitzgerald

A lot of people—not to mention the federal government—are apparently unhappy because practically all car dealerships in metropolitan Detroit are closed Saturdays.

They should write to Ann Landers.

There are allegations that the dealers got together one dark night and agreed Saturday closings would be a dandy way to cut overhead and limit competition—and to hell with working-stiff customers who want to spend one of their days off shopping the dealerships.

But so what? Ann Landers would advise you it's easy to buy a car even if the dealerships are closed everyday.

I'll admit it used to bug me that Detroit area dealers were the only ones in the nation to close en masse on Saturdays. Although it probably should be noted that I get even madder at bankers' hours.

My bank—and many others—is not only closed Saturdays. It is closed until 9:30 A.M. and after 4 P.M. every weekday. This is in a world where normal working hours are 9 A.M. to 5 P.M. So, besides Saturdays, people also can't do their banking before or after work on Monday through Friday. (Some branches extend Friday hours if you don't mind driving that far.)

However everybody is free to spend their payday lunch hour lined up in front of twelve teller windows, six of which are closed.

Why doesn't the Federal Trade Commission investigate banks as well as car dealers? Perhaps because of automatic tellers. You can use them twenty-four hours a day but you can't get similar service by sticking a plastic card into a car dealer's mouth.

Automatic tellers are fine for withdrawing cash if there's some in your account, but don't try to borrow any. And I'm afraid to make an

---

Reprinted with the permission of the *Detroit Free Press*.

automatic deposit for fear I'll make a mistake and send my money in the wrong direction, creating a computer glitch that will take the bank sixteen years to untangle.

But you don't care about that. You want to hear Ann Landers' advice on buying cars. She gave it in Ralph Nader's latest book, "The Big Boys," recently excerpted in the Free Press. She described how easy it is to buy a Cadillac:

"In 1983, I called and said I had a 1980 Cadillac limousine. I wanted a new car. Baby blue, everything on it. A glass window separating passengers from the chauffeur. He said, 'They're hard to find, but I'll get you one.' The next morning—and I had called him late in the day—he had a car for me. A 1983 Cadillac. He said it was in a suburb and that he could have it to me by 3 P.M. . . . . It was perfect. He phoned all over the country and found precisely the car I wanted."

Who was "he"—the car salesman Ann Landers phoned? He was Roger Smith, chairman of General Motors. I don't know if she phoned on Saturday.

That's why I'm no longer concerned about when car dealerships are closed. I'm sure Roger Smith is no elitist. He has a feel for the ordinary guy working on his production lines. He wouldn't do anything for Ann Landers that he wouldn't do for me.

So the next time I need a new car, I'll just phone good old Roger and tell him exactly what I want. He'll deliver it to my door the next day, along with the payment book. You can do the same thing, and the dealerships won't ever have to open.

While I have Roger on the line, I'll ask if he agrees with the FTC that Detroit area dealers got together one dark night and conspired to increase profits by closing Saturdays.

Also, I'll ask what he would do if all cities and states got together one dark night and conspired to help ordinary taxpayers by no longer giving tax breaks and free lollipops to auto manufacturers looking for the cheapest place to build a factory.

If that happened, would Roger Smith write to Ann Landers?

Interview with Kathleen Stocking

Root. What does *Detroit Monthly* ask of you? Is there any set thing about length, regularity of deadlines, style?

Stocking. They don't specify a lot of that except length, and I spend a lot of time putting stuff in and taking stuff out to make it exact.

Root. What is the length?

Stocking. The length is about fifteen hundred words; there's a little play with that—it could be twelve hundred or eighteen hundred. I usually write about eighteen hundred and then I edit from there. I've found that editors like to play around with your copy. If I give them a little more, then they have something to play around with. I'm better off writing long and taking stuff out than writing short and putting stuff in.

Root. You write on a typewriter. How long does it come out in pages, double-spaced?

Stocking. Double-spaced, sixty characters a line, six and a half to seven and a half pages. Usually before I edit, it's about ten pages.

Root. Is that different from what *Metropolitan Detroit* wanted?

Stocking. *Metropolitan Detroit* was the one that gave me the original charge. It was something like fifteen hundred to eighteen hundred words and a topic about this area. *Detroit Monthly* wanted a similar thing. They don't really tell you what to write about in terms of topics at all.

I couldn't get the original editor at *Metropolitan Detroit* to tell me what to write about. She would say, "Well, tell me about your neighbors, tell me about real people," but probably she didn't want reality. She wanted what she thought was reality. I had to try to figure out what that might be and come up with the idea that reality to her was some kind of counterbalance to the things about urban culture she didn't like. She kept saying, "Write about your neighbors." There's an assumption there that I *have* neighbors, which I don't really anymore than she does. Does anyone have neighbors anymore? So I had to extrapolate from the few little clues she was giving me, do a little psychology, imagining that she imagined she wanted a slower-paced life, for instance, or more contact with people on a daily basis in a presumably more natural way. She wanted *cousins,* probably.

There's an infinite amount of psychology that goes into writing, into closing the gap between writer and editor, writer and reader, and the most awkward part for the writer, morally, is that you always have to start from where they're starting from and kind of work them over toward your way of looking at things, little by little. Every writer dreams of a perfect audience, but that rarely happens. The challenge in writing is to find something that connects to as many people as possible without getting down to the lowest common denominator: sex and violence.

Root. Do you see what you're doing for *Detroit Monthly* as different from what anyone else is doing in the magazine?

Stocking. Oh, it's quite different. I don't know if you're aware of this, but my columns deal with ethics and morality and basic philosophy of life and what we would call basic truths. I don't think people know it yet, but I think the sense of values and a real philosophy of life have kind of been leeched from the culture since, say, the American Revolution when people had a clear sense of who they were and their purpose and knew they didn't want to be governed by a monarch. They wanted freedom and that sort of was a guiding principle in their life. Now, people think they want money but I don't think they really do. So I have to meet emotional needs with that column that people probably wouldn't be able to articulate and wouldn't be able to own.

I don't really tell my editors what I'm doing and why. I find if I do that they get preconceived ideas. They get too involved too early.

Root. How often do you have to do this? Once a month?

Stocking. It was once a month at *Metropolitan Detroit* and every other month at *Detroit Monthly.*

Root. What other kind of writing are you doing?

Stocking. I'm doing a travel piece for *Travel and Leisure* on the Leelanau Peninsula and I'm doing a piece for *Diversion Magazine* on American Spoonfoods up in Petoskey, who forage wild plants for very trendy, expensive New York restaurants.

Root. Do you very often have things of that nature to work on?

Stocking. Yeah; that's real common. If I weren't doing those two pieces, I'd be working on a piece on open adoption for *Detroit Monthly* and a piece on Leelanau County hippies' children and what the values of these children are toward their parents for the *Detroit News.* And if I weren't working on *that* I'd be doing a book proposal with all the columns that I've done. I've just done a Michigan Council for the Arts

53

grant proposal as a book proposal. I want to write about one specific place.

It just sort of goes on and on. It's like housework. If you aren't cleaning the refrigerator you're doing the stove, and it doesn't matter what you do first, it all has to be done. I try to balance that with the kids, who really come first.

Root. What's your background? You've been writing about this area for ten years. How long have you been writing?

Stocking. I've been writing since I was a little kid. I went to Glen Lake High School and flunked everything my junior year on purpose and stayed home and drank bourbon and read James Joyce. My parents finally got the idea I wasn't happy with school, so they sent me to Buffalo, New York, where I lived with my sister and I did very well and got into the University of Michigan where, again, I think, from a big backlog of really poor teachers in a rural setting, I was not predisposed to love academic life.

At Glen Lake I had an hour and a half bus ride each way, so basically from 7:00 A.M. to 5:00 P.M. every weekday I was bored to death. I remember hours and hours each day of sitting. The teachers had little or no background or interest in their subjects. I learned how to daydream. When pressed I could do well on I. Q. tests, college entrance exams, that sort of thing, which is how I got into the U of M. I didn't do very well. They threw us all into an anthropology class with five hundred kids and it seemed beside the point to me. It wasn't until my junior year when I met Donald Hall that I really started writing. He was just a marvelous teacher. He was encouraging and he had a fine sense of writing.

I was an English major by default, not by design really, because I couldn't do anything else. Until I met Don Hall, I didn't work in school. English was just so easy for me. Then I wanted to please him. He was clearly working hard to help me learn to write better and so it was incumbent on me to respond in kind. I recognize, in retrospect, that he was a gifted teacher.

I was really self-taught and I had no background in science or math or perhaps no aptitude, but academically the high school I had gone to had been so poor that I wasn't able to do anything except English, and if I had had any decent guidance counselor I probably would have become a reporter then but I didn't know that was a career option for me, so I got a teaching certificate because I thought I could teach English, and I wrote poetry in both high school and college a lot and continued doing that and continued writing voluminously, letters, not just "writing" writing, and raising kids. Then, when I got divorced and moved back from New York City to Glen Arbor again, I got a job as a reporter for the Traverse City paper and I worked there for two years from 1977 to '79 and then met my present husband, got married, and have been just writing about this area ever since.

Root. Let me ask you about "Dreaming Detroit," a fairly recent column. I'm interested in how you happened to write that piece. Give me an example of how a typical column would come about. What's the process you go through? How does the idea come about?

Stocking. A typical column has its genesis months and even years before I actually write it. Sometimes . . . it's kind of like developing a friendship, particularly a male-female friendship where you are both very interested, almost psychic about each other, and very conniving at the same time, capable of arranging chance meetings, that kind of thing. That's the kind of relationship I have with my readership where just as if I were having a relationship with a man I might arrange to wear a dress in his favorite color or be playing a symphony that he loved at some propitious moment in order to intrigue him and bring him closer, the relationship with the reader is such that you're thinking, What are *their* needs? What are *their* interests? So that ultimately you get with them, mentally couple with them, if you will.

Sometimes in order to orient myself to my readers, I try to imagine that they—and I—all live in a little cave community on the shores of Lake Michigan—or anywhere, really, but I usually imagine some place I've seen—but imagine it a million years ago, in a primitive/basic setting. And my role is that of storyteller. They catch fish for me on the basis of how good I am. And how good I am depends on how well I connect with them, how much I give them for the long haul. So there's entertainment while we're sitting around the campfire after dinner, but I also have to give them hope, even when the physical rigors are awesome, to feel they can transcend. In order for entertainment to be any more than a sugar high, it's got to have something in there that will stay in the belly for a while.

I was very aware of the fact that Detroit has an inferiority complex. For awhile, the last five years, it was obvious to anybody who read the papers or read about the high murder rate, that Detroiters are always trying to puff themselves up and say, "Well, it's not that bad, we have development, we have the Renaissance Center, and gee, have you ever been on the Detroit River?" Obviously it's a very insecure, defensive kind of population—maybe for a good reason, you know—and so knowing that and knowing that's my audience, you sort of pulse with that information.

One very bleak period in the winter I thought, God, wouldn't it be great to go to Detroit and go to a museum and eat in a very expensive restaurant and maybe have $500 to spend and wander through Hudson's and maybe buy perfume and a silk dress and meet some mysterious, exotic stranger in a bar and have a conversation about poetry. And I kind of thought that and that's when I wrote the first sentence: "Detroit looms in the dead of winter up north like an oasis of civilization somewhere to the south of us." I had that line and I just scrawled it down. I thought, Well, maybe I'll never do anything with that.

Then last year *Michigan Quarterly* came out with a thing that Ovid wrote when he was in exile on the shores of the Black Sea. First of all, it was marvelous writing, as you can imagine. But it was real whiney: "Nobody understands me here" and "These people stink and they don't appreciate me," and he obviously didn't appreciate them either. At the time I found Ovid's writing about his exile I was having real feelings of alienation from the culture here, and I read that and laughed and gave it to friends of mine who were writers and we all laughed because writers feel like they're in exile no matter where they are. It was taped up on the window by my typewriter all winter.

An essay always has to have a counterpoint, a contrapuntal rhythm. You have to take two opposite perspectives and mirror them or mesh them or twist them in some way. So in "Dreaming Detroit" I took the Detroiters' feelings about themselves, their inferiority complex, my feelings about longing for contact, and mirrored them in myself for awhile. And yet there was a basic connivance in this too, in that I knew that Detroiters needed to feel good about themselves and I knew too that they would be receptive to something about them—everybody likes to hear about themselves so this is talking about them—but also in the process making them feel good about themselves by making them realize that the alternative to where they are is not so great either.

Root. Did you pick that out because you were moving to *Detroit Monthly* from *Metropolitan Detroit*, and this would be introductory?

Stocking. No, it just turns out that it was introductory. The way I moved to *Detroit Monthly* was not by design or choice, really. *Metropolitan Detroit* was having what they call "cash flow" problems and they were three months behind in paying me. I wrote a series of whiney letters and then basically I xeroxed the contract they had given me originally. So they were real miffed with me and I hit the streets and went to all the other Detroit publications. *Detroit Monthly* was delighted to have me, and they've actually been very good about paying and very easy to work with and they actually pay me more, so it's been a better place to work. Freelancing is like that. You'll burn yourself with an editor in some way; you'll burn a bridge and think, this is the end. Why did I ever do that? Now I'll never be able to write for anybody again. That sense of anomie: "If I don't get ink, do I exist?" And it's always happened that something else turned up. It is a lot like dating too, where you think when you break up there will never be another person but of course there always is.

Root. In "Dreaming Detroit," I noticed a couple of things about the structure of the piece. There's a sort of introductory passage which contains five paragraphs where you make that contrapuntal business there—you talk about life in the Leelanau in winter, dreaming of Detroit, and then it goes around to the part where you say, "I've spent a lifetime dreaming about Detroit," and then there's a transition paragraph where you set up the rest of the piece—"imagine we're chatting." Then you go through Aunt Myrtle from Detroit, Aunt Carol's shopping trip, Hervey's reminiscences of Detroit history, the Sears man's reminiscences of Detroit, Marianne Russell's longing for Detroit, Sue Kopka and the changes in Bloomfield Hills. And then there's a transition from there going back and talking about the Detroit-North contrast and then you come up with the conclusion, "while dreaming of Detroit, it's coming out to meet me." Okay, that's the way it goes. One question I don't have to ask is why Aunt Myrtle comes first; it's the earliest impression. But what kind of choices did you make there? Do you remember making any decisions about who or what went where?

Stocking. I had a ton of material. I interviewed not only Marianne Russell and Hervey Park but probably ten different people.

Root. Did you interview these people for this piece?

Stocking. Uh-huh.

Root. Out of all that stuff, obviously Aunt Myrtle, Aunt Carol and Mom are things you're calling from memory. Anything else?

Stocking. No, none of the rest are called from memory. I have a lot of memories. I lied. I implied that I had only been there twice. I'd actually been there other times. Writing is contrived, to some extent. You leave things out, put things in. Not always, but mostly it's contrived. There's a fine line between contrivance and craft. I think maybe that's what I call "tone." You "tone things up" and you "tone things down" until it sounds right.

Root. What about the order in which they came? For example, did you say to yourself, "I've got to have Sue Kopka last?"

Stocking. She's talking about the development that occurs in urban areas. I needed to make that transition to the end paragraphs, which I had developed sometime after I developed the first paragraph.

Root. So some part of what you're doing is going out to find data that will fill in a preconceived structure that you already have? You already know the conclusion that you're going to come to.

Stocking. That's right, I do. And it's a difficult practice. It's not always that easy. This piece, to me, seemed very cut and dried, too cut and dried. I felt, Ooo, I'm not going to be able to put this over on them because it's too obvious what I'm doing. I was late meeting the deadline. I wrote it and I didn't have an ending. I knew roughly what the ending had to be, and I tinkered with it, and I let it sit around and I thought, How am I going to end it in such a way that there's a feeling of resolution and completion, and the reader feels that it's come full circle? I really couldn't think of a way. I didn't just want to say, "It's nice to live in a place that's undeveloped." I didn't want to say, "Well, this place is getting to have some interesting people and some development too." You just can't talk like that anytime and have it be interesting. So the endline sort of came to me.

Root. So you're looking for some sort of perhaps thoughtful or peaceful or provocative conclusion that has a certain amount of punch to it rather than simply an ending.

Stocking. Uh-huh.

Root. When you did this, you said you scribbled the opening lines some place, then you saw the connection to Ovid later on, and then you had the conclusion. How much of the stuff do you record, do you write in process?

Stocking. Very little.

Root. Do you wait until you have a lot of stuff and then start writing? Do you wait until you have a full draft that you're intending to do or do you keep a notebook, a journal, a diary?

Stocking. No. Generally I get the idea for a column and then I do the research and then I do the writing and then I let it sit and then I refine it. I always use a long legal pad for the notes and ideas, and then I always use cheap newspaper-print typing paper—reams of it—when I actually do the typing. I'd probably love to have a computer to write on because I will change one sentence in the center of a piece, not like it, and then go back and retype the whole page again. It's really stupidly time-consuming. You want to see it both ways because you want to see how it's potentially going to hit the reader.

I save every draft, because what I have found is something that seems to me like a final draft will not be as good as a first draft sometimes, or I'll have to go back and rework a first draft and throw out what I thought was great a week ago. It's hard to know always. It is a real creative process and sometimes your sense of what's okay is much better when it's sat around for a week and you can look at it. When you write for a newspaper, you just write fast and you give it to the editor and the editor makes these judgments. I have to be my own editor now, so the only way I can do that is let it sit long enough so that I'm detached from it.

Root. Is there a pattern that you follow in the composition, like you have to do it every day, or you have to do it at a certain time of day, or on a certain place under certain conditions?

Stocking. I am happiest when I'm writing a full eight to ten hours a day. If I can get up in the morning and—ideally this is what I'd like—I can come in, sort everything, kind of tinker around, see what I'm going to work on—if I have a deadline, obviously that's what I'm working on. Sometimes it goes really well immediately and sometimes it doesn't, and I like to intersperse the deadline activity with something else, letters, or phone calls, or housework. Basically I like to have a warming-up period, I guess you would call it if you were an athlete, and then by eleven, I'm in gear and I like to just write madly until about six or seven at night with some breaks for coffee and no eating.

But I'm not in a position where I can do that. Usually my day is taken up with a five-year-old now. If she's at nursery school or at the sitter's it's usually only about four hours and if I drive that only gives me about two hours writing time. I barely get into it before I have to get out of it and that makes me very tense and a little like if you were falling asleep and someone kept waking you up. It makes me tense, agitated, distracted; my thinking rhythms have been disturbed a lot and I have learned, to the detriment of other things, to think about the writing when I'm driving, when I'm reading her stories, while I'm doing dishes, laundry, housework, errands, at the dentist's, at the car repair. I can think about the writing and do other things, but I sort of bifurcate and what happens with that is like the week I got back from California, I not only lost the contract for an article but my babysitter gave me the key to get her mail, and I not only lost the key but I didn't get her mail, and we went out to dinner as part of the research for the

Travel and Leisure thing and I forgot the checkbook. The bifurcation probably doesn't work too well for the writing either, but it means that other things just go out the window when they shouldn't.

Root. You said that "Dreaming Detroit" was kind of stilted. Can you think of a piece that's real good, one which, whatever way you got to it, you think is your best writing?

Stocking. I don't know if it's my best writing but it's one which was almost psychically generated, and that would be the one they called "Piecing the Ribbon Together"—that was not my original title—but when a piece is being born through you, not only will the pieces come in spite of you but it's almost like incidents will happen that will feed into it. Like seeing the two nuns chasing the swan across the causeway in Lake Leelanau and this other woman coming down the hill with her basket at the same time, and somehow those images are so strong, you don't know how, but you know it's part of the piece.

A guy who directed at Cherry County Playhouse one summer who sat next to me on a plane said it was uncanny, but whenever he needed props for a play he'd just think about it and, if it was an old black umbrella, he'd invariably find it in a trashcan while he was walking around during the time that he need the props. Some odd thing that he'd never thought he'd find and always it was there. A piece that comes like that you feel that you're being used by the Great Unknown or whatever it is, and sometimes that happens, where something almost seems to be generated by the karma of the planet and not really by you. There are some pieces where you say, "*This* I did." There are other pieces where all you are is a conduit; the piece writes itself.

Usually it's obvious to me when a writer has contrived or crafted a piece—you can see the structure. V. S. Naipul said writing should be transparent and the best writing probably is, but that's not always possible. It comes more often to some than to others. I don't know why. The more structured writing is good to learn from—it's kind of like seeing the "framing-in" part of house building, where you can see the bones or inner structure of the thing. You could really learn on this piece. I have writers I learn from where I know they had a deadline and their heart wasn't in it and it's real structured and that helps me learn how to write. The pieces that might have come through them, where the writing is transparent, you can't learn too much because you can't see the structure.

Root. Take a look at "Piecing the Ribbon Together" and tell me what you remember about the composition of it.

Stocking. This was cut a lot too; at one point one of the images that came to me real strongly on this was a place in France, in Normandy, where, in order to keep the Vikings out—they'd just been victorious in a skirmish—they just cut all those guys' heads off and put them on posts as a warning. I think I'd read about it somewhere but I felt a deep response to that knowing that I could have been either the Viking or the Norman. I thought, We're the people who make the wars because we're the same people who cut off the heads of the Vikings and put them on posts. And my editor took it out because he felt it was too strong—rightly or wrongly, I really don't know.

Root. Did you decide on this topic, as you said before, and then have to go out and research it? Did you go off to the piecing together thinking, There's an article here; I've got to show up for this thing so I can get an article out of it?

Stocking. Right, right. They invited me. My very sweet hippie friend said, "You've got to help us work on the peace ribbon," and my first reaction was, "Oh, you've got to be kidding." They're always doing something like that—they're quilting to save the world or to save the trees or to save the dolphins or something and they always want me to do it with them, and I think they're wonderful people but I know that I'm so cynical, and so busy also, but this, I thought, this is almost like a metaphor; this is going to be great. So, yes, I did. I deliberately went thinking if this doesn't give me a column I'll be surprised.

Root. Did it begin where you say it begins?

Stocking. Actually it did. We went to dinner and my friend was telling me she was working on this peace ribbon and wouldn't I like to work on it with her? And my immediate response was, "Oh heavens, no," and then my second response was, "Yeah." So I began working on the column before we actually ended up putting those pieces together.

The Jehovah's Witnesses had been coming by every two weeks for three months, and at first I had been kind of intrigued by them, but I had been about to tell them to bug off when I started working with the idea of this column and thought, No, I'm going to let them in; I'm going to include them in this article if I possibly can. So I just kind of led them on and led them on and there they were in the column. But I felt it had to do with that because in their own way they were seeking simple solutions to complex problems just as my ladyfriends do with the peace ribbon or just as the people who want to drop bombs are seeking simple solutions to complex problems. That *is* a human tendency, you know. That's what I saw always as so dumb about nuclear war but also, quite honestly, real dumb about the peace ribbon. Again, it was that mirroring effect. This is the polar opposite of this, but they mirror each other in their human quality. You can't come right out and say stuff like that in essays, as I'm sure you know. You offend people. You can't tell them unvarnished truths but you can lead them down the garden path.

Root. The structure of this essentially starts with the dinner and what happens that night—did you actually have a dream about the ribbon?

Stocking. I did. I did. It was sort of a Chagall, where he has the cow going over the church and the same colors—vivid purple and almost a metallic deep navy blue. My body chemistry sort of changed and I knew that this was one of those pieces where all I had to do was be the lightning rod and it would happen. It just felt like that. Maybe that happens because you're tuned in to all those people just like, really, millions of women worked on the peace ribbon. In my own way, although I was responding in a different way, I was also responding to the need to address the issue of nuclear war, and so all I had to do was open up and it was there.

Root. Did the thing about the cat and the rabbit happen too?

Stocking. Well, it didn't happen right then, but it had happened before, and I knew it was part of the story.

Root. What's the time frame between the dinner, in which you say, "This would make a nice column," and the actual day arriving when you're clearing out the Jehovah's Witnesses and going over to the gathering?

Stocking. Probably three months.

Root. Did you write any of that down?

Stocking. No, but what I did—I don't have a bag full of drafts because it just kind of happened.

Root. Okay, there's the dinner and these two examples and then there's a fairly long paragraph about no reverence for life, only drive for life in nature and the unwinnability of nuclear war. The Jehovah's Witnesses thing happens, the morning arrives for it, and you talk to a bunch of people there, and you say, "It would be heartless to pursue this young matron to the other side of the patchwork, asking 'But do you really think this will do some good?'" And then you start the conclusion, I guess: "I picture my husband at work picturing me at home in Leelanau County working for peace. I feel slightly absurd and naive, a little like I'm attending a symposium to ban evil in this group of very sincere and naive ladies. But then I think about the other side . . ." That goes on to the conclusion. Anything about that structure that was difficult?

Stocking. No. That was pretty easy. I just had spent several weeks or whatever mulling it.

Root. How soon after that meeting did you write that?

Stocking. Right away. I probably spent a morning writing it because it doesn't take that long to write that many words. Sometimes I spend a week though.

Root. Did you have to do a lot of revising?

Stocking. No. A lot was cut by my editor because it was too long. I would have preferred to have it longer because it occurred so naturally that I didn't want to mess with it but I've learned to just accept length restrictions and what editors do with your pieces and not get into it.

Root. Are there any topics you've done where you changed things in the middle, where you thought you were going to write one piece and in the course of it you ended up writing a totally different piece?

Stocking. Lots of times.

Root. Can you think of anything specifically?

Stocking. One story I can think about is where my editor said she wanted a story about the coffee club in Lelend and I said, "Oh, that's been done a lot but, hey, there's a coffee club in Sutton's Bay that's pretty similar—why don't I do that?" And I thought it would be just a kind of nice local village people all getting together and having coffee and there would be a routine about it. There would be an emphasis on community and so on. When I got there I really found their values so dated. They didn't really want women in their group and, as someone who grew up in the era of women's lib, I first of all couldn't even understand why they wouldn't also want to talk to women—I mean, just an all-male group of farmers and whatever—and it was a big concession, I think, that they had me there. And one guy who had been in the service talked about how it was great to live here now—for years his wife could never live any place where there weren't black-skinned people who went barefoot and he had been in Vietnam and various places and the racist overtones were pretty clear. I couldn't write the story I'd come to write, about what lovely little small town people they were. They were small town people, all right, but, boy, with a vengeance.

I was having surgery when I was on deadline for that and I was in the hospital. Something about all the morphine they were giving me and remembering that coffee club—you always have to cast things in positive terms for any kind of readership; you just can't come on as negative with anybody, in conversation or anything, so I was wracking my brains. They repulsed me on so many levels that I had to wrack my brains for something that I liked about them, and once I came up with that—that even though they weren't really egalitarian, they were with each other—I had to tell the truth too, you know—so then I sort of worked in the other things but it wasn't the story I intended to write.

Root. Did you ever come up with a piece that you couldn't write?

Stocking. Probably. And I probably barreled through it. This coffee club piece would qualify as one.

First of all, my editor, who had the idea of how sweet and quaint we all were up here anyway, had a perspective that I thought was really a myth about this area, which was, I think, by extrapolation, that we're all real cute and quaint and have cute and quaint country coffee clubs and quilting bees. It's hard to respond to that, to write an essay with any depth about cuteness, quaintness anywhere, and it's hard to write to satisfy shallow notions based on, essentially, clichés. It was exactly as if I had called her and said, "Hey, you live in Detroit. Write me a great piece about the murder rate." And she would groan and say, "I've got to deal with this person's stereotype, in some sense satisfy it and reaffirm it, but why?" So that was the assignment which I didn't really like but I thought I could do and then, as always, you have to tell the truth but you have to do it in a way that sugar-coats the pill.

Root. Do you get many assignments in the column?

Stocking. That was early on, maybe the second column, and she stopped giving me assignments after three or four pieces. She said, "You do better writing about whatever it is occurs to you."

Root. Did you have to check with her on most columns?

Stocking. No, no.

Root. Is there any kind of change that you make from month to month? For example, having done "Piecing the Ribbon Together," next month if a story came up about another nuclear disarmament event . . .

Stocking. I wouldn't do it. I would hold it off.

Root. Is there any pattern that you see yourself following or is it just random?

Stocking. Well, I took them all in to be xeroxed at one point. And the guy said, "Oh, you're doing a series on islands." They were all about islands or isolation. There was a period when I was feeling isolated.

I think probably I still am influenced very much by the humanitarian values that evolved out of the sixties. That is my generation; I can't escape it. But there are lots of other influences too. I think the columns probably reflect a desire still to change the world—I would imagine, although I don't like to see that there.

Root. A lot of your pieces seem not to necessarily take a strong stand, not that there's necessarily something to take a strong stand about.

Stocking. I do covertly, I would say.

Root. Let's look at the reservation gambling story. It ends talking about everyday risks, the sound of ice breaking up on the bay, and concludes: "Gambling is like that sound, I decide, as I get into the car, less mysterious than I had imagined, more basic and recognizable." How did you come upon that ending?

Stocking. That was a super-hard piece to do. I had thought that there would be more atmosphere in the Bingo Palace and the Casino than there was. The scene was real drab, just as if you stopped in a bar in Pinconning expecting that there would be atmosphere and you just found some people there. And the management would not talk a lot about it, which made it hard to get their perceptions. Initially I'd thought I had had this great idea for a piece, thinking, Well, people in Detroit are going to be interested in this because they want to build a casino on Belle Isle plus people are always interested in what happens on those reservations and the idea that the noble savage should be above gambling. Actually the noble savages are into survival as much as the ignoble rest of us.

I thought it had elements for a good story, but it was real hard to pull together and the ending was almost tacked on. I had heard about the ice breaking up on the bay—this winter everything froze a lot. Some friends of mine who lived near the bay said they could hear it at night and that intrigued me, and I thought, if I'm so intrigued by the ice breaking up in the bay, other people will be too—I mean, it *is* a primal sound—but how can I make this into a story? The ice breaking up is interesting in and of itself and I just kind of threw it in there at the end to give the piece some heft, some weight. It was a real hard piece to do because it didn't have the elements in it that I had expected to find there. So that was just a hat trick.

Root. In some of the pieces it strikes me that what you end up doing is sort of walking out of wherever it is—"Back on Division Street I remembered something Sara said . . ." and rather than coming to a conclusion it comes to an ending.

Stocking. The woman in the column on iridology I just thought was the biggest phony in the world. I couldn't say, "Oh, come on," about her or to her or to the reader. I had to kind of imply it. So the thing about "I thank God for this gift" is sort of tongue in cheek.

The iridology piece, by the way, was written in about two hours. That was real fast. I just flew into Traverse, saw this woman, flew back, probably took four hours for all the research and writing.

Root. Just connecting the notes together?

Stocking. Just connecting the notes together.

Root. Very often in here you tell this in a narrative way. You're not telling this as a reporter who's merely a bystander. A reporter of the peace ribbon would say, "There was a meeting at a certain house and here's what some of those people had to say," and you never get a sense of who the reporter is. Is there any kind of role that you give yourself or persona that you want to convey to the reader?

Stocking. No. I try to stay out of the pieces as much as I can. I just did the piece on the two black musicians, "Mozart and Ace." I say that we don't have any black people up here, which we virtually don't, but at one point I had a line in there about my five-year-old daughter seeing two black women on the streets of Traverse and saying, "There's some people from *The Color Purple*." I thought it was very evocative. She had no reference for people like that except for a movie. But I took it out because I didn't want too much of myself in there. I think it detracts. I also took it out because I didn't want to overstate the case and have too many cute little anecdotes because I knew I was treading a very fine line between accusing people of being racist and being too cutesy naive and isolated.

If I have a persona in the piece it's as the alter ego part of the reader. It's the part of the reader who—maybe you've seen *Annie Hall*, where they're making love and she gets out of her body and sits on the chair and watches them. It's that part of the reader that can walk out of himself, his or her life, and go sit on a couch in a house in Leland and watch what's going on. I try to be Everyperson to the extent that I can be, just an impression absorber.

Root. What kinds of revision do you do? more structual things? more stylistic things? Do you worry a lot about style?

Stocking. Oh, yeah, all the time. I change words constantly. The tone is so important, and I've read E. B. White a lot for tone. I think he gets a wonderful balance between not being too hoky and yet being just a little folksy. Joan Didion I read because she is able to just immerse herself in her subject. She's just a marvelous writer. Calvin Trillin I read a lot for structure. I find his pieces a little formulaic, but that's good to read for structure. I read E. B. White to get a sense of what he puts in and what he leaves out and how he handles really delicate subjects. He handles things with such a deft touch.

So I copy people. I read Ellen Goodman for topics a lot. She has a sense of what's interesting to people right now. And I read the *New York Times* and *Esquire* and *Newsweek* and everything I can get my hands on, both Detroit newspapers and the local paper, to get a sense of what's impacting people, what their concerns are now, what the media is giving them to be concerned about and what it reflects of their concerns.

Root. Do you think your style is like anybody?

Stocking. I've been told that stylistically I'm very good and I'm not like anybody, although I don't have a real sense of what style is. I don't get it sort of about style. It must just happen. It must be like the color of your hair or something, not something you can do a whole lot about.

Root. Do you have a model for these columns? When you started doing this how did you know that this was okay as a column?

Stocking. I didn't. *Metropolitan Detroit* called and said "We want a column about up north," and I had thought about doing it before but the idea of a first-person column about an area and what people did— I didn't have an idea for it, I didn't know what a column was. I hadn't really read any Joan Didion, Ellen Goodman, E. B. White or Calvin Trillin at that point.

Root. Did you then go out to look at their stuff and discover what they did?

Stocking. Yeah, to find out what a column was. One of the biggest influences on my writing is my friends. I'm good friends with three writers and there are a couple of other people too who don't write but they think a lot. I feel that some people more than others are somehow tapped into the collective unconscious. Those people, either because they also reflect the things I'm thinking about or because some cata-lystic event in their own personal lives has put them in touch with something, are real good resources for just the mood of the country.

Root. What kind of things do they do?

Stocking. Of the writers, one woman is an academic like yourself, who taught at Purdue and is now doing carpentry; she does real academic writing on how the media influences society. Stephanie was editor of *CoEvolution Quarterly* and she does essays, such as what it's like to have herpes or to be an alcoholic. She's not afraid to bare her soul and she does it very well. Gloria Whelan is a short story writer. She is a little more controlled in how she relates to the world but even in her control I think are revelations.

Root. What's the effect of being a writer with a monthly column or trying to make a living as a writer on the way you view your life?

Stocking. My husband and I were just talking about that this morning. It's just, as you know, no way to make a living. I'm committed to my family and I'm committed to this area, but I hope in my next incarnation that I can do nothing but write. Nobody got me pregnant by immaculate conception—I was there and participating and wanted children and wanted a family—but I just hope that next time around I don't so badly want all of it. Because there's no way that you can have the time and the energy to write and do that. It's a constant schizophrenia. It's real difficult to be a full-time writer in your whole being and a flesh and blood person at the same time. I don't know what the balance is.

Root. Do you find yourself looking at the world as a writer because you're thinking, I've got a column to do?

Stocking. Is everything grist for the mill? Yeah. You bet. And I don't feel badly about that. I'm grist for the mill. Why shouldn't everything else be? It's all community news. I'm no holds barred, whether it's information about myself or seeking it. Everything feeds into the writing process. It's all usable, and I don't feel at all bad about that or apologetic.

Root. Has your writing changed over the years?

Stocking. Hopefully it's gotten better.

Root. Have you looked at stuff that's ten years old?

Stocking. Yeah. I would say it's the same person writing it to the extent that I can recognize the style but I think it's gotten smoother and cleaner and the perspective is more mature, a little more surefooted, a little wiser.

Root. What do you think accounts for that?

Stocking. Age. Practice. Just doing it.

Root. Has doing it regularly or frequently changed the way you write?

Stocking. It's exactly like playing the flute. If you can afford the time to do nothing but that, you'll just get better; even if you're awful when you start you'll get better, and hopefully if you're at all talented to start with, you'll get much better.

Root. Are the columns coming more easily?

Stocking. No, I wouldn't say so, they are sometimes more easy and sometimes real hard. I still have to work with them the same way. They aren't any easier. I'm more sure of myself in this sense, that sometimes I used to send things out hoping that the editor would know what to do with it. Now I know that I'm going to know better than the editor and I let it sit there and I get back at it. I am more sure about what to put in and what to take out. Like the line about "There's some people from *The Color Purple*"—I would have wanted to bounce that off an editor before or left it in hoping if they had the same reservations about it, they would just take it out. Or I just agonized about it. Now my sense of it is much clearer. My editorial sense has improved a lot but the writing process never gets any easier. It's easier or harder from piece to piece but it doesn't get easier with time.

Root. When Tom Wicker was writing three columns a week, he said about a third measured up to his personal standards and the rest were professional but not first-rate. What percentage would you give yourself?

Stocking. I wouldn't say that at all. I feel that I'm still learning. Maybe I'll never be completely satisfied. I understand the distinction he's making. This is professional and this is something that, because it came through me, I'm just so pleased that it did, like giving birth. You just feel so pleased that you could be part of the process of creating something larger than yourself. But I don't take credit. I try not to measure, myself against myself, myself against other writers. I just try to keep doing it, hoping God or whatever the magic is will let me keep connecting to other people.

It's like living itself. You don't try to get it right. You just try to keep doing it. And you're led by your desires, I think, not by some ultimate standard. You *want* to walk to the top of the hill or you *are* falling in love. The craft part of writing can only improve with time, but the connecting part is a gift.

Dreaming Detroit

Kathleen Stocking

Detroit looms in the dead of winter up north like an oasis of civilization somewhere to the south of us. Whatever Detroit's image is to the rest of the country, or even Detroiters, to a northern Michiganian with cabin fever, Detroit is a fantastic city filled with possibilities.

There's a certain time of year up here when there is nothing to do and nowhere to go, nothing but bars and basketball games and more of the same. If you aren't ready yet to drink your brains out, you stay home. Snow extends for miles in every direction and one lives literally in a vacuum. A new curtain of snow descends hourly around one's small house, and the sense that there is, three hundred miles to the south, a city, is the one counterbalance to gaping infinity.

I cannot complain, as Ovid did when Caesar exiled him to the remote shores of the Black Sea, that I am trapped among the barbarians, "those gross tribes that sweep down from the steppes." I am, in some sense, one of those barbarians, having grown up here in tiny Glen Arbor on the shores of Lake Michigan. In the vernacular of the summer people, I am a "local." And while I may have been trapped here as a child, nothing forced me to come back here as an adult.

My roots drew me back here, but no sooner was I here than I longed for everything I had gone away to find: jobs, money, education, art, people like me, people not like me, drama, diversity, energy; in short, civilization. Civilization, I've come to understand over the years, is having enough people interacting in one spot over a period of time to give life definition and make it interesting. Living in the vast north country, you face one awesome truth: When a tree falls in the forest and nobody hears it, nobody cares.

Reprinted with the permission of *Detroit Monthly*, Crain Communications, Inc. Also appears in Kathleen Stocking, *Letters from the Leelanau* (Ann Arbor: U of Michigan P, 1990). Reprinted with permission.

As a child living on a high hill above Lake Michigan, I would watch the freighters go by on their way to those distant cities known collectively as civilization. Just as Detroiters fantasize about the piney Michigan that stretches due north of them and come to view it— romantically and somewhat erroneously—as a world of wood stoves, log cabins and trout streams, I have spent a lifetime dreaming Detroit. Mainly my impressions of Detroit, like a kindergartner's ideas about where babies come from, have been garnered secondhand from books and ex-Detroiters, a fanciful amalgam that most real Detroiters probably would find amusing but unrecognizable.

So let's imagine we have just met, at the trout stream in front of my log cabin, and are becoming fast friends. Let's throw another log on the fire, put a pot of coffee on the wood stove and I'll bring out the vignettes and freeze-frame images of Detroit I've collected over the years the way a tourist collects Petoskey stones.

Aunt Myrtle provided me with my earliest impressions of Detroit. She was a redheaded woman who had chartreuse Chinese coolies on her what-not shelf and who painted her nails. Aunt Myrtle knew how to play canasta, and once played it with me for a week. "She's from Detroit," my mother said often about Aunt Myrtle. I didn't know what this meant, exactly—that Aunt Myrtle dared to be different because she was from Detroit, or that everyone in Detroit painted their nails and played canasta—but I wanted to find out.

Another time my mom and my Aunt Carol packed about six of us kids into the station wagon and went on a marathon shopping trip, less to Detroit than to downtown Hudson's. After a whirlwind tour of a dozen floors of goods, by escalator and elevator and with all of us in tow, we ended up waist-deep in a city pool in hot July, my aunt and my mother remarking on how much they'd had to pay for all of us to go swimming. What possessed these two women to drive almost three hundred miles to look at towels and why they didn't leave us home, I will never know. I suppose they had no choice but to take us, and it was simply "the call" of Hudson's echoing back past Clare and rippling over the cedar swamps that finally made them get in the car and go.

Detroit is a place where people either made history or were aware of it being made and therefore participated vicariously in events beyond themselves even when they didn't participate directly. I still can see old Hervey Parke, a relative of the people who owned the old Parke Pharmaceutical Company in Detroit, sitting on the porch of his Lake Michigan home, telling me how his great-uncle, Captain Hervey

Parke, had walked out from New York State to survey along the Detroit River. "He walked with a forty-five-pound pack on his back," Hervey said. "People walked then, you know."

I cultivate Detroiters, which isn't hard to do in an area to which they all seem to be moving. One day my stove broke and the Sears man came to fix it. He was and is a real Detroiter whose grandfather was a motorman on the Detroit Street Railway in the days when you could go anywhere in the city on the DSR for a nickel. "I grew up on Detroit's East Side," Ken Dezur says, "Linnhurst. Fairmont, when the streets were gravel. From Fairmont to Eight Mile it was all open fields. We could sit on the upstairs porch and watch the fireworks at Eastwood Park on the Fourth of July. On warm summer nights my folks used to take us kids out to Belle Isle to sleep in the grass. Tashmo Park. New Baltimore. It was like the wilderness. We used to swim off the dock in the St. Clair River. The current was real strong there." He draws an impromptu map while he waits for the timer to go off on my stove. "You have the Detroit River, then Lake St. Clair, Lake Erie, the St. Clair River and Lake Huron." The drawing is gone, but the place that stays in my mind is this city, where a kid could go anywhere for a nickel, a city surrounded by a river with a strong current. The excitement of participation, that's what Detroit had to offer, and maybe that's why my aunt and my mother drove three hundred miles—to be caught up in the current of others' lives.

Marianne Russell is a friend of mine and grew up in Detroit: "I remember riding in the elevator at Hudson's," she tells me one gray November day in Glen Arbor, when we are trying to think of ways to keep her magazine afloat in an area where there are no people to buy ads. "I remember being 4 feet tall, and all I could see were rear ends and the bottom buttons of people's coats. I remember art classes at the Detroit Institute of Arts, Saturday morning, huddled in the cold outside those wrought-iron gates. I remember the man in the Kern block on Woodward, standing on a crate, quoting from the Bible, dressed in a big black topcoat and a white silk scarf." Detroit was a place with enough people, she seemed to be saying, to allow characters and creativity to flourish, to allow art and culture to flourish, to be crowded in an elevator—enough people to buy ads.

At a party one night recently during an early spring thaw, when the water was dripping rhythmically off the eaves and the melting snow seemed to make the air heady with oxygen, Sue Kopka tells me about growing up in Bloomfield Hills. "When my parents moved there in the 1950s," she says, "Bloomfield Hills was the country. It was woods and farm fields and swamp. Now I go back there and it's gone. It's city now. There was a huge twisted tree, like a serpent, that we played on as kids, next to the swamp. Now the tree is gone. The swamp is gone. I came north to find country, to come home. But sometimes I wonder what would have happened if we had all stayed living where we grew up. We would have felt more attached to the land and we might have fought to save it."

In some ways we are all a nation of nomads—restless, displaced, haunted by memories of trees and men with Bibles, yuppies looking for the perfect place—not realizing we create our environment as much as it creates us. The difference is that here in the north country all the ingredients are raw, like a new bolt of cloth, whereas in Detroit it's a matter of remaking what's already been done. In the north we have to figure out ways to create civilization without destroying the wilderness. In Detroit the dilemma is to recreate some wilderness without perturbing two million people.

The proper balance of civilization and country living seems to be what everyone is looking for. And almost in the space of time that we've been talking by our imaginary trout stream, or certainly since I was growing up here forty years ago, civilization, with all its paved roads, water pollution, traffic, condominiums and hundreds of people, has moved north. As I watch the wilderness vanish, it strikes me as odd that in all my dreaming of Detroit, I had always imagined I would go there; I never dreamt it would come to me.

Mozart and Ace

Kathleen Stocking

This is a story about two elderly black musicians who came to the remote Leelanau Peninsula last summer and won the hearts of the people through their charm and their music. It begins in a little honky-tonk bar on the shores of Omena Bay.

The Harbor Bar sits in a tuck of the bay, a place where the bay curves in and the highway curves out so the two almost touch, except that in between is the bar. Its patrons usually have consisted of a few Omena regulars and people from the nearby Indian community. It's a plain bar with a rickety wraparound porch and a good view of the water. Old gas pumps, not out of use, are on the highway side, and on the other, boats are docked so close to the bar they almost seem tethered there.

The bar is one of about five commercial buildings in Omena, the others being a false-fronted country store, an ancient U.S. Post Office, a grocery store converted to an art gallery and the fire station. There are about a dozen villages like Omena, give or take a few buildings, scattered over the Leelanau Peninsula, a county of rolling hills, cherry orchards, sand dunes and two hundred miles of Lake Michigan shore—with an indigenous Indian population, several generations of Polish, French and Norwegian immigrants, about twenty years' worth of hippies and several thousand summer tourists. Except for the tourists, we are an isolated, unsophisticated population. We do not, as a rule, have live music in our bars, nor do we ever see many black people.

In the beginning, some people say they heard the music floating out over the water from the Omena Harbor Bar. Others say they heard

Reprinted with the permission of *Detroit Monthly*, Crain Communications, Inc. Also appears in Kathleen Stocking, *Letters from the Leelanau* (Ann Arbor: U of Michigan Pr, 1990). Reprinted with permission.

it when they were walking by on the road. After that it was word of mouth in a county with only fifteen thousand people, most of those either related or friends, or people who know each other from work or church.

By late July, farmers, bricklayers, wealthy lawyers, poor artists, librarians and summer visitors all were flocking to the bar to experience what had become a Leelanau County cultural event. By August, some local people had taken out an ad in the Leelanau Enterprise "to thank John 'Ace' Davis and Mozart Perry for the fine entertainment and wonderful summer." By September the owner of the Harbor Bar was running "held over" ads.

It was a warm Sunday in early September before my husband, our two daughters and I got up to the bar to hear the two people whom everyone by this time was calling simply, "the musicians." We had heard Sunday was the day they played from four to midnight with an open mike. Other families like ours were already there when we arrived, giving the place an oddly innocent, after-church air.

Ace is a tall man with a wide smile who stands with his arm around his bass and talks to the audience as if they were at a family reunion. Mozart is shorter, quieter; he sits at his electric piano, peering down through his glasses like an owl, with a look on his face of some-one about to smile. Ace announces to the audience that they have seven song books with a thousand songs each, dating back to 1895 and up through the 1940s. He invites requests. They begin playing Cole Porter's "Night and Day."

It is pressure-cooker muggy in the room—pickle-canning weather. The bay is clouding over and it feels like it might rain. Ace takes a request on a cocktail napkin and turns to Mozart, "Mozart, what can we play for Chubs on his birthday?" He could be talking about his cousin.

"We'll think of somethin'," Mozart says, and in a moment has launched into a surprisingly wild and joyful version of "When the Saints come Marchin' In," his fingers a blur over the keyboard, his eyes ruminant, half-closed.

At six they take a break, and under the wisteria vine over the steps of the Tamarack Craftsmen Gallery across the road, Mozart says he grew up in Toledo in the 1920s, when it was a little like Leelanau County. "There was no dope. You could leave your screen door un-locked and sleep on your back porch. All people had was church and the picture show. That's what made good musicians. People took patience with their music."

Mozart says he got his nickname from an aunt who "played a little piano," and that he was influenced by Art Tatum, another Toledo jazz pianist. Both Ace and Mozart say they are primarily self-taught and were in their late forties before they became full-time musicians. They've been working together nineteen years. "We don't drink, we don't smoke and we eat right," Ace says. "We want to be able to work the next morning. Mozart and I, we're on the bandstand for the art of music, for the joy of it. The joy of music is built on love—love of life, your fellow man."

Back across the street they open with a cool, light version of "Take the A-Train," and then go into a rousing version of "Route 66." A Lake Leelanau mason, LaVern "Zip" Flees, is waiting with his concertina to sit in with them. Ace introduces Flees as "Zip the Zipper, the Concertina Man." Another man is practicing his trumpet in the parking lot, waiting to come on. Some members of a local dance group have come up from Traverse City "just to dance to music you never hear anymore," Darcy Cunningham, one of the dancers, says. An Indian is dancing by himself. Ace says, "Wonderful music. Wonderful people, people enjoying themselves." I overhear someone behind me say, "If I ever have to go to Mars, I want to go with those two guys."

Not everyone appreciates it, however. "I like music with a message," says a disgruntled woodcutter at the bar. "The music of the sixties had a message: Bob Dylan." A woman sitting next to him, a musician herself, says, "They miss notes. They aren't as perfect as everyone says they are."

But Rick Shimel, manager for the Detroit-based rock band, the Buzztones, says, "I like to see the life musicians bring to their music, and those two cats bring a lot. They come and plug in on a Sunday afternoon and play for eight hours, and that's unheard of in this business. They do it because they love it and the audience knows it. There's a hundred years of rich musical history behind them, and the audience feels that. Those guys are packing a bar that never had anybody in it—that's a valid act."

Mozart and Ace stayed through the fall. They played at the Harbor Bar on weekends, and during the week they sometimes played free for schools and local civic groups.

One winter day I called a friend in Boston, Berrien Thorn. Berrien had come to Leelanau County last summer and walked into this little bar in Omena and heard Ace and Mozart and asked them if they knew a song his father had written, "I Hear a Rhapsody." They knew it and played it. Berrien and I talked about music and perfection.

"Basho," Berrien says, "the Japanese haiku master, sometimes wrote haiku with either more or less than the perfect number of syllables. When asked about it, he said, 'It's not the syllables of the haiku that's important, but the syllables of the heart.' People who complain about Ace and Mozart's notes have little hearts. Besides, lots of nights I'm sure they are perfect." Then Berrien talks about a student of Basho's who came to him and said, "Master, if you take the wings off a dragonfly, it looks like a salt shaker. That's a great haiku, right?" And Basho says, "No, no, you idiot. You put wings on a salt shaker so it looks like a dragonfly; that's a great haiku."

It is now spring on the Leelanau Peninsula. The leaves on the trees are the size of mouse ears and the morel mushrooms are coming up in the woods. People are talking about Mozart and Ace coming back again this year. Word is they'll be back at the Harbor Bar the first of July, and local people are polishing up their instruments and getting out their dancing shoes in preparation for the event.

For my part, I can't get that haiku out of my mind. I keep seeing Leelanu County as a salt shaker with wings on it. And I keep seeing Mozart and Ace—weightless silhouettes floating over Omena Bay with their instruments—like light-filled holograms.

Piecing the Ribbon Together

Kathleen Stocking

It began over dinner with friends in the warm, early spring that has now passed. Something about the night—my friends being very much in love, the spars of northern lights through their dining room window, the gentle way our kids played together and then fell asleep in front of the TV—gave a tender feeling to the entire evening. And it was this evening I learned about the peace ribbon.

Women from all over the United States, my friend said, were embroidering pieces of ribbon which would be wrapped around the Pentagon on August 4, 1985, in memory of the bombing of Hiroshima and Nagaski and in protest of all nuclear war. Already, she said, they had more than ten miles of ribbon at the ribbon center in Denver, and it was going to take a semi truck to haul it all to Washington. She invited me to join a group of women working on the ribbon.

That night I fell asleep dreaming of this truck, trailing ribbon, making its way across the night landscape of Iowa, past farmhouses sleeping in the violet starlight and cows in back pastures chewing in slow rhythm.

But when I awoke an hour or two later, it was to the sound of shrill little screams. It took a minute to realize the screams were coming from a rabbit the cat had apparently trapped in the woodpile. Sleepily I got up to go release the rabbit and corral the cat.

The night was still warm and I sat on the picnic table in the backyard thinking there is no reverence for life in nature. Drive for life, yes. The cat kills the rabbit. The owl kills the cat. The Russians kill us, or would, if we didn't have enough nuclear warheads. I

Reprinted with the permission of *Metropolitan Detroit*, Crain Communications, Inc. Also appears in Kathleen Stocking, *Letters from the Leelanau* (Ann Arbor: U of Michigan P, 1990). Reprinted with permission.

wouldn't be sitting here at this picnic table thinking about this, I thought, if hundreds of aboriginal ancestors before me hadn't been willing to kill someone or something in order to live. The instinct for war was in me, too. I preferred confrontation to compromise. I relished a good fight. It occurred to me that there was such a thing as fighting where life, liberty or principle was involved, where not fighting would be worse than dying. It wasn't so much that war was wrong, but that our weapons had outstripped us. A nuclear war was unwinnable—unless the other side decided not to fight back, which was unlikely.

Time went by. Early crocus spring gave way to buggy near-summer. The Jehovah's Witnesses got me on their calling route. Teresa from Kentucky sits on my living room sofa telling me about Armageddon. "This will not be man's war," says Teresa, who once had a guru in Cincinnati and who looks uncannily like Diane Keaton in *Mrs. Soffel,* "but God's war. We are in the last of the latter days when evil spirits, which we know are fallen angels, are trying to take over the world." Teresa is accompanied by Dena, a teeny-tiny mail-order bride from the Philippines (I picture her arriving in an envelope) who has married a local farmer many years her senior.

Like Madame Defarge, I embroider while Dena peppers me with heavily accented quotes from the Bible, and Teresa tries to cut Dena off with her own rote-like quotes from the Bible. I am fascinated by these women, by their faith, by their aggressiveness, by their prissiness. "What are you working on?" Teresa asks me with a slightly forced smile. This is my moment, "I'm working for world peace," I tell her, "the end of all wars." Perhaps it's the way I say it, or perhaps the actual absurdity of this strikes them, or perhaps it's simply that their proselytizing time is up, but they leave then.

The morning all the ladies for the peace ribbon are supposed to get together, it had rained hard the night before, then cleared slightly, with a fierce wind. By the time I drive through the village of Lake Leelanau at 9 A.M., the air is gray and humid and the trees are a glittering chartreuse.

Two nuns, their black dresses whipping around them in the wind, are trying to chase a wounded swan back across the bridge and down off the causeway. The white of the swan matches the wimples around the nun's faces and the swan's black beak matches their dresses. The proportionate colors and the shooing motions make it all seem oddly choreographed. Meanwhile, an old woman winds her way down the hill by the steepled church, a wicker basket over her arms as if she were going to some past century's village market. For a moment Lake Leelanau seems to exist not only in its own time warp, but in a time warp that is also a vortex that will suck me down into it.

When I finally cross the bridge it is as if I am accepting the present century with its potential for nuclear holocaust.

Bev Cheadle, the woman who has organized our particular group of ladies, has a house high on a hill with a narrow view of Grand Traverse Bay through the trees. She is a woman in her early thirties with a halo of pale, wispy blond hair and a soft voice. "In the winter," she says, "I had dreams of mushroom clouds, of nuclear holocaust. Working on the ribbon project is my way to do something positive, and show my children I am doing something and so are our neighbors."

As the house begins to fill with women and children, Laurie Davis, Bev's neighbor and my friend who first told me about the ribbon project, comes over with a pot of coffee. Trays of warm apple-bran muffins are being pulled from the oven. Children flit in and out of the kitchen. "To me," Laurie says, noshing on a muffin, "the whole idea of thousands of women all over America creating something beautiful with their own needlework that is also a political statement for peace, a spiritual statement—that's quite a piece of the collective unconscious, if you ask me. And the more people who think about peace, the stronger the idea gets. Love *is* stronger than death."

"It's a feminist statement," says a hugely pregnant Gerry Simkins. "Men make guns, women make babies. It's time for the women to be heard."

Mavis Bottenhorn, a young mother of a toddler and an infant, between changing diapers, wiping noses and kissing "hurts," is scrambling across the floor, pins in her mouth, trying to pin the pieces of the peace ribbon together. It would be heartless to pursue this young matron to the other side of the patchwork, asking, "But do you think this will really do any good?"

I picture my husband at work picturing me at home in Leelanau County working for peace. I feel slightly absurd and naive, a little like I'm attending a symposium to ban evil, in this group of very sincere and naive ladies. But then I think about the other side, the Pentagon with its gold NORAD phone that doesn't work—the one they're supposed to use to communicate on in case of nuclear attack. I think about Reagan's "joke" about bombing the Russians. I think about American presidents generally—Carter prattling on about lascivious thoughts in an interview with *Playboy*, Andrew Jackson who thought the world was flat—and I come to the conclusion that the little group of ladies embroidering for peace is not so absurd by comparison.

It's just that human life, in the face of nuclear threat, takes on a surreal quality. It is then we realize our duality, how recently we evolved from the muck and acquired—somewhere along the mucky way—a soul. Willy-nilly, pursuing our animal instincts for survival, for killing, like the cat with the rabbit, we have, at the same time, bozo-like, created the means for our own annihilation on a hair-trigger. We are at a point in our history where we can now see with breathtaking clarity how experimental the union of body and soul has been.

3

Writing Political Columns

In the preceding chapter, two essayists described the process of association by which their articles evolve, the connections they make that first prompt and then help develop their essays. In writing that is more specifically topic-centered, the connections formed in context are equally important to the writers, and their composing processes are likely to be more similar to one another. This is true for the topic-centered writing of political columnists and critics.

Tom Wicker and Richard Reeves are both political columnists. Wicker is a columnist for the *New York Times* and Reeves is syndicated by Universal Press Syndicate; both write two columns weekly, Wicker's running 750 words, Reeves's running 650. Both started their journalism careers in small newspapers, Wicker in the *Sandhill Citizen* [NC], Reeves as editor of the *Phillipsburg Free Press* [NJ]. Both have been reporters as well as columnists. They also write in other forms besides the column: Wicker has written several novels of varying types and several nonfiction books, including works on John F. Kennedy, the Attica Prison uprising, and the press; Reeves has written not only books on American politics, Pakistan, and Tocqueville's travels in the United States but also television commentary, an Emmy-winning documentary, and other scripts for television.

Both Wicker and Reeves see an opinion column as, in Reeves' description, "one idea expanded" (*Jet Lag* 123). In *On Press*, Wicker explained that, while

> news stories are restricted primarily to facts . . . opinion
> columns necessarily deal also with ideas. I learned early that I
> could accumulate a lot of facts on a given subject, and still not
> be able to put together a useful column on that subject. (150)

He also distinguished between editorials and opinion columns, arguing that "the editorial writer's function . . . is basically that of reasoned advocacy" (150) and illustrating the difference between the three forms of journalism:

> For example: an article detailing how the two-party system works is a factual report; if the writer states that he is for it or against it or favors modification, it is an editorial; but if the article assumes that everyone knows what the two-party system is and that most Americans favor it as an instrument of political stability and moderation, then goes on to argue nevertheless that the two-party system is an instrument of the economic status quo—that's an opinion column . . . an *idea* calculated to offer a different perspective on some known facts, arouse intellectual interest, produce discussion, maybe even affect thought and attitudes. (151)

Like Reeves, Wicker feels that "an opinion column needs an *idea*—rarely more than one, given length restrictions" and insists that "an idea does not require acceptance to justify its existence; nor does it necessarily exist to achieve anything other than an intellectual end" (150).

Athough both would agree that a column is neither an editorial nor a news story, neither feels inhibited from pushing the column toward the other forms when appropriate. Wicker acknowledges in the interview that his column, "Recycling an Idea," about a proposal for a new variation on the Civilian Conservation Corps of the Roosevelt administration, is "like an editorial. It's a piece of advocacy." He points out that, while he feels no responsibility to "sit down and figure out exactly how" to create and operate such a youth corps, he does think "it is my job to throw out ideas like that."

Similarly, Reeves was more interested in the news value of his column "What is Ted Kennedy Running For?" than in the analysis it might include. As he says in his interview, "I thought since this isn't an analysis of something, the major thing about it is the . . . news value . . . so it was a pretty straightforward structure, figuring I'd want to get the news up top." Although Wicker's piece is not strictly an editorial and Reeves' column is not strictly a news story, both writers stretch the boundaries of their own definition of the opinion column form.

Since both men write political opinion columns, they are limited in subject matter to public affairs. Wicker's column has somewhat more constraints than Reeves' because its title, *In the Nation*, theoretically restricts him to matters that affect national interests; he doesn't feel justified in writing about foreign affairs unless they have strong connections to national affairs. As he says in his interview, "I probably wouldn't write about the Iranian-Iraq war, unless there was some good reason; for example, it was causing some problems with our oil supplies." Within those strictures both men have a great deal of latitude. Wicker routinely writes about criminal justice, transportation, and nuclear disarmament; Reeves has ranged from media to religion to education. Both regularly write on political campaigns, legislation, and the economy.

Both vary their writing habits with the writing task. When writing the column while traveling, both write in longhand on yellow legal pads (or whatever is handy—the manuscript of Reeves' column, "Why We Are in Afghanistan," was written in pencil on the back of a copy of Senator Daniel Evans' testimony to a Senate subcommittee), and both dictate their columns over the telephone for transcription. About half the time, Wicker's columns are written on a computer terminal in his *New York Times* office; his books are written in longhand. Reeves tended to work on book-length manuscripts on an electric typewriter but eventually changed to a word processor; for a time he wrote the column in longhand for a secretary to type up in his home.

Both men are, in Wicker's term, "assiduous string-savers" (*On Press* 49). Wicker keeps files of information and notes as well as scrapbooks of his past columns that he sometimes uses as resources; Reeves keeps manila envelopes stuffed with notes and clippings, much in the way that Jim Fitzgerald does. Both take such materials with them when they travel, since most often they will need to write a column on the road in order to meet relentless deadlines. Nonetheless, they are most apt to write on topics that have an immediacy for them. In *Jet Lag*, his collection of columns with a running commentary on the columnist's life, Reeves gives an example of how a chance conversation on a plane led immediately after the flight to a column about the career of the person with whom he had been talking (201–203). Similarly, Wicker's column, "Reagan's Apple Pie," grew out of remarks he'd read in a local newspaper while visiting in Vermont.

The pressure of regular deadlines aids both writers in discovering topics. As Wicker says in the interview,

> It's a relentless task; it's like a clock going on. I have to do it
> sooner or later, so it's always going through my mind: What'll I
> do next? It's never very far off my level of consciousness that

I've got to write a column, and by the day before I've got to do it it's very high on my consciousness, and the day I've got to do it, I wake up thinking about it, because that's my work.

Reeves writes of the experience in *Jet Lag*:

Like the prospect of hanging, to paraphrase Dr. Johnson, columning has focused my mind wonderfully. I found myself alive and alert to my surroundings, to what I saw and heard and to what it meant; I was desperate, of course. Twice a week, rain or shine, sleet or snow, I have to deliver a readable thought. And I have to deliver it on time—if I'm late the syndicate (aptly named) charges me about seventy-five dollars. (42)

Later he points out that, "with your mind focused on the next dead-line, you notice what's happening around you" (72). For both writers, then, the frequent deadlines help keep them alert to the need to gather information, and they "assiduously string-save" any material that might potentially make a column.

Like Jim Fitzgerald, who writes twice as many columns annually as either Wicker or Reeves, the political columnists also depend upon being able to draw on resources they have drawn upon before. As Wicker puts it in the interview,

No columnist can afford to be a Johnny One-Note . . . so I have a fairly wide range of things that I write about . . . But you find also—it's true for every columnist—you keep coming back to a lot of the same subjects time and again . . . a certain amount of what I do can be recycled. That is to say, if I've used certain facts in one column, there's no reason I can't use those facts again.

Reeves treats the same issue this way in *Jet Lag*:

A column, usually, is one idea expanded. That, to me, means having at least two ideas a week, 104 a year. I don't, of course. But I do have several that I feel strongly about and don't have any compunction about repeating them. Over the years you learn that in a media-bombarded society, you have to repeat and repeat to get through—that's what commercials are about. (123)

The recycling or repetition sometimes draws upon the same informa-tion or returns to the same themes. Neither writer assumes that any readers are reading every column and keeping track of topics, and the repetition not only gives them a chance to reach other readers who may have missed earlier columns on the subject, it also gives them subjects to work on about which they have some prior interest and experience. This gives the column not only more authority but also greater ease of composition.

It is also likely to give the article more immediacy. Jim Fitzgerald, discussing the compilation of his collection of columns, *If It Fitz*, pointed out during the interview that

> so many [columns], particularly the way they're written, are based on a big news item the day before. You don't have to explain the news item because people know what you're talking about *then*, but not five years later.

His collection omits time-bound columns in favor of those that are timeless, but at the same time the columnist knows that a certain number of columns each year will inevitably be time-bound. In fact, Wicker explains in the interview that "something that you do now, this week, may be really good in the context of this week and a year from now have no relevance to anything"; for that reason he has never published a collection of his columns, "because there's just too much there that was topical at the time." The immediacy, the topicality, is important to the article at the time it is published, but the columnist knows it may be irrelevant or outdated quickly.

To some degree this explains why both Wicker and Reeves give their columns a lower priority in their writing than some other columnists do. Wicker says in the interview, "I've almost gotten to the point where I regard the *New York Times* work as secondary to other writing . . . I think of myself fundamentally as a writer" rather than as a reporter or columnist. Reeves lists his priorities in writing as, "in descending order, the books, work for *The New Yorker* and other magazine pieces, the column, the films." When he rises at five-thirty or six o'clock in the morning to work without interruption while he has his greatest energy of the day, he works on a book or magazine piece, if one is in the works, and puts the column off until later, unless he has no other, more pressing business.

All of these factors—the shortness of the column, the immersion in context, the regularity of writing, the ability to make connections between past columns and current events, the sense of the column's importance both to its audience and to its author's writing priorities— as well as other factors of the task environment and stored knowledge of the rhetorical dimensions of the writing aid in preparing and drafting the column. Some further sense of what happens during the composing of these two writers can be had by examining manuscript evidence.

Wicker's column, "Reagan's Apple Pie," discussed in the interview, was one of those he composed on a legal pad and phoned in to the *New York Times* from Vermont. The first page records a number of changes:

ROCHESTER, Vt., Sept. 9—The leaves are turning early
this year in the White River Valley and on the slopes of the
Green Mountains [above]. Brandon Gap (elevation 2,170 feet) is
[already a (faint) harbinger of (the summer) autumn, the red and gold]
already a harbinger of autumn, beginning shades of red and gold
[patterned] glowing richly against summer's (with) fading green.

                (too, in)
Children are going back to school, [in] this most tranquil
of states, lining up cheerfully by the roadside to wait for
[the buses that are commonplace here. The[y] make[s] fall the
true season of renewal; and the timeless (new school year)
ness of both the turn (that annual recycling of the generations,)

          new [illegible] growth
ing of the leaves and the [illegible] {children}]
(beauty and)
[the buses that are commonplace here. In their be]
[the buses that are commonplace here. In this beauty and
timelessness, the new growth of children—that annual recycling of the generations—as well as the turning of the leaves

                They also
make fall the true season of renewal ₓ [and] suggest how
much nonsense the world more commonly covers itself with]

                This new
the buses that have long been commonplace here. [In their]

  growth of   the
[beauty and] children, [that] annual recycling of the generations, as
well as the turning of the leaves—in the beauty and time-

  (of both)
lessness—make fall the true season of renewal.
    [They also suggest how]
              More 11

This representation gives some sense of the nature of Wicker's revisions. For one thing, he tries to write a sufficient number of words to the line so that he can predict the length of the piece, and his changes often involve interrupting one line with new words to be inserted at a point in the line above, as we see by the circled material. Arrows indicate where new information is to go—"new school year" between "They" and "make" on the line above (with appropriate changes to "The" and "makes"), "that annual . . . generations" into the space after "year." "Timelessness" and "turning" are broken off in midword to keep the line count reasonably accurate. Eventually the number of changes, circling of phrases, arching of arrows, insertions, and crossings-out make the section hard to follow. Wicker begins again at the left margin with a phrase he will keep through two more rounds of revision, "the buses that are commonplace here," at first quits on it and crosses it out, and then copies it over and tries to sort out the previous revisions into a flowing series of lines. This too he abandons with a large "X" through the section, and then he starts at the left margin a third time with "the buses . . ."

The changes the third time are much slighter, and he is able to observe in all these changes that he has so far produced eleven lines. On the second page of the draft he writes a circled "12" in the margin of the first line before he begins with the new paragraph and the very phrase he had crossed out at the bottom of the first page. In the pages that follow he keeps a running line count, and at the bottom of one page, after he has completed the page but gone to the middle to delete two sentences, notes "–2" to remind himself to adjust the count in the remainder of the manuscript. That deletion is of a statement that brings in tangential, marginally important information about Mr. McGregor, the man whom Wicker is using for comparison with President Reagan. From that point on, the draft makes only minor revisions until the end, when he adds a new paragraph to be inserted before the concluding two paragraphs. This is the single draft of the article, and Wicker phoned it in to New York reading from that manuscript.

The manuscript of another article, "There He Goes Again," shows far fewer revisions of substantive or stylistic kinds, but it does have at the top of the first page an example of the kind of outline Wicker provides himself for "a sense of how you're going to proceed." It reads:

Reagan quote
Regan   "
This overoptimism events
    Investment
    Int rates
    Fed
81–82 Tax Bill Contradix

The guide is not followed faithfully, although all of these points are touched on in the order indicated, and, except for one paragraph in the middle, the piece moves much more smoothly through initial drafting and minor revisions to a final draft.

The evidence of Richard Reeves' manuscripts reveals a similar approach. One, originally titled "What's Wrong With the Senate?" and printed as "Fixing the Broken Senate," is accompanied by a preliminary sheet that reads:

```
            (1) "Process"
Lede?       (2) No one controls        (4) Unanimous Consent/No Debate
End?        (3) RARE OPPORTUNITY [DOLE]        [QUAYLE]
            (5) WHAT TO DO?
            (6) Reduce Staff      1,176-   595 in '68
Sched         (5X)- Scheduling Weeks, Days
Rules         (5A) Committees      (5Y) 1,2,3,
Committees------------------------------(5Z) Rules          (5C)
      [(5B) Debate]              (TV availability)

      A- Quayle      Democratization      CHOKING


                     Mail –13,000   HHH
                          1964 [illegible]
                  161   O'Neill   [illegible]
                     [illegible] doubled in
                     1970              10 yrs
                         2.8- in 5
```

Although some of these items are numbered to indicate their places in the article, a comparision of the preliminary sheet with the actual draft, which is very close to the published article, demonstrates that here Reeves is brainstorming more than outlining. Many of the references never make it into the article, and some that do are in different locations than this worksheet would lead a reader to expect. For example, the prospective lead and prospective ending are both replaced by other material. In the case of the ending, a comment on allowing Senate activity to be televised, considered as one of a series of paragraphs on changes, ends up concluding the article as a sardonic quote from Daniel Evans rather than a recommendation.

Moreover, it is clear from the manuscript that these decisions are made in the course of drafting. The single draft begins this way:

> Wash, D.C.—Daniel Evans became a U.S. Senator on _____ and then he found out there was no Senate.
>
> That lead may be an exaggeration, but it is only a slight one. "I was shocked when I got here and that hasn't changed," said the former gov of [W] the state of Wash, [wr] a Republican appt'd (Insert: and [later] elected _____ months later) [when] after Sen H Jkson died [and then elected last month _____ (when?) _____ "We've got a lot of stuff that's broken here and we should fix it before we try to do anything else."
>
> "Process," he said, is the problem. The Senate is broken because old, cumbersome, elitist procedures and traditions have collapsed—and, so far, no one has been able to get the 100 Senators together to fix up new ones. ["The World's Greatest] [The Senate] What used to call itself "the World's Greatest Deliberative Body" is so democratic and individualistic now that it no longer deliberates at all. Senators don't even meet each other, much less deliberate in comm or debate on the floor.

The changes that Reeves makes in this text are chiefly questions of style—how to phrase a sentence, where to put information—not substantive changes of content. Once he establishes his lead, moving the idea of process from the start of the piece to the third paragraph and using the quote from Evans about the "broken senate" to replace the idea that "no one controls" it, which he had considered for the lead, the draft continues without significant shifts in direction to the conclusion. Items on his preliminary sheet are discarded and new items are generated, such as when his note about "unanimous consent/no debate" becomes this paragraph:

> There is usually no one there. [Senators speak to] A Senate "debate" is one senator orating to an empty hall. ["Committee hearing"] A Senate "hearing" is a committee chairman popping

in and out of a committee room while staffers listen to witnesses. [The] And where is everyone else? At their own "hearings" or back home [in the district] telling Rotary Clubs how important Senators are.

The sardonic tone of this paragraph is not indicated in the preliminary sheet, and the revisions clearly attempt to replace straightforward, declarative phrases with ones more critical in tone. In the last two sentences of the paragraph the edge to these remarks is clear. Clearly Reeves is relying here on the text produced so far to help generate text.

A different column by Reeves was written on the back of a copy of Senator Evans' testimony on the Senate committee system, a background source of the previous article. In this article on the U. S. involvement in Afghanistan, the revisions—this time made either in pencil as the original draft was being composed or in red ink during a later reading—are again chiefly directed at tone or clarity and are relatively minor. The draft leaves a gap intended to be filled in from another source already in finalized form. In the same way, Reeves leaves spaces in the Senate piece for information he needs accurate data on and, in an article about the meaning of the outcome of the 1984 presidential election, makes a note to himself referring to a passage in an article he had recently published in *New York Times Magazine* that he later inserted verbatim into the column. Since in such cases he is usually phoning in the column for transcription, he feels no obligation to prepare a final draft for publication since the text he is working on is one he himself will be dictating from.

The election column was written on the plane flying to a speaking engagement at Central Michigan University and dictated over the phone from the airport before he was driven to campus. He had carried the *Times* article with him intending to use it as a resource for a column; he was also speaking on the election results the day after the election. The next morning he rose early to work on his filmscript of "Red Star over Khyber" for the PBS program *Frontline,* and then started a round of activities with faculty and students that lasted until he was driven back to the airport. That kind of schedule is fairly typical of the circumstances under which Reeves regularly works, with a number of projects under consideration or in progress at any given time. Since a good many political columnists need to be actively engaged in gathering information as well as following public events, such a schedule is not atypical for others as well.

Moreover, the demands of constant composition force columnists of all kinds to be more pragmatic and less demanding about their work. In *On Press*, Wicker writes of

> the columnist's relentless routine—for me, three articles a week, at the fixed length of 750 words each (about the equivalent of writing a magazine article every week), the three pieces due on certain days of the week, rain or shine, ideas or no ideas, hangover or no hangover. (148)

The relentlessness of that routine necessitates standards of professionalism that stop far short of perfection. Frequently in these interviews, as the writers are asked to examine specific articles, they are moved to point out that some are not examples of their best writing but are merely adequate or not completely satisfying. Wicker explained the problem well in *On Press:*

> Just as Detroit sometimes has to recall its cars, not everything I or any columnist turns out is up to scratch. For myself, I estimate—and talks with colleagues suggest that my experience is not untypical—about one-third of my columns come reasonably close to meeting my personal standards. I don't mean one of every three or one a week, either; sometimes a long period of intellectual aridity afflicts anyone who has to keep turning out articles week in and week out . . . I mean roughly a third of the total over the years may have been the kind of work in which I could take real satisfaction.
>
> As for the rest, some aimed high but missed the mark, which is neither surprising nor deplorable; but more have been the kind of hackwork any demanding schedule is likely to produce—compilations of fact without illumination, old ideas rehashed, easy pieces of advocacy, slick repackaging of someone else's news story. Ideas worth writing about don't come all that easily or often; or maybe they just aren't recognized. (160)

Most of the regular columnists and critics in these interviews acknowledged that some portion of their work did not come up to their personal standards, although most would assert that the work was acceptable or professional or sufficient. Most could cite work of which they were especially proud.

One aspect of the work of Wicker and Reeves that should perhaps be stressed, then, is the difficulty of maintaining a consistent level of quality over a large number of compositions. Related to that is the importance of setting priorities for the work a writer does, to channel the most productive energies into the most important work and to hold the less important to a standard of acceptability rather than perfection. These are aspects of composing that affect the outcome of the writing but may not always be taken into consideration by writers without deadlines, multiple assignments, and conflicting obligations—or by the people who study them. However, they are aspects of composing that columnists face regularly.

Interview with Tom Wicker

Root. What exactly are your working conditions?

Wicker. I write two columns a week—up to about 1980, it was three columns a week. Until the schedule is changed, which it could be, my articles appear in the *Times* on Tuesdays and Friday.

Ordinarily, I sit over there and work on my computer terminal, I would say half the time. When I'm traveling, I write in longhand and we have a very effective dictation system; you just pick up the telephone and dictate into a tape recorder and then someone else transcribes it into the computer terminal. I no longer have to carry a typewriter because no one has to literally read my copy; I put it in the telephone. And I much prefer to write in longhand anyway. I've written all my books in longhand. But for traveling, it's really a great boon not to have to carry a typewriter. I can take a yellow legal pad, and my handwriting is such—I learned to do it—that a line of my handwriting is roughly the equivalent of a typewriter line. So, just as if I were working on a typewriter, I would count seventy-five lines or 750 words and it comes out with considerable accuracy. With the computer terminal you don't have to do that, because it counts the words for you.

Root. So you're supposed to come out with seventy-five lines, at average?

Wicker. Well, I just used that as an example. My columns average about eighty lines. Sometimes there's a difference depending upon the makeup of the page. A column straight down the page, which is the most common form, is eight hundred words, and that leaves room for the headline. Sometimes when they back it up all the way across the page or in three columns or something like that it's different; usually you lose a little space on that.

Root. Do they edit things out for space?

Wicker. No. If the column is too long—that's what happened yesterday; they called me and said I was one line over—then right on the telephone with the copy editor I work out what's to be taken out. But, unless it's circumstances in which I'm traveling and they cannot reach me, they don't cut the copy on their own. They might call and say, "I really don't quite understand this sentence and maybe we can clear it up some," so we might do that sort of thing. Or if I misspell something, or more commonly if I've written it in such a way that doesn't conform to *Times* style—sometimes I might capitalize something or not capital-ize something that our style calls for—they'll make those changes, but they won't change the text in any way without clearing with me unless I'm not reachable, and then they only do it for length.

Root. What essentially do you see as the charge you have for the column?

Wicker. There are two ways that I see that. First is my literal charge to the *New York Times* which is in the title of the column, "In The Nation." I began writing that column when I was bureau chief of the Washington Bureau. But my basic assignment is to write about national affairs, which could be Washington affairs but is not limited to Washington affairs. And it can even be foreign affairs as long as it has some really strong interest here. I probably wouldn't write about the Iranian-Iraq war, unless there was some good reason; for example, it was causing some problems with our oil supplies. Most national columnists write about politics and economy and that sort of thing. I write about that too, but I'm the only columnist I know of who writes at all frequently about criminal justice, for example—I'm very interested in that. I write about transportation; it just happens to be an interest of mine. So I interpret that very broadly as writing about national affairs.

Another way to look at that is, what is it you're trying to do for readers? The *Times* didn't tell me anything about that—they just rely on me to be a reasonably good columnist—but I have a few ideas for myself. I go into it in some detail in *On Press*. I don't try to persuade a reader; I don't try necessarily to achieve some purpose—get a bill passed or something like that. More than anything else I want to cause people to think about a subject, to generate some consideration of a matter, maybe to put it in a light people haven't perhaps thought of before or, because they're not in my line of work, don't have an opportunity to see in that fashion. I don't in the slightest mind, or have it anger me, if people don't agree with me. I'm not trying to get people to agree with me. I'm trying to get people to think about what I'm writing and to feel that what I'm writing has somehow advanced their own knowledge or broadened their way of looking at it. If in fact it makes them angry, that's good—somehow it's got through.

Root. Do you have a sense of who the reader is? I mean, for example, that the *New York Times* reader is different from the reader of the *Sandhill Citizen*.

Wicker. I try not to think that way. The shortest answer to that is that I write to please myself. I figure that anything that interests me is likely to interest enough other people to be worth doing. I don't figure that I'm smarter than a whole lot of other people, and I certainly don't figure that a whole lot of other people are smarter than I am. I do think that, on occasion, because of the nature of my work, and because I work for the *New York Times*, I have the opportunity to talk to people or to learn about things in a way that even a very intelligent, well-informed person who is working in some other field or living somewhere else doesn't have. But I would say that I write to please myself; if the subject interests me, then I figure it's well worth writing about.

Root. When you're writing, do you follow the same procedure? Plan it, draft it? You said the procedure would change if you're on the road or if you're here. But do you essentially take the same amount of time to write it each time?

Wicker. The actual literal writing of the column is about, I would say, two to three hours. It varies somewhat. The better prepared you are when you sit down, the easier it is to write the column. But being prepared doesn't necessarily mean just having a whole hell of lot of information; sometimes that can hinder you with all this great stuff you're trying to get in there. But when I say being prepared I mean having a coherent idea, one that you can state rather briefly and simply, having the information to substantiate that idea, and having in your head or on paper or outline—I usually outline things—a sense of how you're going to proceed, a beginning, a middle, and an end. It's one of my theories—I won't say rules—for a columnist that you're dealing with ideas, and all the information in the world won't make a good column unless there's an idea in it. If you've got an idea, then all you really need is just enough information to plausibly state your idea and support it. Flowing out of that is another of my theories— the word that I apply to myself, if not to anybody else—I don't think you've got an idea unless you can sit down and state it in a relatively short paragraph. If it takes you more than that, you really don't have an idea, you're just fumbling around. Or you have a whole lot of corollaries and you haven't settled on that one theme that you want to put through. I often find that that one paragraph where I simply state my idea, my theme, often turns out to be my lead. I just state it and there it is and that in effect is the content of the column. Then I take seven hundred-odd words to support it, with fact or anecdote or analysis or whatever, state it again and quit.

Root. Speaking of that, I was looking at several of the columns and one that struck me is that one, "Reagan's Apple Pie," about the school kids. The structure starts with the lead about enduring values, children going back to school, autumn coming to Vermont, contrasts that with the nonsense that's prevalent in the world, the first example being McGregor of Vermont and the second example being Reagan on two issues. Then the article talks about Reagan's view of abortion and his view of school prayer, and how they are actually contradictory things that he is doing which are both attempts to get on the bandwagon. There's an analysis of Reagan's motives, then you go back to that lead again, as you suggested. Let me ask what you felt you were trying to accomplish with that and what started you working on it?

Wicker. I have a house up in Vermont and had been up there about a week; I had not really done any personal work, calling anybody or doing any interviews or anything of that sort, but I was following the newspapers, knowing that I had to write a column at some point, and was struck by how early the leaves were turning up there, as everyone was. I wanted to say something about that—autumn in New England is a mellow time—and I wanted a mellow feel to things. At the same time I didn't feel justified in just writing at that time a kind of scenic, don't-we-all-love-nature piece. So one way or another I just sat down and it worked out this way. Exactly how those connections get made in your head is hard to trace. The business about the children going back to school—I can tell you that my children are all grown now or at least college age, but I have several times over the years as a columnist used that notion because, having been a father and raised children, children going back to school always seem to me to be the true beginning of the year. If you researched my whole file you'd find that I've used that notion a lot of times. People have an inventory of ideas and you keep calling on it every so often.

Root. In *On Press* you said you'd written fifteen hundred articles in ten years.

Wicker. I started in 1966, and from 1966 to 1980 it was three a week, you see, so it mounts up.

Root. I know you've made reference to Reagan's position on abortion and the Jesse Helms bills other times.

Wicker. None of that would have been new to me. I would have written that all before in some context.

Root. Was it that you started in this mood and then found something to contrast with that mood?

Wicker. No, I decided from following the news that week that these topical matters were what I was going to write about. As one of the things you do, I think I mentioned before, you need a way to proceed, a beginning, a middle, and an end. I mean, what are you going to start with? On occasion, I start with just a flat statement of my idea, whatever it is. In this particular case, as I say, I was influenced to see if there was some way that I could use all of that. I would tell you frankly and I thought at the time—I'm a professional writer and I can do things—that's a fairly weak connection. I wouldn't regard that as one of my strongest pieces by any means. There are times when something that you have as an observation will lead you on quite naturally and easily and even powerfully. The "Apple Pie" piece was acceptable. I wouldn't say more than that for it.

Root. Did you do an outline of that?

Wicker. Only the most cursory kind of outline. When I said I outline pieces, what I consider an outline is just a guide to myself. It's really not in any detail at all. That's what I usually do, almost always. I suppose sometimes if I'm really up against deadline or I've got something that I'm writing at "white heat" so to speak, I might not outline but I can't remember an occasion. It's just easy to have a little roadmap.

Root. Essentially, then, you were interested in Reagan's making the political moves. How did you decide to put in the piece on McGregor?

Wicker. I read it in the paper up there and it struck me as funny, as being the kind of political nonsense you get this time of year. There's a mistake in that, I found out, the *White River Valley Herald*'s mistake. He's a Democrat rather than a Republican, but I didn't find that out until a week later. I was just sort of cribbing from the local paper.

Root. The amount of time that you had this idea wasn't very long, was it? You said you were sitting around reading the paper and noticing what's going on in the world.

Wicker. The way it works, it's never really far off my mind that I've got to write a column, even if it's Sunday afternoon and I don't have to do it again until Thursday afternoon. It's a relentless task; it's like a clock going on. I have to do it sooner or later, so it's always going through my mind: What'll I do next? It's never very far off my level of consciousness that I've got to write a column, and by the day before I've got to do it it's very high on my consciousness, and the day I've got to do it, I wake up thinking about it, because that's my work. I have to do it, so I don't exactly remember now but I know that all through that week I was up in Vermont, it would recur to me: What am I going to write about?

When I go off on a trip like that I take lots of material along with me because more and more in recent years I find myself writing without any particular reference to the headlines. I don't mean just ignoring the headlines but, when I first began as a columnist, particularly doing three a week—and that's a lot more than two, you'd be surprised, it doesn't sound like it but it's a hell of a lot more—I used to write a lot right out of the headlines. I mean, you get up one morning and Reagan has said so and so and you sit down and do a piece about Reagan saying so and so. I do that a good deal less than I used to, say one-third less than I used to. When I say without reference to the headlines, I don't mean without reference to what's happening in the world. But, for example, I'm writing my next piece about a question having to do with nuclear weapons strategy and that sort of thing. It's not in the headlines as such, but it's part of the currency in the world at the moment. When I went up to Vermont that week I took a briefcase full of stuff like that, so it was not a question of, "Oh, my God, I don't have anything to write about." I had plenty to write about, but I also kept watching the news—is there something topical that seems to me more timely, more instant, or more useful than this material I have in my briefcase which after all I can do next week or the week after—maybe not anytime, but perhaps sometime or another? That sort of triggered me off. Had that not happened, I might have very easily pulled out the stuff out of my briefcase that I'm now writing for tomorrow. I don't think that's quite true, but could've been.

Root. Was there anything in it that you changed radically, or is this pretty much what came out? Was there an earlier draft that was much different?

Wicker. No. This would have been a longhand piece. I remember sitting out on my open porch in Vermont on a beautiful fall day and writing that. I do not at this moment remember whether I had more or less trouble than I usually have, but I do remember that I didn't have to rewrite it. Sometimes that happens; sometimes you get into a piece and any number of things can happen. First place, the news can change; you never know how it might blow up. Happened to me recently. I was writing a piece about the Middle East and fortuitously I turned on the cable news and I found out Reagan made a whole new peace proposal right in the middle of my composing over there; fortunately I had time to adapt to that. Or you can get into something and decide your one point is a little weak and call up somebody or check your references or something and find out that you're all wrong, you're operating out of an assumption that is not correct. That can happen too. Or you get into a piece—and this has happened to me a number of times—and decide that, by God, this is just not good enough; I thought there was a column here but there's not. Sometimes you're stuck but you have to go ahead anyway, it's too late, but other times you rewrite or change your approach when it happens.

Root. That reminds me of a couple of things. One is that you talked about being a string saver in *On Press* and the importance of that— how much do you draw on that for your writing as opposed to, let's say, when you started out and didn't have any string?

Wicker. A great deal. I have an elephantine memory and I don't think anybody could function in this business without it, or not very well. I have really a strong memory for that kind of thing, and I think it helps a great deal when something happens to be able to flip through the files of your mind and say, "Yeah, yeah, right, Eisenhower did something like that in 1958," and have just that much of memory to go and look it up, if you don't have the full memory and such. Not only just historical stuff like that but, for example, I collected a lot of material to write a piece about Marcos while he was here, the Phillipine president. I'm very critical about him; I've read about him before. Somehow while he was here, I never quite saw the opportunity to do it. I didn't want to just write a "Marcos is bad" piece—it's kind of like criticizing the Ku Klux Klan, and anybody can do that. I really didn't have an idea for it. But I collected a lot of material and I'll hang on to that and sooner or later that particular material is going to come in handy. There'll be something in the news, some reason that'll give me reason to dump on Ferdinand Marcos, and I've got a lot of material there to do it. I've got in those stacks clips of stuff I've pulled out, I couldn't list for you what's in there now, but if I picked up the paper this morning and read a particular story, it might very well trigger something and I know I've got something in there that pairs up with that, or contradicts it or whatever, and pull it out.

Root. What kind of thing have you thrown away?

Wicker. I can't think of anything quite recently. I've thrown away a lot of ideas at one time, pieces that I was going to write and presumably could have written but ultimately just didn't because something else came along that was better or I thought was better, or else I delayed it long enough to where it was no longer really relevant or whatever.

Just for example, the *Times* did a piece about the majority leader, Jim Wright, who fancies himself a barbeque cook, as indeed do I, and I know a good deal about barbequing and Wright's recipes are, in my judgment, just barbarous. So I was going to write a funny piece and say, "This man might be a good majority leader but he's a terrible cook." Well, I never got around to it and it's probably not a good idea anyway. And then I saw a reference about some big to-do at the Kennedy Center where Jim Wright was going to cook barbeque for them. And I was going to write a piece that all those people are going to be poisoned. But I haven't done that and I probably won't.

Sometimes you do things like that when you're doing even two a week and particularly when I was doing three a week. I really notice it and I notice it several ways. When I was writing three, for a good many years, I was frequently really stuck for something to write about, not that there wasn't a topic but there wasn't something that I felt was good enough or interesting enough or that I wanted to do or that Reston hadn't just done, or Tony Lewis hadn't just done, whatever. Many's the time I would find myself, two o'clock in the afternoon and four o'clock's the deadline, saying, "Jesus Christ, I gotta do something." That almost never happens any more with the cutback to two. Almost never. As I said I find that very many fewer times I write out of today's headlines.

The third thing is, and I find this is really the most serious—I rather like three—I would in many ways rather go back to the three. I don't write a lot of pieces I'd like to write, because there's just not time to do it. It affects the travel too. If you go somewhere interesting for a month, like I traveled in Africa for nearly six weeks in 1978, you'll stack up a hell of a lot of column material. I was then writing three columns, and my Africa columns stretched out long after I got back from about the first of November until after Christmas. Well, now, comparably they stretch out from about the first of November to about the middle of February, and you just really can't do that. So if I went to Africa for a month now I would wind up writing many fewer columns than I did before just simply because of the time it takes to get them in the paper. Ten columns then would get in in three weeks; ten columns now would get in in five weeks.

It makes a difference when you're traveling. This is the first election that I have covered really with just two a week, and I drew up extensive travel plans and I'm going to be gone for three weeks in more than a dozen states or so, but all that is is six columns. I thought to myself, is this worth it or not? It is because I'll have that knowledge and that fills up my inventory up here which I need even though I don't write the piece.

Root. Let me ask you about another article. The structure of this is basically going off of what Ariel Sharon said about Jerusalem not being Saigon. This is one where you have that structure you were talking about—the Jerusalem and Saigon quote, the argument that America is not the one who's got difficulty with that, the U.S.'s position, the statements that we *haven't* done these things that we did to Vietnam but we *have* expected these things, and here's what the Israelis did, and then the conclusion that Jerusalem is behaving like the Saigon government did and that's where the comparison is. So in fact what you do is take this from their interpretation of the quote to a new interpretation of the quote. How did you arrive at that structure? Do you remember anything about composing this?

Wicker. Yeah, I do. I remember reading the Associated Press story, obviously in the newspaper which I was getting, and that's one those things—I often react this way—that angered me. I thought that really a reprehensible thing for Sharon to have said, and I think he's a reprehensible man anyway, and if you recall at that period—this was right at the time when the Beirut massacre was being disclosed and the Israeli responsibility, to the extent that it is a responsibility, was headline news. So I was really writing off the headlines that day. But now, the background, the side of the record of what the Israelis did and all that, I tell you that came right out of my head, and that's what I'm talking about having a memory. I can remember all that; it's not difficult, it's just this past summer. It's my business to know things like that, and then I'm backstopped on that, if I felt at all shaky on it. I could have called up here and had my research assistant check every line of that column and make sure. I didn't because I was really sure about it, but I could have.

Root. So you worked out an outline that covered that. You've got the U.S. position and the expectations of the U.S. and then you've got all of that stuff, and I'm wondering which came first. I mean, your reaction, as you say, was to the quote.

Wicker. Well, I had the almost immediate idea; as I say, reading that quote angered me and I thought that's a terrible thing for him to have said. Then I immediately thought of what seemed to me the irony that in fact they're acting like Saigon used to act. So the genesis of the column was an almost immediate reaction to what I read; then it's a fairly simple step from there that we're not treating them like Saigon, they're treating us like Saigon used to treat us.

Root. What do you think of that piece?

Wicker. I think that's a pretty good piece. I got a lot of critical mail on that; the Jewish groups and so forth didn't care for that. That burned them a little. But I think it's a legitimate piece and I'm very careful in here on these things, as one should be. My criticism is of the Begin and Sharon government, not of Israel. I'm a strong supporter of Israel.

Root. You said in *On Press* that about a third of your articles met your personal standards.

Wicker. That was when I was writing three a week. I'd like to think it was higher now. I hadn't really thought about it since I wrote that. Clearly it ought to be; if you're writing nearly two-thirds as many you ought to have more that are up to snuff. But I think I used the one-third figure in there—obviously I didn't go through and count them, anything like that—because I figured that was about right. At least once a week in those days I wrote something that I considered reasonably weak; it might not have been every week, but I mean it would have averaged out to about one a week.

Root. You mentioned that you talked to other people and that figure seemed to be about right for them.

Wicker. I think something that you have to remember too is that something that you do now, this week, may be really quite good in the context of this week and a year from now have no relevance to anything. That's why I have never collected any of my columns in a book; I would be reluctant to do it unless somebody paid me so much money that my principles would decline. But I think that collections of columns are rarely if ever very good because there's just too much that was topical at the time.

If you were going to do that you'd have to pick out some kind of a theme for your book or two or three themes and try to use columns that illustrated something. For example, I thought at one time of doing a book in which I would publish all of my journalism during the Vietnam war—I wrote a lot of news stories in those days too—and try to show through what I had written how one man's view of that whole episode had changed through the years and then do some commentary on what I had written to try to identify the influences that were causing the changes. Now I think something like that could have value. Or for another thing if someone had written, and in fact I have, a lot, about a couple of issues that I've seen just come almost full circle over the years. Environmental questions—I used to write a lot about clean water and clean air, you know, and nobody'd listen. About bulldozing down the buildings, dumping the DDT and all, well, all that's changed and come full circle. People thought I was crazy. I was the only person in the entire country, as far as I know, of anyone writing, who opposed wire tapping. Nobody uses wire tapping any more except the FBI catches a few bookies that way and foreign intelligence work where everybody's tapping everybody else. But Frank Hogan, the district attorney of New York, tried to get me fired because he used to tap everybody; he never caught anybody, but he tapped them. So I think you could do a book like that showing how things have changed over the years, but just to throw in two hundred columns back to 1966, who gives a damn? Whole pieces denouncing Nixon and all . . . I don't find anybody knocking down the doors to publish mine and I'm certainly not anxious to do it. I'm usually working on some other kind of book anyway.

Root. Let me show you another article of yours. This is the one, "Recycling an Idea." It's about the Conservation Corps. Again, I guess the reason I picked this one out is that I noticed a couple of things here—one, that it starts with talking about the C.C.C. and North Carolina and then talks about FDR and the Conservation Corps and then goes on to talk about Moynihan and Mathias' proposal, how it's going to be backed and paid for and so forth, the Reagan administration's objections and the fallacy that you find in their objections, the success of the California Conservation Corps, and the final note on Reagan's Ecology Corps which preceded the California Conservation Corps. There seem to be a lot of parts to this. How did that come together?

Wicker. I didn't know anything about the Moynihan proposal, but some reader wrote in and said I should support it and my research assistant, who opens my mail, said, "I think this is a good idea; why don't I follow up on it?" I have always supported and been in favor of things like C.C.C. and maybe national service for young people. So I said fine, go ahead, and he did most of the reporting on the actual bill that is before Congress and gave me a very good memo on it. And then there was a newspaper article, "The Senate subcommittee will open hearings on the Moynihan-Mathias bill September 22." This column appeared September the 19th, so that was the timing of it. And the way I wrote it is just because there are plenty of people like me who remember the C.C.C.—they did do a lot of work around my hometown—so it's just kind of an anecdotal lead to get into the subject.

This is the kind of column that I don't do too much of. In many ways this is like an editorial. It's a piece of advocacy. You don't find too many articles like that in my scrapbooks, but I occasionally do them and I do think this is a good idea. It leads to an even better idea I would like, and have advocated before, a much broader scale youth corps that would do several things: primarily, take a hell of a lot of unemployed kids off the street so they don't mug you at the drop of a hat and put them to useful work that will stick with some of them. And then we've got lots of things in this country that could be done; we could rebuild the railroads that way—we built them with Chinese and Irish immigrants before and we could do it with black kids from Harlem now. We could have a tremendous impact on our energy usage if every house in America were insulated. Installation of insulation again is something we could do if the unions wouldn't kill you for it. There are a lot of things like that. You begin to see stories now about a really serious problem in this country which is the deterioration of our infrastructure, roads, bridges, sewers. Again, a hell of a lot of that could be done that way. I don't think it's my job or my business to sit down and figure out exactly how you would get a youth corps at work building the railroads and how you would get around all the problems and how much that would cost, but I think it is my job to throw out ideas like that, so this is really part of an ongoing approach that I've had. I've written that a lot of times about the railroads and the insulation and that sort of thing. The beauty of that is you get something done—I do not honestly know if it would be cheaper that way than by hiring skilled laborers; I think it probably would be—but I'm almost certain it's maybe the nearest thing you could have in this country to a real anticrime program.

Root. What about "Enough Is Enough," the one published today? It's fairly fresh. Can you tell whether it's a good column or not?

Wicker. I think it's a good column; it's useful. This quickly I couldn't evaluate it beyond that. Of course, that was inspired by Reagan's remark the other day, but I was less interested at this point in bopping him one for McCarthyism, although he certainly deserves it, than I was in trying to develop the other ideas that are in here, the subject of ideas, not the mere fact that he's misrepresenting things. Because I do think that the freeze movement is important. I specify that the movement is more important than the freeze. In my line of work for years somehow I never felt it necessary to get much into that. I don't exactly know why, but I left that to other people; I didn't write much about these things. Beginning about the time that Carter proposed that whole big MX thing, I began to get interested. It was just a natural interest to begin with; I didn't say to myself, "Gee, I ought to go and learn about that." I got interested in that and then one thing led to another, and by now, insofar as a newspaper man ever does, I consider myself as fairly authoritative on those issues. I've learned a lot about it, read a lot about it, talked to a lot of people. I regard it as profoundly important, nothing is more important, and I think the advent of Reagan has been salutary in the fact that it woke us up out of about a twenty-year sleep to the importance of nuclear arms control. So that's one of many columns that I've written on it. And I look for opportunities to write about that subject, plausible opportunities.

No columnist can afford to be a Johnny One-Note. You can't write about the same thing day after day, week after week, and so I have a fairly wide range of things that I write about. I keep a chronological scrapbook out here. If you went through it for, say, two months, and counted the number of topics in there, I think it would be fairly wide most of the time. But you find also—it's true for every columnist—you keep coming back to a lot of the same subjects time and again. I keep coming back to certain subjects; Tony Lewis keeps coming back to the Middle East, for example.

I don't assume that somebody—you have because you had a purpose—reads all of my columns. Therefore, I assume that a certain amount of what I do can be recycled. That is to say, if I've used certain facts in one column, there's no reason I can't use those facts again. I wouldn't necessarily do it on consecutive days, but in fact I often use my own columns as a resource. I have a pretty long memory for these things; I know that back there in 1980 I wrote something or other. I'm getting ready to write another piece, and when the hell was it when I wrote that about so and so, and I know that it was roughly in the summer of 1980 and go to my scrapbooks and find that column and there's my research for me, I use it all over again. I do that a lot, I'm doing it now. That's why my scrapbook is over there, for the column I'm writing now.

Root. Do you ever feel influenced by anybody? In *On Press* you talked about the influences of Philips Russell and Worth Bacon and I'm also wondering about someone like Arthur Krock or other people who are writing. Do you ever, say, read William Safire and say, "Gee, that was a good piece"?

Wicker. Sure, I often do. I read the other columnists fairly widely. Of course, I read all of our paper and I read the *Washington Post* op-ed page very religiously, and that pretty well covers the waterfront for the leading columnists right there, with rare exceptions. Then I read the *Wall Street Journal* pretty regularly, particularly their editorial page spread—I don't read the rest of it—and I'm often influenced. I try to be careful not to repeat what some other columnist has done, but on the other hand I think it's fairly frequent that out of Joe Kraft or Tony or Reston or somebody I get something that fills in an idea of my own or maybe sets off an idea of my own or sometimes I see things that I disagree with very strongly in other people's columns. I think this is a strong influence.

Root. Are you ever influenced by their style of writing?

Wicker. No, I don't believe that. I've almost gotten to the point where I regard the *New York Times* work as secondary to other writing. I just finished a novel I've been working on for four years, *Unto This Hour*, and I'm getting ready to start a nonfiction book on Richard Nixon. Beyond that I've got two other novels blocked out. So more than most of these guys—I don't mean to imply that I'm a better writer than most of them—I think of myself as fundamentally a writer, and I think with rare exceptions—George Will might be one—most of those columnists would think of themselves as columnists and reporters. Look at Tony. Tony Lewis is my age, he's written one book, I've written eleven. I don't mean to draw any other comparison 'cause he does what he wants and does it brilliantly in my judgment; his stuff on the Middle East has been incredible. But I'm saying that my whole line of work is focused on writing. Most of those fellows are much more focused on journalism than I am. And so therefore I would doubt very seriously that any newspaper writing has ever been any influence on my literal composition. Now there would be novelists who have certainly influenced me as a writer.

Root. Like who?

Wicker. Faulkner, Graham Greene, two very different writers. Joseph Conrad in particular probably more than anybody else.

Root. What things about them influence you?

Wicker. Well, that's hard to say. It's hard to define in that sense, but I could go into some of my books and identify a really Conradian sentence here and there. Ways of telling a story, in effect. I think all good writers, speaking now of novelists, really learn the trade by reading and there are very few just natural-born storytellers. If they are, that's much more likely to be oral than written, and oral story telling doesn't work on the page or doesn't often work on the page. So I think almost every good novelist today, and there aren't many, is shaped by two things—one by reading and the other by the movies. You can look at post-1920 fiction and fiction pre-1920 and there are real differences because writers now look very much out of a camera's eye. They look in a way that they've seen things depicted on the screen. Take the opening of *The Heart of the Matter* by Graham Greene. Scobie is sitting on a balcony over a street in an African city and he's looking at the street life and you've seen that opening in a thousand movies where you see all this swirling and finally the camera moves in on the sign that says Cairo Hotel or something. And you can find that in fiction all over the place today, to the point where it's possible to take a novel and translate it almost literally page for page to the screen because it's written like a movie. For example, *The Spy Who Came in from the Cold;* go to that movie sometime and then read the book.

Root. The movie was very close to the book, and in fact there are a lot of people who seem to write scenes that are obviously only there to go into a movie.

Wicker. If not that, they're done because the only way the writer knows to construct a scene is the way he's seen it on the screen. With older people like myself, I believe I'm more influenced by reading than by movies. You'll notice that of the three writers that I spoke of, Faulkner, Conrad, and Greene, Greene I think is the only one that is a movie-style writer. Conrad probably never saw any movies as far as I know, only the earliest ones, and Faulkner was himself a screen writer, and a damn good one, but that doesn't mean he wrote his books that way. Most of his best work was done before he went to Hollywood.

Root. When you're revising something, how much is revising for style and how much is revised for clarity and accuracy?

Wicker. That's hard to say, and it's redundant a little bit because style is clarity and accuracy.

Root. Yes, but sometimes when you read a sentence, you think, People aren't going to understand what I'm saying.

Wicker. I try very hard; I'm limited now to newspaper work. It's true also writing in books but that's a different thing. One of the things I try hardest for is absolute clarity, to be understood, to make things clear. In fact, I think that's one of the things a columnist should set himself to do, to make complex things clear to the reader, but I mean even in addition to explaining something as complex as, let's say, this morning's column—trying to explain why there's no real advantage in having a hundred nuclear bombs if the other guy only has ninety—that's a difficult concept to grasp so you want to make the concept clear, but to make the concept clear, the sentence has to be clear. One thing leads to another, and others may not agree and probably you're the worst judge of your own work, but I pride myself in writing clearly and, even if someone else disagrees, I pride myself in making exceptional effort to write clearly. I feel that's very important. Christ, if you're not understood, you could be brilliant, but it doesn't do you very much good.

Jerusalem and Saigon

Tom Wicker

Israel's muscle-flexing Defense Minister, Ariel Sharon, has declaimed in the Knesset, apparently in warning to the United States:

"This is Jerusalem, not Saigon. It would be well for you to remember this."

But it's Mr. Sharon and his supposed leader, Prime Minister Menachem Begin, who most need to remember that. Washington has not, after all, sent five hundred-thousand American troops to Israel, nor overwhelmed that country's society and economy. Neither the Reagan nor any predecessor Administration has carpet-bombed an enemy capital to placate a petulant Israeli government.

Despite dark insinuations from Jerusalem, Washington has not tried to destabilize the Begin-Sharon Government and certainly has instigated or supported no coups. Even the Reagan peace proposals, far from being a dastardly undercutting of Israel's rights and prospects, represent what has been basic American policy for decades—and sometimes Israel's.

On the other hand, the United States has been generous in its aid to Israel, even if no more so than deserved. But in return for the one-quarter of its total foreign aid that goes annually to Israel, and for the weapons that have—together with Israeli resolution and ingenuity—made Israel the strongest nation in the Middle East, Washington has no right to expect and has not demanded the subservience of a client state.

Washington does have a right to expect, however, that in return for its long and generous support Israel will deal with it fairly and squarely, and that Israel's own actions will reflect not only a decent respect for American policies and interests but also for the opinions of mankind.

But that is not what the United States has been receiving from the Begin-Sharon Government in recent months, as the following record shows:

The Israeli invasion of Lebanon was timed, purposely or not, to embarrass Mr. Reagan during his European tour; and the stated reason for it—to bring peace to Israel's northern border—was flimsy. That border had been quiet for a year, owing to a cease-fire negotiated by Philip Habib, under Mr. Reagan's auspices.

The originally announced invasion objective—a twenty-five-mile zone north of the border—was discarded by Israel as soon as its forces penetrated twenty-five miles into Lebanon. Cluster bombs were used, in defiance of American restrictions.

After the Israelis invested Beirut, and Mr. Habib began trying to arrange the evacuation of Palestinian guerrillas, Israeli forces—in the opinion of most observers—repeatedly broke the cease-fires Mr. Habib devised. Whatever the Israeli purpose, these tactics tended to undermine Arab respect for Mr. Reagan and the United States, hence to undercut not only American standing in the Middle East but also Washington's prospects as a peacemaker.

The subsequent Reagan peace proposals were spurned in the most vitriolic and abusive fashion by Mr. Sharon and Mr. Begin, who said it would be "treason" for any Israeli to support them. Nothing could have made clearer the Begin-Sharon Government's intention to hang onto the West Bank, in contravention of U.N. resolutions, American policy and most of the world's interpretation of the Camp David agreements that Mr. Begin signed.

A strong case can be made that, following the assassination of Bashir Gemayel, the Israelis entered West Beirut—again sabotaging an agreement devised by Philip Habib—to undermine the credibility of the Reagan proposals. In West Beirut, they signally failed their self-appointed mission of maintaining law and order in another country, and even Ariel Sharon admits that Israeli forces introduced vengeful Christian Phalangists into unprotected Palestinian camps.

That amounts at least to a complicity of incompetence and/or blindness to danger that Mr. Sharon would pay for with his office in most countries. But not only is he defiant; he and the Prime Minister will not even tolerate an independent investigation of what happened in West Beirut. Such stonewalling shows contempt, not just for world opinion but for all those American Jewish leaders who have been pleading with Washington to "wait for all the facts" before condemning Israel for the Beirut masssacre.

So Ariel Sharon is right that Jerusalem is not Saigon; but it isn't Washington that needs to be reminded of that—it's Jerusalem. For if the United States has no right to expect of Israel the subservience of a client state, it has every right to expect that the Government of Israel will not conduct itself like the militaristic, dictatorial and untrustworthy Governments that ruled in South Vietnam for so many years, to such bitter effect.

Reagan's Apple Pie

Tom Wicker

ROCHESTER, Vt., Sept. 9—The leaves are turning early this year in the White River Valley and on the slopes of the Green Mountains. Brandon Gap (elevation 2,170 feet) is already a harbinger of autumn, with beginning shades of red and gold glowing richly against summer's fading green.

Children are going back to school, too, in this most tranquil of states, lining up cheerfully by the roadside to wait for buses that have been commonplace here. This new growth of children, the annual recycling of the generations, as well as the turning of the leaves—in the beauty and timelessness of both—make fall the true season of renewal.

They also suggest how much nonsense the world more commonly works itself up about—the 1982 elections, for example, which are being waged here as everywhere else. In Tuesday's primaries Vermont has a Republican candidate for the United States Senate, Thomas McGregor, a pharmacist, who has confided to *The White River Valley Herald* that his decision to run was impelled by God, who he said appeared to Mrs. McGregor in a dream.

With such an endorsement as that, Mr. McGregor naturally opposes abortion *and* sex education, gun control and secular humanism, while favoring prayer in the schools and a strong military buildup. That puts him right in the footsteps of President Reagan.

Mr. Reagan, while claiming no heavenly backing, did his part for "family values" this week by strongly endorsing Senator Jesse Helms' anti-abortion proposal, and offering no opposition to the same Mr. Helms' plan to bring prayer back to the public schools by emasculating the Supreme Court. In both cases, a President—even one who shared

Mr. Helms's attitudes—who respected constitutional precedent, orderly procedure and the equality of citizens would have insisted instead on a constitutional amendment.

Mr. Reagan was apparently willing to put such conservative principles aside because, as an unnamed White House official put it to Steve Weisman of *The New York Times,* issues like abortion and prayer in the schools are "motherhood and apple pie to this Administration." Translated, that means that with an election coming up, the President is trying to please the radical right, his base of support, by showing that he's one of them—that Ronald Reagan is still a Reaganite.

In the one case, the President of all the people urged senators to support the Helms proposal that Federal funds may never be used to pay for an abortion unless the life of the mother is at stake—not even, for example, in the case of a rape or incest victim or a woman too young to provide adequate care for a child.

This is not only senseless public policy—particularly for people like Mr. Reagan and Mr. Helms who bitterly resent "welfare mothers." It's also patently inequitable, leaving women able to pay for an abortion free to have one, while decreeing that those too poor to pay either have to bear unwanted children or have the job done by a coat-hanger artist in a back alley.

A constitutional amendment, on the other hand, would at least impose a uniform rule on rich and poor alike and would have the virtue, if passed, of demonstrated national approval. And it would openly repeal, rather than deviously undercut, a constitutionally reached Supreme Court decision.

Mr. Reagan's political grab on the Helms prayer bill is even more opportunistic and less principled, since his own Attorney General has already cited the plan as an "undesirable" attack on the Supreme Court; more eminent legal scholars—for example, Robert Bork, Mr. Reagan's appointee to the District of Columbia Court of Appeals—called it unconstitutional.

The Helms proposal—like his anti-abortion plan, a rider on a debt-limit measure—would strip the Supreme Court of jurisdiction in school prayer cases. Therefore the Court could not enforce its 1963 ruling that such prayers are unconstitutional; and a hodgepodge of state laws, making prayers in school legal here but illegal there, legal in some forms but not in others, would be bound to result.

Even worse, the Helms plan would effectively amend the Constitution by majority vote of Congress rather than by the votes of two-thirds of each House and three-quarters of the states.

Mr. Reagan is supporting a constitutional amendment on the prayer issue, but his statement made clear that he would sign the Helms court-stripping bill despite the Attorney General's opinion, despite its probable unconstitutionality and despite the radical precedents it would set for getting the Supreme Court's authority and amending the Constitution.

So praise be for the children going back to school and the leaves turning in Brandon Gap. Some things endure, even if nonsense prevails.

Recycling an Idea

Tom Wicker

Near my hometown in the sandhills of North Carolina, stands of tall pine trees line the roadsides, the gray earth beneath them richly carpeted with brown needles. The trees grow in straight rows, as if planted that way by human design.

They were. I well remember from the 1930s the young men of the Civilian Conservation Corps setting them out, in row after row of pine seedings across the eroded old fields. That kind of thing made the C.C.C. one of the most useful and successful projects of the New Deal.

President Reagan, sometimes an admirer of Franklin Roosevelt, has a good piece of evidence close at hand. Camp David, where he spends weekends and entertains foreign visitors, was built by the C.C.C. as a low-cost resort for Federal workers.

The C.C.C. lasted for nine years, employed over three million Depression-age youngsters, planted 1.3 billion trees and carried out conservation projects worth $1.5 billion. Much of this work, like those North Carolina pine forests, is still visible and still environmentally valuable nearly fifty years later.

There's no way to measure the other achievements of the C.C.C.— the hope it gave to the hopeless, the skills it taught the unskilled, the social dynamite it defused by providing alternatives to idleness and resentment, even the quasi-military field life to which it introduced a generation destined to emerge from Depression into World War II.

Senator Daniel P. Moynihan of New York and his Republican co-sponsor, Senator Mac Mathias of Maryland, now propose a rebirth of this proven program—proven not only in the old C.C.C. but in more recent examples such as California's flourishing Conservation Corps.

The House already has passed its own bill setting up a National Conservation Corps; a Senate subcommittee will open hearings on the Moynihan-Mathias bill Sept. 22.

The idea is simplicity itself. About seventy thousand to a hundred thousand unemployed young people—aged sixteen to twenty-five, men and women—would be paid the minimum wage to fill conservation-related jobs. An additional summer work force would be recruited among those fifteen to twenty-one. Preference would be given to the disadvantaged, or to those who live in areas of particularly high unemployment.

What would they do? One idea comes from the Office of Management and Budget and the Interior Department, although the Reagan Administration so far opposes the conservation corps concept. These agencies want to use revenues earmarked for new park acquisition for the rehabilitation of existing parklands—many of which badly need it. Mr. Moynihan sees this as a project that could be carried out splendidly by the proposed corps of young workers.

There's no lack of other suitable and needed tasks—reforestation, road-building, bridge and dam construction, cutting fire trails and fighting forest fires, drainage and flood control projects, land reclamation, to name only a few.

The program would be paid for by earmarked Federal revenues from various leasing and permit activities on Federal lands—oil and gas leasing, for example, or timber cutting.

The House-passed bill, principally sponsored by Representative John Seiberling of Ohio, provided for $50 million in fiscal 1983 and $250 million in each of the following five years—an affordable total of $1.3 billion between now and 1989. The House bill requires the states to match fifteen percent of these funds; the Senate may increase that requirement.

The Administration opposes the legislation on the grounds that two smaller conservation corps programs, now defunct, were not effective; but that's a weak case.

Mr. Moynihan says that in New York State alone, the former Young Adult Conservation Corps returned $2.83 in appraised work for every dollar spent; the costlier Youth Conservation Corps returned $1.04 per dollar invested. And those figures don't measure the job skills, character development and sense of self-worth imparted to many participants, or whatever reduction in youth crime and delinquency might have resulted.

The California Conservation Corps, functioning since 1977, costs

$36 million annually and pays the minimum wage to a turnover of about four thousand young people a year, for an average of six months each. In 1981, the corps logged three million hours of work, a third in emergency situations, the rest in home and forest improvement, conservation and historical preservation. Three million trees were planted that year.

The California C.C.'s slogan—"Hard Work, Low Pay, Miserable Conditions"—suggests that it is not a picnic or hiking trip. A Federal version could be just as demanding; and, among other things, it probably would do more to diminish street crime than any of the dubious crime-fighting proposals President Reagan recently unveiled.

Just in case he thinks he has philosophical objections, he might remember something called the Ecology Corps, a forerunner of the California Conservation Corps. You guessed it. The Ecology Corps was launched by Governor Ronald Reagan, and a good day's work, too.

Interview with Richard Reeves

Reeves. I have learned over a lifetime my own energy curve and I know about myself that my energy is highest in the morning and then declines until about six o'clock. Between four and six it plummets. Given my druthers I'd sleep between four and six everyday. Then my energy begins to come back up through dinner and the evening. If I am doing real writing—a book or whatever—I will get up as early in the morning as I can and that tends to get earlier and earlier as it nears completion. I start by getting up at six, then I get up at five-thirty and five or whatever my wife can tolerate. It's the work that requires the most concentration and the most effort and is the most painful. At that time of day and before any distractions start, I want to do that work at the time where I've no other options. There's no one I can call, there's no one calling me, there's nothing happening. And then I get this almost euphoria because at eight-thirty in the morning I am beginning my day but I've already done my work. I have accomplished the real work and I will then go about the business of getting the kids off to school, of handling the phone calls that come in, of my secretary coming in and telling her what to do, of scheduling, going to lunch, then—I hate to admit this for anyone who reads it—I would write my column. If I were not working on a book or on something else I would then do the column earliest in the day, and then I kind of skip through the day thinking of myself as a normal person, to begin the routine again.

I'm very sensitive to where I work, what I work with. I got my first magazine assignment in 1966, which was a profile of John Lindsay, then the mayor of New York. I was living in a house in New Jersey and I had all these visions about what writing was about, that writers had their own offices. And I built myself this small office in the basement with that little window above the ground and it was very small. I also had this vision, for some reason, that real writers—because now I was going to become a real writer as opposed to a newspaper reporter—that real writers wrote everything in one burst; it was some sort of ethic, that you sat down and began writing until

119

you were finished. As I look back on these pieces, of course, their energy curve goes like my days. The endings sometimes seem to me barely comprehensible, because I was exhausted by that time. I have since learned how many words I can write of each type during the day.

I had lived in California and we moved back to New York into an apartment on Fifth Avenue, on the twelfth floor overlooking Central Park, and I couldn't produce. Nothing was happening. It was beautiful—you could see all of Central Park and New York City, over into New Jersey, Pennsylvania. I thought I was living in a painting. There was no noise, no nothing. So we moved to Fifty-second Street on the third floor because I came to realize that I needed that energy and interaction with people and I needed light and a room and noise to work and then I could work again.

Writing is the same as basketball or tennis or football if you're a writer; I mean I think about these things the way a professional athlete thinks about his body. These things really are important to me and the way I "play" tonight depends on what kind of conditioning I have, what kind of exercise, and I take it all very, very seriously to the extent that to write or not to write or like to write in a lifetime you have to take it seriously. It's a very difficult thing to do. People who say they like writing are liars. No one "likes" writing as I'm sure no one "likes" lifting weights or doing other things but they do it for a reason. I like being a writer which doesn't mean I like writing. Everyone likes being a writer—it's a terrific thing to be. It's the thing in life where you are most allowed to wear corduroy jackets, or so I've always thought, but actually doing it is painful.

The worst thing that can happen to you in writing is getting in the position where you can get stuck. I read a lot about writing and I think most writers like to read about writing. Hemingway wrote standing up; many people do, because they find that in the same way that I have to have noise, their bodies are alert standing up. It focuses their concentration. Hemingway, who always worried about that problem, said that you should never write yourself out at a sitting, or in his case a standing, that you should always know the next thing you're going to write. Believe me, if you get up at four-thirty or five-thirty in the morning as I do to write, I get up knowing the next sentence or paragraph or subject that I'm going to write on. I use that concentration of the day before to know where I'm going. Writing is all about knowing where you are going next. I didn't think about it until your question, but all of it is devices to avoid getting blocked, to avoid running into that thing where you're sitting—standing—at the paper not having any idea what to do next.

I'll talk about the way I work, but it took me twenty-five years to figure out that this works for me—it may work not for any other human being in the world. I was up at five o'clock this morning, writing a film script for a film called "Red Star over Khyber," about Afghanistan and Pakistan, which will show on public television December 11th. I'm the chief correspondent of the *Frontline* series, and I'm writing the script of it which I will record next Tuesday.

Script or book, whatever, it's no different. Partly because my education was as an engineer, as was Norman Mailer's and a lot of other writers, I break it down not much differently than Henry Ford broke down the assembly of an automobile. I don't consider myself an artiste in a room with harps while I'm waiting for the muses to come. I am the muse and the muse breaks it down in sections that he comprehends so that in the end what I am doing is writing words to fill eighteen seconds, and almost anybody can do that. And when I've written all those little eighteen second segments I can write a film or a book. Books I write essentially the same way.

If you look at the film—the filmscript means nothing since they are words written to be spoken and not words written to be read—I have got this organization for a work—this also could be the first draft of a book or an article—then you look at it and it looks, I suppose, something like the clay models of automobiles where the people keep carving away. It's a process very similar to sculpture; like sculpture it's not what you put into it but what you leave out that's important, and the difference between the people who are good and the people who aren't is what they leave out. It's much harder to write short than it is to write long.

I then have this rather bulky thing where you can see the wires and you see the bolts and whatnot, and sometimes the transitions from section to section don't work very well, and then you begin to take out the internal contradictions, you look and you take out the material you've repeated which you inevitably do. Basically you begin to do the thing that makes the difference between good writers and bad writers in terms of style and in terms of grace, and that is, you work on the transitions. Most of the things that you think are terrific in writing, it seems to me, are probably insight—that is, "Wow, I never thought of that before"—which is not a writing technique, it's a thinking or observational technique that doesn't strictly have to do with writing; it has to do with your visual sense or your mental electricity—how your circuits are wired. What is really the writing technique that shows, that you remember, has to do with transitions—how you get from one point to another. And that's really where you, as it were, smooth out a piece.

And with books it is not greatly different for me. It's a question of organizing a work, getting it done; it's a component not only that you can deal with but that you can put whatever your own full mental capacities are. I mean, you can focus your energies—I know that I sound like a mystic on some of this—it takes enormous concentration to write. For that moment, like John McEnroe hitting a tennis shot, for that moment in the world there can't be anything but the ball and his relation to it. The rest of it has to come from that focus, that concentration. And writing is like that. You don't concentrate on a whole tennis match. You concentrate on that ball and that moment; you can't concentrate on a whole tennis match. It's too awe-inspiring to even think of everything that's going to or might happen. The smaller you can get your focus down and apply the energy and the concentration and the intellect and the creativity that you have on it, the better the work will begin to build, I think. It's easier to talk about than to do, sometimes. If I leave you with one thing it should be that the things that are most important to you and the most difficult you should time for the moment when you have the maximum powers of concentration whether that's at 5:00 A.M. or at 4:00 in the afternoon.

I live in a neighborhood with a lot of writers and a lot of them are friends. I, like many writers, when I'm really writing well, will write two thousand words a day, and I am almost a physical wreck and in a kind of stupor when I finish doing that, it's so difficult writing. I tend to look around for friends to have lunch with but if none are around, I end up walking. One of the reasons writers like to live in places like New York and Paris is when you've drained your energy you can walk around and there are always other people—you don't know what they're doing but they're doing all these things, and you can just feel that energy. You don't have to live—you can just let yourself get lost in that feeling.

Anyway, one of the writers who lives near me and is a close friend is Kurt Vonnegut, and he mentioned to me one day, "I was at a writers' conference the other day." Writers' conferences, I had always thought, were about writers coming up and asking, "What do you do in the afternoon?" In fact, Kurt said he had been to a conference in Europe where there were a number of Eastern bloc writers and he thought their writing habits would be different, being state-controlled and so on. But a writer from Bulgaria or some place was introduced to him and the first thing he said was, "Mr. Vonnegut, what do you do in the afternoon?"

I use a variety of tools in writing, depending on the work. I have very McLuhanesque feelings that the medium has something to do with the message. I only a couple years ago switched to an electric typewriter and found out I doubled my output because of physical fatigue. I also had some back problems and neck muscle problems, which are very common to writers. I began using a computer in 1987—a Toshiba—and my output may have doubled again.

I still often do my columns in longhand on a legal pad with a pencil. Any work beyond that, book work and whatnot, I do on the computer. This script I'll do all in longhand simply because it's not worth the trouble. I first tried a word processor in 1983 and I had a bad experience. I went back to it because everyone I know swears by it. The word processor's ability to make changes, which is what writing is about, is so much easier than retyping a whole page. I used to have a secretary who could read what I do, so that she was the word processor, in the sense that I said, "Move this around; put this here," and I marked this "A" and I said, "Put 'A' there," then she retyped that. Then I edited that retyped version and gave it back to her to do again and maybe to do again and again. The word processor is a secretary. That's what it does. It does all those things which are so physically wearing and unpleasant to do.

A student asked me if I get reports back on who's reading my articles so that I know who to adjust them to. I have no sense of audience. I don't think writers have a sense of audience. Good writers do not have a sense of audience. Years ago, when I was the political editor of the *New York Times,* I was quoted in a journalism textbook or some kind of thing as saying, in answer to the question "What audience do I write for?," that I write for my peer group, that I am interested in what the other people, the other political correspondents, columnists, etcetera, the boys on the bus, think of what I do. I said that in 1972. I no longer think that and I wish I had never said that, because in my own life I went from not knowing who or what I was writing for, having no sense of that whatever, then went into the newspaper business and, because part of the training was to give you a sense of who you're writing for and what you're writing about, began to understand more of who the audience was I was writing for, went into fairly high-level selective magazine business where still partly because of the daily interaction had an idea of who I was writing for and was probably affected by what those people thought.

I came to believe, ten years ago, that I was limiting myself as a writer, that that was a big mistake, that in the end I should be writing for me. Much more now, I feel that freedom of feeling I'm writing for myself. I'm lucky enough to be either well-enough known or well-enough paid that if I go to Afghanistan or Pakistan and want to write a book about it, someone will publish it. That wasn't true ten years ago. But now that I'm used to it, I like it just fine, thanks. I think my writing is better and I hope is getting better because I'm writing for me. I don't think anymore in terms of audience because thinking in terms of audience puts a limitation on me, and I would like to break away. The truth is, the answer to "Who do I write for?" is "I don't think in terms of audience anymore," unless I happen to be working for a journal that is so audience-conscious that they impose audience on you—that is, *Travel and Leisure Magazine,* if I am writing about Lake Dahl in Kashmir, is not interested in my views—or anybody else's—of the political volatility of Kashmir. They are interested in whether the wine is good or if in fact there is wine at the hotel. I like to do that kind of travel writing—it also pays the bills to travel. So I occasionally do things in terms of audience, but that to me is a certain kind of craftwork. I could do that kind of work in my sleep, but I don't think that people in college who are really learning to write, unless they are really, really gifted, can transcend audience at this point.

Root. What is the charge specifically that you have from the syndicate?
Reeves. Two columns a week every week. The charge is principally financial. They get half and I get half for whatever they sell it for. They don't edit it. They only make suggestions and only under the strongest urging from me to say, "Can you give me any indication of what people like and what they don't like?" It's more a commercial relationship than editorial.

The standard length is around 650 words. I think the reason for that is the end point, the newspaper can use whatever they want. The traditions of the business are such that, if they want to edit it down to 100 words, they do it, or if they don't want to use it, they don't. It's never been a subject of discussion. The recommended length is 650 words and that's the last conversation I've ever had about it. It's three pages in a long length legal pad, four in a short length.
Root. You're going to write 104 of those a year. Do you have any pattern for selecting what you're going to write about?

Reeves. Nothing. I'm sure that I'm different from some people. I treat it like letters home. I tend to think of it as what am I doing or thinking about at the moment. I wrote one yesterday and dictated it in on the way here. I won't think about the column again, other than the fact that I'll read a lot of newspapers and if there's something interesting stick it in my pocket, until next Monday morning.

Root. How much is the column on your mind, at least under the surface, knowing about that deadline? In *Jet Lag* you say you always have to be alert.

Reeves. It's probably somewhere under the surface all the time. Obviously the reason that all those papers are stuck in my bag is because I may come across something for the column. I have one column subject that I'm thinking about that I happened to carry to read out here, which is that Ypsilanti study of young black students that they feel Head Start worked well for. I've got other things stuck in that bag at one point or another that I might be able to get a column out of if I get desperate. So yeah, its obviously somewhere on my mind.

Root. How much research would you do for the column?

Reeves. It varies totally. Often none and often quite a bit in terms of reading or calls or covering an event. If there are a hundred a year, only fifteen or twenty—twenty-five?—I cover something specifically for the column. I might be doing something else. To a certain extent I recycle myself; the same thought that appears in a magazine piece I might also use in a column. I think of a column, by the way, as one idea expanded and so I try to come up with a hundred ideas.

Root. Let's talk about how this piece came about, the one on Kennedy syndicated in the Sunday *Detroit Free Press*.

Reeves. Okay. I don't know if it's of any interest. My guess is, even as I did it, that this is a little shorter than normal, but I also thought, it didn't matter, that more and more newspapers seem to like short columns, that *this* column really had one *very* specific thought that nobody was ever going to have any trouble figuring out what it was about, and that there was no use to pad it. I could have padded it with other stuff.

A friend of mine, a man named Mickey Kantor who is a lawyer in Los Angeles and a former neighbor and chairman of Mondale's campaign in California, was in New York with his wife. We had dinner and he asked me what I had heard about Kennedy. I said I really hadn't heard anything. He said, "He's really around, beating the drums. Not only is he doing it, he's hitting a new group of young fund-raisers." I said, "No kidding." He said, "He's got the new people, the young bankers and whatnot in their late thirties and forties and he's having little lunches with them about the future." I said, "When are you going to be back in L.A.?" He said, "Monday." I said, "Let me give you a call."

Between that date, which was I think Thursday, and Monday I made three or four calls on my own. One to Kennedy's office, to find out what his schedule had been during the campaign. One to his principal speechwriter, who is a good friend of mine, who did not return the call, which I also took to be slightly significant. This is a guy I could call to say, "Let's have a drink." We'd been friends a long time before he worked for Kennedy. I had a funny feeling he suspected what the call might be about and didn't want to talk about it. One to a pollster and one to a political consultant asking them what they'd heard about Kennedy. Two to two fund-raisers in Chicago. They may have been it. This was before the weekend. They all gave me various bits of what's in that column but they all said, yes, they had seen this activity. The political consultant said he'd already been indirectly asked to work for Kennedy in the campaign and said that, in addition to that, Kennedy is looking at *these* people, who are very expensive staff-type political people. He said, "It's also been made clear to them and made clear to me that we're not talking about a Massachusetts-type Senate race here." Then on Monday I called Mickey who was back in L.A. and asked, "Would you call your friends you know who were at those Kennedy luncheons and dinners and ask them if they would talk to me? I'll protect them and I won't pinpoint what state it was in." And he did it and I called them and they told me what had happened and then I sat down and wrote the column.

There were two thoughts on my mind. One was my own personal opinion, which was the structure of it all, that it would be a disaster for the Democratic party if Teddy does this. And two, that I wanted it to come out that Sunday because I figured as soon as the election was over everybody was going to begin writing about the prospects, etcetera. And they were going to pick up the Kennedy thing. It wasn't hard to pick it up once somebody mentioned it was happening and so I wanted to get it out before the election rather than after when I thought everybody else would be on it.

Root. The initial impulse came from casual conversation where you picked up on something because you're attuned to what's going on, what's current, and it struck you that there was a potential column in that.

Reeves. Right.

Root. Where'd that part in here about Mario Cuomo as an alternative come from?

Reeves. It came from a conversation with another writer, a friend of mine named Ken Auletta, who did the series on Cuomo for the *New Yorker*. We're very close friends. We talk together about most of what we do. And I mentioned to him I'm working on the Kennedy thing and he said, "It just kills Cuomo." They have basically the same constituency. So that's where the idea came from.

Root. When you started writing this how did you get the structure that you get in this piece? Did you plan this out at all?

Reeves. Let me see what I have. I've forgotten how I structured it. In this case what I remember of the structure was—I'm going to mention something else to you here if it's of interest—was that I thought since this isn't an analysis of something, the major thing about it is (and I see the *Free Press* used the headline that way) the reprinting had news value and I thought that would carry it, so it was a pretty straightforward structure, figuring I'd want to get the news up top. You're always the victim in newspapers of what headline they put on you—and that's what they take away, so if you're writing the column to an audience it's the editors and what you're saying to the editors is, "This is news, if you want to use it that way."

The other thing I was going to say, by the way, was my friend with Kennedy is Robert Shrum. He's described here as one of the most talented staff men. I would guess he won't like this column. He won't like it, Kennedy won't like it, and "one of the most talented staff men"—it happens to be accurate but is also a way of saying, "I know this pisses you off, Bob, but we're still friends, right?" That's literally why that line is in there, although it's true—he's an extraordinarily talented man.

Then beyond that what I would tend to do in a column like this is, on the side of the sheet of a yellow sheet of paper, mention the names of the people I'm going to quote even although I'm not going to use their names because the name will remind me of the quote. Like many people when I don't quote people by name I am sloppier in the relationship between what is printed and what they actually said than otherwise. So I probably wouldn't write the whole quote—I'd write their names and the key words on the side of the paper; I would write whatever other thoughts, like the numbers—the twenty states, the two million dollars—on the side of the paper. In the Cuomo thing I wanted to let him know that I knew that he is already traveling out-of-state and also tip off other people that no matter what Cuomo now says he has already begun the process, and then would have used phrases like "bloated," "eight-hundred-pound gorilla" because I knew I wanted to make reference somewhere in the piece to the thoughts that come to my mind with those things and then I would write it free form. I mean, I didn't know how it would end when I started writing it or in what order I would use the stuff.

Root. But what you're doing in effect is creating an outline in the margins and then trying to write prose that fits that, write yourself right through that.

Reeves. I have one of those here. Yes. Now in this case—I often put the outline kind of in the order that I'm going to do it. In this case I didn't. This was, in terms of writing, a particularly simple column, only because the information was more important than what I said about it, I thought. I didn't always think that. This is a column I did for next Sunday.

Root. The one you sent out last night?

Reeves. Yeah. There's notes down the side where this part just came to me, it just flowed. I wrote it late in the day and I was tired and I actually stopped. That's the reason I put the outline on the side and then went to other things. It's basically my analysis of the election in terms of my own feeling that it was not an accident that Reagan was reelected and Reaganism was rejected. I wrote my thinking about the new consensus and recycled material.

Root. From the *New York Times* piece? Is there any way in which you looked at the *New York Times* before you wrote that? Did you carry it with you?

Reeves. Yeah, there, where it says "A," that's a paragraph in the *Times* piece, so that when I was dictating it I didn't rewrite it, I just looked in there and dictated that paragraph out—I carried it with me— I knew when I left home that I was going to write the column about that subject and that I might refer to the magazine piece.

Root. Do you keep files of material or notes?

Reeves. Not really. I keep folders that I keep stuffing things into that might lead to future columns. At points where I feel barren or at points where it seems advisable I'll flip through and there'll be twenty notes to myself or clippings. Of those twenty my guess is that one out of four—might even be less than that—eventually becomes a column. Usually I keep them there because I'm waiting for one other thing to happen that I think relates to them—something interests me but I'm waiting for one other piece of information to go.

Root. When do you have enough for one idea, one column?

Reeves. It's a mechanical thing with me, I don't know if other people do it—I will very often seize on two things happening in different parts of the country to back up an idea I've already had or had part of. I did that in the column that would come out about now. There was a shooting of a woman they were evicting from a public housing project in New York, sixty-seven-year-old woman who was shot down by a police SWAT team; at the same time friends in Nebraska had called me to tell me about a farmer who was shot down by a police SWAT team when they were trying to serve bank papers on his home when the bank was thinking about foreclosing on his farm.

Those two incidents together, both local stories, stories that had not gone out of their local areas, I wanted to use to show in my own feeling that in two very different places what the kind of new law and order can lead to and the fact of what the winners-losers politics the President likes to play leads to. We're just blowing away a couple of more losers so we don't have to pay for them. In the column I said that I may make too much of these incidents but there is a meanness that goes with this law-and-order, winner-loser attitude and that maybe it was more than a coincidence that on the same week more than fifteen hundred miles apart the same thing happened.

Root. So one of the things you're doing in that piece is clarifying those examples in order to get to some kind of point at the end.

Reeves. Yeah.

Root. Do you find yourself having a typical structure? For example, I've talked to people who say they always work from a general idea and then move right down to something really specific and then end it talking about something as specifically as possible.

Reeves. I don't do that. Now I often must use that technique but I think that in fact I am equally likely to begin with the small incident and go to the idea. I tend to do it—I think about it like a newspaperman. I want to have the best first paragraph I can in the column. This belies some of the things I said earlier. I have this sense of people at a smorgasbord or a salad bar and they don't have much time. If somebody buys a book I write, they want to yield to that book and I know there's something going between us in the sense that in making the financial commitment they've also made a time commitment in terms of they're going to find out what this is about, so I have great luxury with them, great freedom. In the column I don't feel that way at all. I don't think that I have readers. I don't think about this a lot—I don't want to contradict what I said earlier—but I do think they're very busy people, they're doing things and whatnot; the most important paragraph in a column is the first paragraph or maybe the second that plays off the first in a certain way. At least in terms of that general methodology I would probably reject it. I would go either with the incident or the big thought depending upon which I thought was most likely to hold the reader for a moment.

Root. Would you make any distinction between a column that's going to come out on Sunday and one that's going to come out on Thursday?

Reeves. No. No. I might in relation to timing of events, say, an election or something, but no.

Root. Would you then write quite differently for the *New York Times Sunday Magazine* not only because of the format but because you know it's coming out on Sunday, you know it's coming out in a specific kind of magazine that is going to be bought by a specific kind of people who have the time on a Sunday to be sitting there reading something as opposed to the person in the salad bar with the paper open, flipping through things?

Reeves. Right. The answer to the question is yes but not for those reasons. I write differently for the *New York Times Magazine* because it is a heavily edited bureaucratic product (where the column is an unedited product and I am going through a process which can be painful sometimes, simply annoying others), and since I know the rules of the game—and if I don't know them I'm reminded of them during this endless editing process—I adjust to it. I do not make adjustments in terms of audience; I do make adjustments in terms of medium, in the sense that it is a six or seven thousand word piece and the exposition is going to be much different and a lot of things are going to be much different and the piece itself is going to be much different because it is going to go through a rather tricky maze before it gets anywhere near a reader. So, yes, there is a great difference but it is not for reasons of the reader; it has to do with the institutional process it has to go through and that the medium itself is different—not the medium of the *New York Times* but the medium of a six thousand word piece as opposed to six hundred word.

Root. Would you say there was any difference in your writing where you were writing for the *New York Times* and your current writing for Universal Press Syndicate?

Reeves. They're very different. I'm doing a very different thing; I'm not repeating news as I was then and I'm not working under a series of rules and restraints, different for the newspaper than for the *New York Times Magazine.* I am much more colloquial, I have a much more varied voice. The *New York Times* is designed so that everyone tends to speak in the same voice.

This is the difference between writing a magazine piece and writing a column. It's not true of the daily story in the *New York Times*. I write 104 columns. I know at the beginning of the year that twenty— I don't know what number—ten? twenty?—aren't going to be very good. You're hitting on the average of things. You're speaking with different voices, different levels of energy, all sorts of different things. I think sometimes about experimenting and it usually doesn't work. You wish you were able to do things like suddenly write satire or parody or something in a column because something strikes you that way. You can't do it. You find out from the letters and whatnot that people take you seriously or they see you as a certain kind of person. But, within the range of that, I can speak with different voices.

Root. Does it help you to have a set length and to have a sense of regularity about when you have to have it in? Does that help your process?

Reeves. Well, it makes it easier. Do you mean does it help your creative process? I think frankly it doesn't. It just makes it easier. I'm a professional. I could do the same thing in two hundred words or twelve hundred; twelve hundred is a little long. Two hundred or a thousand. The same amount of information I could make go in either direction.

Root. Did you feel that way when you were doing the two-minute spots on television? Is there any way that starting out in something that's new for you makes you change the way you work, change your thinking about what you're doing?

Reeves. Yes, I think that happens and when you particularly go into those kinds of media, you tend to want to get too much information into it. You tend to want to make a more elegant—or at least more coherent—argument, and then you quickly learn how to sell out. In fact the big danger is that you become so facile at it that it starts to slop over into the work you temporarily abandoned to do that stuff. It becomes so easy to do the very short form stuff, because you hold yourself to lower standards, that you then resent the work of doing things in a longer form and, for instance, demonstrating if not proving what it is you're talking about. I find it—I wouldn't use the word "seductive" but I find it dangerous; "tempting" is the word I'd use. It takes an extra level of discipline to be able to switch back and forth.

Root. Where do the columns and a book like *American Journey* or *Passage to Peshawar* fit in your life?

Reeves. In descending order, the books, work for the *New Yorker* and other magazine pieces, the columns, the films. It's so clear in my mind that that's the order. When I talk about my energy curve, if I had to do the four things in a day—no, that's not true, the three things in a day, the books, the magazine pieces, and the column, I would do it in that order. It takes physical energy to do the film work which would necessitate doing it early in the day. But it's not a creative kind of process.

Root. Would you say then that your best writing is a book like *American Journey?*

Reeves. Yeah. I may get lucky and say things, you don't know, but there's no question about a sustained effort. There's no comparison in the work. You're also harder on yourself. In any work there's a certain game between the seller and the buyer and if I'm writing for the *New York Times Magazine* and they want certain changes or they have certain questions there comes a point where if you're sane, fine. If that's the way they want it, that's the way they want it. And I'm not going to say anything I don't believe in or I'm going to do something to get around those strictures and at that point their satisfaction makes it okay. But when I am my own editor on my own book it doesn't work that way. You can't play the seller-buyer game with yourself. You've really got to deliver to yourself and yourself doesn't accept shoddy goods. Maybe someone else does and there comes a point where you figure, screw it, if they want it that way, fine.

I mean, I am a professional writer and I don't think that I'm doing it in stone. I have occasionally written—and would again—for *Parade Magazine* and that kind of thing, and obviously I know I am not going to be judged by that work. There you also find yourself more flexible because it's their magazine, they know what they want, they have that sense of audience, and anyway the fact of the matter is that they pay you and whatever contracts say and whatever people say, except for *The New Yorker*, every publication in this country that I know of changes your words when you aren't looking anyway. Some of them even feel bad about it and apologize for it, but of course its always too late and it's out there.

Root. How would you describe your development as a writer? You started out with the *Phillipsburg Free Press.* How would you compare yourself as a writer to the person who started at the *Phillipsburg Free Press?*

Reeves. Well, I'd hope I was a lot better but I think that I probably wasn't that bad. I occasionally see that stuff. I was very skillful. I had great skills. I look back at the stuff I wrote for the *Newark News* [NJ] and it's well-written.

Root. Would you say it's also as insightful?

Reeves. No. I've developed in two ways. One is the simple mechanical thing of how much you can keep in your head. It's like exercise. There was a point where I could keep a four hundred word newspaper story in my head. Everything else had to be notes. By that I don't mean I could keep every word but I could keep the organization in my head and I went to the point where I could do that, and can do that now for seven thousand, eight thousand word magazine pieces. The book, *Passage to Peshawar*, is seventy-five thousand words. It might be more. But it's all in my head. Everything that was in that book— I mean, I sat at a lakeside in France and outlined that book on a single sheet of paper, a small sheet at that, and I knew every single thing that would be in that book and where it would be. I was very proud of that. I knew that for that kid from Phillipsburg that was a tremendous breakthrough. I could have stood there and recited the book. That level of development, of expansion, is really exciting in the sense that it's really hard work. It's like building up your muscles. It's a muscular thing, not an intellectual thing.

The other development, it seems to me, has been terribly slow. It is probably the evolution from not only reporting other people's words but not really being very far ahead of their thoughts to more and more eliminating them from the center of your work. In some of that *New York Times* piece the quotes are there for decoration, because of the *Times* style and the question of backing up, as you would for an academic paper. The thoughts and the perceptions were mine, and basically I had to go out and get them out of other people because that's the way the *Times* deals with the world. But the evolution of the point from where you are reporting other people's words, not capable of reaching much beyond their thoughts and their view of the world, and gradually moving from that pole to the pole where it's all your thoughts, it's all your words, that your thoughts are moving beyond those words someplace else—I think I've gone through that but it seems a fairly plodding process. I keep waiting for the breakthrough, the epiphany, and it doesn't happen. I look at my work and I have more insights, more perceptions. A big part of it is I have more confidence in my own perceptions and insights than I used to and therefore they can get to appear, but it seems to me a painfully slow process.

Fixing the Broken Senate

Richard Reeves

WASHINGTON—Daniel Evans became a U.S. senator on Sept. 18, 1983, and then he found out there was no Senate.

That lead may be an exaggeration, but it is only a slight one. "I was shocked when I got to Washington, and that hasn't changed," said the former governor of the state of Washington, a Republican appointed (and elected two months later) after the death of Sen. Henry Jackson. "We've got a lot of stuff that's broken here, and we should fix it before we try to do anything else."

"Process," he said, is the problem. The Senate is broken because old, cumbersome, elitist procedures and traditions have collapsed— and, so far, no one has been able to get the hundred senators together to fix up new ones. What used to call itself "the world's greatest deliberative body" is so democratic and individualistic now that it no longer deliberates at all. Senators don't even meet each other, much less deliberate in committees or debate on the floor.

There is usually no one there. "A Senate debate" is one senator speaking to an empty hall. "A Senate hearing" is a committee chairman popping in and out of a committee room while staffers listen to witnesses. And where are the other senators? At their own "hearings" or back home telling the Rotary Club how important the Senate is.

The new Senate, in fact, is not powerful at all, although it is indeed more democratic than the tight ship run by powerful people such as Lyndon Johnson in the past. Freshmen (like Evans) can speak now whenever they want to, and they even have their own subcommittees to impress the folks back home. But there is no one to listen to them, and some of those impressively titled subcommittees never meet.

Unfortunately, the new Senate is like a developing nation, with all the problems of democracy and few of the benefits.

So, I asked Evans, what would a former governor (and former minority leader of the Washington state House of Representatives) do about such procedural problems? He had these answers ready:

(1) Go to a five-day workweek instead of the present Tuesday-to-Thursday schedule designed to allow members to get back to their states for perpetual campaigning. But recess every third week. Senators could then take one round trip instead of three, and get more time at home and more time in Washington.

(2) Reduce the number of committees and committee assignments so that each senator would serve on one of the "Class A" committees—Armed Services, Foreign Relations, Finance or Appropriations—and one each of the less important "B" and "C" committees, such as Indian Affairs. With each senator restricted to three committees—some now serve on as many as fifteen—hearings could be scheduled in the mornings and early afternoons in separate "A," "B" and "C" time slots.

(3) Schedule important debates at prearranged times in the late afternoon when there are no committee meetings. And, require senators to vote from their seats (instead of walking into the chamber and nodding) so that they would have to hang around and eventually get to know each other.

Simple. Or it should be. But nothing is simple with a hundred prima donnas. Still, the Senate is so embarrassed about how foolish those hundred looked in their chaotic rush to approve a budget and adjourn last month that there is some movement toward repair work. Sen. Dan Quayle, R-Ind., is chairman of the Temporary Select Committee to Study the Senate Committee System and has been focusing on ways to cut the procedural possibilities of endless filibusters in the Senate.

"The time may be right," Evans said. "We may have the right combination of old frustration and new leadership."

"What about televising proceedings?" I asked.

"I have an open mind on television in the Senate chamber," Evans answered. "I suppose it will come someday. But right now there's nothing worthwhile to televise."

What Is Ted Kennedy Running For?

Richard Reeves

WASHINGTON—Sen. Edward Kennedy campaigned for Democratic candidates in twenty states these past four weeks. And everywhere that Teddy went this thought was sure to go: He has begun
running for president in 1988.

What bad news for the Democratic Party!

"He's going," said a political professional who considered himself
asked recently to begin work for Kennedy now. "They're talking to
people about 'the campaign' and 'the future,' and they're making it
clear that they're not just talking about another Senate race."

"Kennedy's gotten a few of us together twice to talk about 'the
future,'" said a financial executive who raises "important money" for
national Democrats. "Politicians don't invite people like me to dinner
because we're such nice guys or because they want our advice on arms
control. He wanted money, and I don't give money in Massachusetts."

The senior senator from Massachusetts is making all the moves.
He has distributed $2 million to Democratic candidates around the
country through his personal political action committee, the Fund for
a Democratic Majority, and has campaigned for many of the congres-
sional candidates he's giving money to. The chairman of the fund is
Kennedy's speechwriter, Robert Shrum, one of the most talented staff
men in politics. And Kennedy has also begun recruiting other heavy-
hitters around Washington.

All this has been going on while the senator has been campaigning
loyally for his party's 1984 candidate, Walter Mondale. But politics is
nothing if not endurance and pragmatism: 1984 may be over for all
practical purposes, including the most practical of all, winning. Kennedy is not the only Democrat thinking four years ahead. New York

Gov. Mario Cuomo has already given interviews regarding his own 1988 prospects and has also begun violating his own rules about traveling out of state, going as far afield as California to shake hands.

The future as seen by Kennedy must involve a collapse of Reaganism and its current popularity during four more years in the White House by its namesake. Then, the theory goes, there would be a return to old-fashioned liberalism—to Kennedy dreams such as national health insurance.

"Dreaming" seems the right word to me. Even if a plunging economy and anti-war demonstrations dominate a second Reagan term—and that could happen—it is still questionable whether the nation would then turn back to what Gary Hart calls "the solutions of the '30s." Fairly or unfairly, Edward Kennedy and his Massachusetts fellow, Tip O'Neill, have become the physical symbols of a bloated, blustering big-government party.

What is far more likely to happen is that Kennedy—the eight-hundred-pound gorilla of the party—will crush the hopes and plans of younger Democrats by grabbing the money and publicity of pre-primary campaigning during 1987 and early 1988. His bulk could block the light that might shine on newer possible candidates with strong appeal to old Democratic constituencies—Cuomo, say, or Sen. Bill Bradley of New Jersey.

That destruction done, Kennedy, I think, would lose in the primaries anyway. Edward Kennedy for president is an idea whose time may have passed—more than once.

4

Writing Criticism

If you asked Walter Kerr, drama critic for the *New York Times,* David Denby, film critic for *New York Magazine,* and Neal Gabler, formerly film critic for *Monthly Detroit,* what steps each of them follows in composing a review, you would be given a familiar description of a linear process. Each attends a theatrical performance or cinematic screening, takes notes on what he sees, transcribes and organizes the notes, creates an outline of some kind, and begins drafting a review that he will later revise before submitting to an editor. Thus described, the process of critical writing seems direct and logical; however, so bald a description leaves out some essential elements in composing criticism that a closer examination of the earliest moments of that process, as practiced by these critics, reveals.

For example, the critics give evidence of going through such sub-processes as planning, translating, and reviewing. In the interviews that follow, each talks about taking notes and examining, transcribing, or arranging them to create a tentative outline or sense of structure. Neal Gabler claims to write on cards and pads and to outline the piece carefully before he writes; from that outline he writes a review of about sixteen hundred words in three sessions, a few hours at a sitting, writing, rereading, adding, and revising as he rereads and writes.

David Denby's heuristics are even more systematic: from notes taken in the dark while viewing a movie, perhaps on a Tuesday, he sits down on a Friday with a notepad, examines his notes, and makes fresh notes under specific headings until it is "broken down for purposes of analysis into separate topics in front of me," and then he makes an outline. He drafts the twelve hundred word review on Saturday, rewrites on Sunday, and takes it to his editor on Monday.

Moreover, the rhetorical situation affects their processes. At the time I talked to them, Gabler was writing ten columns a year for a monthly magazine; Denby, forty-eight columns a year for a weekly magazine; and Kerr, a weekly Sunday review for his newspaper. Their writing was scheduled to the deadlines of the publications with some awareness of the audience for that publication. More important, all three gave evidence that the "text produced so far" influenced the text to follow; all three worked a great deal on the lead of the article. As Kerr says in his interview, "there're many times when I have to tear up page 1, or a first paragraph, or three-quarters of a page 10, twelve times before I'm satisfied it's rolling." Sometimes the whole of his first day—he starts Fridays at 1:00 P.M. and hopes to finish on Saturday or Sunday so he can phone it in and proofread the transcription over the phone on Monday—is given over to producing a "lead, a first sentence."

Similarly, Denby uses the outline less as a strict structure to fill in than as "a safety net" as he calls it, a way of knowing what the major points will be and staying on track with them. Otherwise, he depends on his lead to direct the article: "I'll try to write my lead to see where that's going to go and see the way the piece is going to develop." Gabler tries to organize so well in the initial processes that the piece follows systematically from his lead with little opportunity to deviate as he writes; the text extends itself like a legal brief.

Finally, all of these critics give evidence of the role that long-term memory plays in the cognitive process of writing by the automaticity of their decisions about format and audience, which are negligible in any overt sense, and the obvious storage of data related to their subjects of film and theatre from which they routinely draw. In this area, as in others, the critics' experiences support the reliability of the cognitive process model as a paradigm of composing.

Walter Kerr's notes for the review he wrote of Henrik Ibsen's *Ghosts*, a revival with Liv Ullman and John Neville, demonstrate the process he usually undergoes. His original notepad from the theatre contains a phrase or two per page, many of them barely legible except to himself and often cryptic in reference for another reader: "as watery as the wallpaper," one reads; "this not moody it has no air of living about it," reads another; "hands together, almost seem extra," reads a third. Such notes he then organizes and recopies, categorizing them into such groups as, in the case of *Ghosts*, "Gen.," "Lang.," "Liv," "Neville," "Oswald."

The "General" category may contain observations about the whole production, quotes, plot explanations, reactions to set design, lighting, production values, record of audience reaction, and the like. Some examples:

—Lot of light considering only 2 oil lamps in place (slender) R brings 1 later
—Ghosts grown lightweight in my lifetime
—AUD laughs O's description of illness
—incurable syph, incest, blackmail (refrain from calling BI arson, but I think Ibsen burned that place down
—Light lavender wallpaper, furn not as overstuffed as usual
—"Social convention! Do you know I think that's behind all the mischief in the world today!"
—"What about truth?" L
"What about ideals?" JN

In the general category the focus is broad; in the other categories it tends to be more narrow. In the case of *Ghosts*, most of Kerr's comments focused on Liv Ullman's performance and character, which already began to foreshadow the greater weight he would give general production values and her part in them in his review.

The notes influence the direction of the text. Some of his attention to the details of set design have arisen because of familiarity with earlier productions—*Ghosts* is one of the classics of modern drama and frequently revived, particularly in repertory. The set is the center of his concerns in the first part of the review. Midway through the second paragraph of his first draft, he writes:

The wall paper was a very light lavender—it seemed to reflect all
ˆnothing but sunshine
[of the {old} cheery sunlight that Norway could muster up in a year]
(in spite of the fact [that] it was now [supposed to be raining] raining heavily outside and the room boasted no more than two slender, at present [unlit] unlighted lamps), and the furniture it surrounded was not only characterless stuff but surprisingly spare. Mr. Neville,
ˆacutely
[looked (actually) uncomfort] locking and unlocking his fingers, seemed acutely uncomfortable everytime he was required to lean [forward] forward in a chair that was [clearly] clearly never [desig] selected to [accomid] accomodate his lanky frame.
Wallpaper and furniture aside, the building doesn't
seem structurally sturdy. I don't mean that [so] it wobbles if some stagehand opens the stage [odo] door and lets a gust of air in,

or anything like that; I can't even remember a door shaking on being shut. But [does anyone here know] I do expect, on a stage or off, that whenever [the] two walls [com e tog] come together to make a corner, the walls will meet. It is highly probable that [si] no one trying to make his way through this column knows what a "dutchman" is. it is possible that the strips of cloth I have in mind are no longer called "dutchmen"; they were when I was a lad, coming peri- lously close to failing Scene Construction 2. Anyway, a "dutchman" is—or was—a narrow band of [canvs] canvas painted the same color a [   ] the two wall pieces that could pasted over them, at meeting-point, so that the join would not show. I think Mr. Kupnik should get himself some dutchmen, or at least one to pull the down- stage edge of the dining room together. God [knows whyt] knows what might get through that crack. [In any event the setting as a whole is just not moody. I hav]

In any event, the setting as a whole is just not moody. It has no stain of living about it. Surprisingly, neither does Miss Ullman's performance. Miss Ullman is playing a woman

In this passage are several elements to note about Kerr's compos- ing. For example, like a lot of writers who compose on the typewriter, he types a row of X's over material he wants to delete. (The deletions are marked by brackets here.) In some cases these are merely misspell- ings or typos ("canvs" for "canvas"); in other cases they are phrases he intends to delete and then reinstates, or in the case of "In any event . . . moody," the deletion has come about because he has elected to start a new paragraph with that sentence. Elsewhere the change is one of tone—"does anyone here know" is the start of a scolding question that Kerr immediately softens into "I do expect . . . the walls will meet." These are features of embedded revision in the midst of drafting.

We can also recognize from this passage instances where material from the notes is incorporated into the text. The items about the lamps, the texture of the wallpaper, the lack of "moody"-ness, the stain of living, and Neville's handling of his fingers are all from the notes. It is also apparent that the "text produced so far" has an influence on the text being produced. The paragraph beginning, "Wallpaper and furniture apart," is an example of text generating itself—none of the comments until the very last sentence are taken from the notes, and the repositioning of that sentence as the start of the next paragraph suggests that it is really a shift in direction. The earlier comments about furniture and set design have triggered a stream of consciousness that leads Kerr to focus for a time on the physical problems of the set and to free associate stage terms and personal history ("dutchman" and "Scene Construction 2").

This draft continues for five pages. When Kerr returned to it, his revisions made him create two major inserts into this text with accompanying deletions. The insertion that has a bearing on the passage we have been examining comes as a half page in between original pages 2 and 3 (original page 3 is now renumbered as page 4). Kerr deletes virtually everything we have been looking at, from "The wallpaper was a very light lavender" through "It has no stain of living about it" and substitutes the following:

> The wallpaper was a very light lavender, it gave off
> a sunshiny glow that was positively blinding (in spite of the fact
> that it was reported to be raining outside and in spite of the further
> fact that there was no interior illumination except two spindly kerosene
> [gas] lamps, economically unlit), and the furniture it
> [surrounds]surrounded
> was not only characterless stuff but surprisingly spare [to boot]. Mr.
> Neville, locking and unlocking his fingers, seemed acutely uncomfortable
> everytime he was required to lean forward in a chair that was clearly
> never selected to accomodate his lanky frame. [Let us say that] {*the
> room*
> > [let us say]
> ambience of the production as a whole is just not moody. It has
> no stain of living about it.}
> *as a whole is a room without a past. It has no stain*
> *of living about it.*

The last two lines are handwritten, as is the word "room" to replace "ambience of the production," and an arrow extends down the page and through part of the next page to indicate the start of a new paragraph at the existing typescript line, "Surprisingly, neither does Miss Ullman's performance," quoted above. Out of two paragraphs, together a page long, Kerr has distilled one paragraph little more than a third of a page long, both finding focus and polishing language as he does it. Later in the draft he writes a final page to follow the renumbered six pages, then revises the first paragraph on that page and inserts it before the final paragraph. In that revision he expands on his analysis of the reasons for Liv Ullman's performance. This is the draft that was phoned into the newspaper and printed.

Writing Criticism

The example of Walter Kerr's composing just illustrated is one more demonstration of the reliability of a model of composing that takes into consideration the recursiveness of the elements in the process. In that regard Kerr's drafts are similar to other examples we have looked at already. However, something in the composing of critics separates them from essayists and opinion columnists, something about the intersection of long-term memory and the writing process just at the juncture where the commitment to composition begins. To draw a metaphor from computers, there is a moment in the composition of a review where the critic selects the configuration of his criticism, initializing the composition, as it were, by generating the patterns by which it can store and process information. That moment is not exclusive to criticism, but criticism can focus our attention on it because the point at which an author's predilictions and the context of his composing meet is more transparent in criticism than in more personal forms of writing.

In a sense, an important key to what happens in composition can be found not in what the writer does after the discovery of a topic but in the ways the writer decides he has any topic at all. The critics all talk in terms of the ways they are moved to write about a film or play. Gabler says his first decision in choosing what to write about is to look for "a film that interests me so deeply that I feel the compulsion to write about it." Denby's decision lies in "whether I have an edge on the movie, have something I really want to say about it. The intensity of my feeling about a given movie is very important in determining how much I'm going to write about it." The clues to sources of such compulsion lie in the notes taken in the theatre or in response to the experience.

Part of it comes from a state of constant receptivity. Gabler says, "I'm always scribbling things down on cards and pads, whenever anything occurs to me that I think I might someday write about, even if I think it's not going to happen until a year from now." The notes are an ongoing idea-gathering, the "assiduous string-saving" other writers like Tom Wicker refer to when they discuss folders of ideas, clippings, and memos. But in the context of the critical act, the notes are considerably more.

Denby explains that when he sits down to write the first draft, he will

> try to replay the movie in my head using my notes as a
> memory aid, literally think it through, think what happens. In

other words I might write down in my notes some reaction to a
scene or something or just even a few elements or the visual
components or even plot elements in a scene, and then I will
try to reconstruct at home when I'm sitting there what it was
that made me feel at that moment whatever it was I felt.
When you're sitting there in the movie, there are really two
media: the medium of movie that's playing on the screen, and
then there's yourself which is kind of a receiving medium, and
you want to recreate what it was on the screen that produced
those feelings in you that you had at that moment.

Similarly, Walter Kerr's transcription of his notes written in the dark
in the theatre is not just a way of organizing or making legible; as he
says,

What happens for me is that by going through all the notes I
put myself back in the mood of the play, as I felt when I was
watching it. It becomes more real. I may have seen two other
plays since that one, which tends to blur things, or neutralize
them, but if you sit down and spend forty-five minutes writing
down everything that struck you in the theatre, then by the
time you're through with that you're sort of close to the
experience again.

For both critics the notes are not merely memory devices but ways of
reliving the experience palpably enough to generate responses to it in
an environment where composition is possible; they are no longer
writing in the dark.

But a more fundamental consideration would be the question of
how the critics decide what notes to take in the first place. In other
words, what causes the responses they take notes on and attempt to
relive for reviewing? The evidence from these three critics suggests
that the answers lie as much in the context of the viewing and the
connections the critic makes between the background he brings to the
performance and the film or play he's viewing as it does in the content
or competence of the work being reviewed.

For example, before Neal Gabler wrote the piece entitled "Beach
Blanket Cinema," he had seen three films—*Porky's* in March, *Diner* in
early summer, and *Fast Times at Ridgemont High* in August. While
watching *Fast Times* it occurred to him not only that the specific film
was different from other films about adolescence, but that there had
been "a fair number of films that dealt with adolescence in ways that

were different than films in the past." Part of what started him thinking about the issue was his negative reaction to the film. As a single film, *Fast Times* would not have been worth reviewing for Gabler, but as he says,

> when you put it in the context of a film like *Porky's* [and its success] . . . these films reverberating off of one another sort of struck something in me and then when I thought of *Diner* . . . and what that says about adolescence, I saw a piece beginning to form in my mind.

After identifying the traditions of teenage movies and comparing past films with the current crop, Gabler decided that the difference between the traditional films and contemporary movies was "the difference between adolescence as a bridge between childhood and maturity and adolescence being no bridge whatsoever." But the impetus for the article comes from the ability to connect one film to trends and traditions in cinema—to relate a current experience to a larger context.

David Denby also wrote a review of *Fast Times at Ridgemont High*, but it was far more positive than Gabler's, taking the view that the film is seen "from a sympathetic but skeptical feminine eye," a reference to the director, Amy Heckerling. In the beginning of the review, says Denby,

> I talk about this girl losing her virginity and she was fifteen and she was lying on a bench in the San Fernando Valley in a baseball dugout and she read what was on the ceiling and how the director, who was a woman, put the camera up on the ceiling which is something a male director probably wouldn't have thought of doing since men generally, when they're losing their virginity, are not on the bottom.

The scene had a strong impact on Denby; his original lead for the review was "Surfer Nazis. That's what it says on the roof of the dugout in which Stacy Hamilton was losing her virginity at the age of fifteen!" Because the sentence structure seemed convoluted, he changed the opening to: "In *Fast Times at Ridgemont High* Stacy Hamilton is busy losing her virginity and she looks up and this is what she sees." His perception of that scene, his strong response to it, and his feelings about the mall environment depicted in the film influenced him to react differently to the film than Gabler did. In fact, where Gabler links *Fast Times* with *Porky's* to condemn a trend in teenage films,

Denby states that *Fast Times* may be advertised as "another raucously blue beer party celebration of raunchy teens like the repulsive big success *Porky's* but it's actually very sweet, a fresh funny exploration of adolescent anxieties and confusion." The difference in interpretation lies in the contexts for which the critics are making connections— Gabler to traditions in film and comparable adolescent releases, Denby to a feminist perspective and a trip to California, including its malls, a few weeks before he saw the film.

Even an idea which seems spontaneously generated is likely to be the result of a long accumulation of context. Walter Kerr observes that in one review the lead hit him "right smack out of nowhere." He says,

> in yesterday's article, the first line was, "The next time I see
> Colleen Dewhurst, I want to see her with her hair combed,"
> sounding like her mother, and that just hit me out of nowhere.
> Because I was going through the play and I was seeing Colleen
> Dewhurst do this, do that, and it just struck me—I kind of liked
> it as an out of place attitude, I guess.

But in the course of conversation Kerr recalled a host of anecdotes about Colleen Dewhurst's "earth mother" image on stage; the context for his spontaneous remark had been building over a period of years and a number of roles on the stage. It was the kind of remark that someone unfamiliar with Dewhurst or indifferent to her appearance could not make. Indeed, it may be argued that none of these critics could duplicate the criticism of either of the others, because the context in which connections are made for reviewing are individual, even idiosyncratic, to the critic.

Obviously, then, the key to criticism lies in connections made in context. Moreover, the act of critical reading, even on nonprint "texts" such as theatre or film, is a prerequisite for critical writing. But critical reading is not simply an act of decoding; it demands a set of aesthetics and an appreciation of the predispositions toward subject, performance, and format that the reader brings to the text; it demands some sort of schema, which the critic has borrowed, adapted, and developed for himself through exposure to earlier practitioners and considerable practice in context over time. Thus, the writing that the critic does in the dark is not a dispassionate and objective evaluation based on more or less universal criteria, but rather a spontaneous response prepared for a host of personal and professional experiences and schemata. Moreover, because it initially occurs during the performance, it makes the actual experience recursive rather than sequential. The viewing/

reading is intensified by the writing, and the entire composing process is enhanced by the intensified viewing.

An interesting point of comparison about these three critics is their early interest in criticism and writing. Walter Kerr remembers writing a movie review column for his hometown paper in the eighth grade; his writing goes back at least to when he was nine years old and his aunt gave him a typewriter. Neal Gabler was working on a high school daily in ninth grade and rose to editor-in-chief his senior year; in college he became a film critic for the university daily. David Denby remembers reading a lot of criticism in college and writing a review for his college paper of critic Pauline Kael's first collection of reviews. All can cite favorite earlier critics, but, although all three come out of a tradition of both academic and journalistic criticism, the main impetus behind their criticism is a combination of personal interest and self-development. The preparation for their criticism extends far back before the specific act of criticism they have to engage in. In a different sense from the ways we have used the phrase earlier, they are hardly writing in the dark at all.

Interview with Walter Kerr

Root. In your letter you expressed some reservations about doing a verbal protocol, talking out loud about what you're thinking as you're writing.

Kerr. Right, I think it would rob you of all the extra little things you get because you don't know where they come from if you're working privately. It would be conscious, and, as I mentioned to you, I was talking to a psychologist once who suggested that all creative work was a form of self-hypnosis. It struck me that that was true, because it explains why some days you sit down and you cannot get going at all and you'll spend three or four hours typing to get a lead, just a first paragraph, and it won't come. That's because you're thinking about the writing, but you have not succeeded in hypnotizing yourself into losing yourself in the process, where you're not thinking about writing, you're just doing it; you're doing what's in your head, and it seems to me that's not a bad way. But that can only take place in privacy.

Root. What are the conditions under which the *New York Times* is asking you to produce what you produce?

Kerr. Actually they're much easier than what they used to be at the *Herald Tribune* or the first year at the *Times.* I used to be under the gun. That is to say, we used to have to deliver that copy in an hour, immediately after seeing the show.

That's gone now, really; but it was something you had to learn, you had to be able to do it. As my then editor, Otis Guernsey, used to say, "You're going to bleed to death on this job, that's all," meaning ulcers or whatever. But you learn to do it even though you're in a busy city room, all the noise in the world going on around you. I used to work under those conditions because I trained myself to, that's all, and it took a while, but I did it for fifteen years at the *Tribune* and just one transitional year at the *Times,* where it was startlingly different. At the *Tribune* we got used to never finding a copy boy, screaming your lungs out because you had to be doing the next page and maybe sometimes running the copy yourself or, if my wife, Jean, was there, she'd run it for me over to the city desk, and then coping with an editor who would occasionally come back asking you about something in your copy—maybe you'd X'd out too many words or something.

But as I say, it can be done. I didn't want to do it beyond the time of the *Tribune*, but when the *Tribune* folded and the *Times* said, "Would you like to come over here?," that's when I said, "Sure, but only for Sundays." I thought, "I can still do the tight deadline now, but for another fifteen years? twenty years? No." So that's when I made the deal; I was in a good position to make it. The *Times* was very generous.

Root. The *Times* asked you for a Sunday piece. How long is it expected to be?

Kerr. Shorter. Actually, even when I first went to the *Times*, I would end up writing quite a bit. Even if I picked, say, *Toys in the Attic* or whatever the important new play I was going to do the main Sunday piece on, eighteen hundred words it usually was, Sy Peck, my editor, would still like some coverage on what was the best off-Broadway work I'd seen last week and what had I seen in the subscription houses and so on and so forth. So for Sy I used to do an eighteen hundred word lead piece and then I would do a twelve hundred word roundup piece which he'd put back on page 5 or 7, so I was winding up doing three thousand words, which is a fair amount. They would have liked it to be at the most fifteen hundred, but I rarely get the total down that far. They will accept it; they'll find room for it. They don't come back and say, "Look, you have to cut three hundred words," or anything like that.

Root. You never have a problem with being cut back on space?

Kerr. Not on space.

Root. You do all your writing here at home?

Kerr. Yes.

Root. What's your normal procedure in the writing? Do you write in longhand?

Kerr. No, always on the typewriter. I was given a typewriter when I was nine years old; I wanted a typewriter, and my aunt gave me one for my birthday and I never looked back. Also I've never learned to get beyond two fingers either, hunt and peck. I go pretty fast, though.

Root. How many drafts usually?

Kerr. Oh, it depends on the piece and how I think its coming along, or if I'm worried about it I'll show it to my wife and say, "How is this coming along?" At the *Tribune* I did daily and Sunday, therefore I didn't have that much time to waste or squander, so once I got through with my two or three dailies a week then I'd sit down and pick the best one to do a Sunday piece on, but I'd have to do it pretty fast because there wasn't any time left. But normally I can do it in one afternoon or at least I used to be able to do it, and that's the ideal. If I worked from 1:00 to 5:00 P.M.—four hours, that should be enough; sometimes I could do it in less—two or three hours.

Now with the pressure off, no one-hour deadline, and really only the one piece to do each week, most weeks, I start Friday at 1:00 P.M. and start transcribing the notes I took in the theatre. I have to do that now, I always did to some extent. I transcribe all my notes from these little booklets. I take the latest one and I copy every single note in it, sorting the subjects into groups having to do with the principal characters or the structure of the play or whatever. When I'm through with a page, I draw a line through it to show I've got that copied.

What happens for me is that by going through all the notes I put myself back in the mood of the play, as I felt when I was watching it. It becomes more real. I may have seen two other plays since that one, which tends to blur things, or neutralize them, but if you sit down and spend forty-five minutes writing down everything that struck you in the theatre, then by the time you're through with that you're sort of close to the experience again. At least that's one of my tricks.

Root. So when you've gone through that, then what happens?

Kerr. Then I hope to God I get a lead, a first sentence. Some days they come easier, some days they're bitches. And there're many times when I have to tear up page 1, or a first paragraph, or three-quarters of a page ten, twelve times before I'm satisfied that it's rolling—I mean that the rhythm is all right, that I'm not embarrassed by this adjective or that adjective, or that I haven't padded here. You either get a sense of that or you feel something is wrong, you don't know what necessarily, but it just doesn't roll right to you or maybe it doesn't lead you to your next paragraph, because you get a paragraph written and you have to work out an elaborate transition to get into the second. When that happens, forget it, it's not going to be any good. So I will redo them ten, twelve times, and maybe by the end of the day I'll have a start and pick it up again tomorrow and go from there. Sometimes I start the whole thing over. I may write the whole eighteen hundred word piece and then start from the first sentence again, if I'm certain it's really bad. Other days I'll be sitting here transcribing the notes and, boom, it just hits me, a line, that's all. It seems to come right smack out of nowhere. I didn't intend to do the review that way at all. In yesterday's article, the first line was, "The next time I see Colleen

Dewhurst, I want to see her with her hair combed," sounding like her mother, and that just hit me out of nowhere. Because I was going through the play and I was seeing Colleen Dewhurst do this, do that, and it just struck me—I kind of liked it as an out of place attitude, I guess.

Root. So you always start Friday at 1:00 P.M. and do the transcribing and you find yourself then working Saturday and Sunday?

Kerr. Almost always. Sometimes I do the notes on Thursday, the day before. If I think the review may be one that's tough for one reason or another, like *Cats*, for instance, I do all my notes on Thursday, because I want more time on Friday to get going. That worked out well from my point of view because I was then able to do the whole thing in one day. But I was worried about it; it's a tricky thing to handle. I didn't like it, but there are good things in it, costumes, some of the staging, setting, lighting, so on and so forth, of a highly professional quality, and at the same time I got very tired of it, very bored in the theatre finally, and when you have a situation like that you have to get it into balance, and that's tricky. You don't want to mislead people, you don't want to do an absolutely half-and-half review, although it will tend to come out that way—you know, "Yes" in the first two pages and "No" in the last two pages—so I wanted extra time on it to see if I could get it right. So, therefore, I did the notes ahead of time. Usually it takes all of Friday and all of Saturday, occasionally something on Sunday if I still have a lot to clean up.

Root. You said, today you usually read proof. Is that your final copy you've typed up and are proofreading for yourself or is that for the newspaper?

Kerr. What happens is I phone it, it's recorded. I type it here—just to show you how messy (it can get a lot worse than this), that's the review of *Cats*—and when I'm satisfied I've made my hand corrections on it—sometimes I have to stop and retype individual pages—then I phone it in late Saturday, early Sunday. It must be in type by Monday morning so they can start to play around with the section. Then on Monday morning, usually it's around noon, one of the girls will call me, Ann Barry mostly. She is the editor of the Arts guide, and she'll call me up and read it to me. She'll read their printout and I'll follow her with my sheets and see if I can hear anything that they got wrong, because words get scrambled in transcription. And that's it. After that they take it away. I don't write my own heads; usually that's the editor's job.

Root. What are these notes?

Kerr. Those are the notes as transcribed on that particular show. The reason I keep the notes is because if I get around to doing a critic's notebook piece for the daily paper, I will need some reminders of shows in order to dig up enough material for them and they like to have three different items in one column.

Root. You just did a piece on *Cats*. Was there anything else that you had seen in the same time period?

Kerr. In that week? No, but usually there would be. There wasn't in this case because the season is so very thin.

Root. If you've seen three in a week how do you decide which one you're going to write about?

Kerr. The one I liked best, I suppose.

Root. The play that you liked best or the one you think you got the best ideas about?

Kerr. You certainly wouldn't skip the one you liked best because you had a better idea on another one. Occasionally, you might see one that's so bad that it strikes you as funny and you have what you think are funny notes that you could use, but I would never use that in preference to the best play, that would be crazy. But I can always hold those back and put them in the critic's notebook for the daily.

Root. Do you ever read the reviews that other people do about the play that you might be writing about?

Kerr. I do now, yes. When you're on daily, of course, there's no opportunity to do it, but then we were so strict we didn't even talk about it at intermissions.

Root. Do you then still try to rely on your notes and your reaction and not talk about it with people or do you talk about it now that you're on Sundays?

Kerr. I won't talk about it much but that's for a different reason. I'll read the other reviewers, though. In fact, it's important that I do, because they will be using up a certain amount of material that I have in my notes. I'm getting in that situation with Frank Rich right now. Just in the last two or three weeks he's used two or three things that I had planned to use, in my head, you know, and I have to scratch it or repeat it or find a different context. That's one reason you have to read your colleagues ahead of time, because you don't want to walk into exactly the same thought or shape.

Root. Do you talk about it with the people you go the theatre with?

Kerr. No.

Root. You're not apt to say to your wife, "I can't quite get a grip on what I feel about this," and talk about it, trying to talk it out?

Kerr. Oh, yes, just in the normal course of ordinary events you do something like that once in a while, but at the same time there's a kind of understanding like, "Don't be too explicit, don't push, don't be dogmatic, be careful not to influence the review or to try to influence the review." That's just an understanding between you.

Root. Speaking of bad plays, I'm thinking about the Colleen Dewhurst piece. When you wrote this, what was the chief thing on your mind? What were you trying to accomplish first of all, the primary thing? I noticed about the structure that it opens up mostly talking about Colleen Dewhurst and the persona that she's able to project and how she has been repeatedly put in "earth mother stuff" and then got into talking about how really bad the play is. I'm curious how you get those pieces together.

Kerr. I forget, how did I? What's the transition? I remember talking about her, because I think that's kind of important. She's got to stop that.

Well, I'll tell you the honest-to-God truth. This is really two leads blended, bled into each other. The first lead is the "hair combed" idea, and the second was, if she's going to keep on doing this sort of thing, at least she can be more careful about the plays. That's the other lead and that's the one I first thought I was going to do, that I wish that Colleen Dewhurst would be careful, more careful about the plays and then go into what's wrong with the Ugo Betti piece that she'll have to fight her way through. More people would be interested, I'm sure, in reading about Colleen Dewhurst and her uncombed hair than in analyzing Ugo Betti's dialogue. I didn't do it for that reason; it just popped as I say. But that would have been the lead otherwise. Sometimes you have to do that. You tie things together.

Root. I'm curious about how the parts of something come together and also about what you suggest, what people are going to be reading the piece for. Do you have a sense that you're doing something different in this column than the weekday reviewers are expected to do? I noticed that often you take an individual performance or an individual play and make that the center of focus for a piece which is a larger discourse on something. I'm thinking of "Screen plays are skimpy for the theatre," the piece on *Inserts*.

Kerr. Well, that's what you want to do. You don't do it as often as you would like. But one reason for going on Sunday only is that you have the freedom of choice; you don't have to cover every disappointing show you saw that week; you can throw three of them away, not mention them at all. If there is one that seems the likeliest to be talked about and if you can think of connections, remember connections, and usually they bounce into your head in the theatre, then you try to do a more general piece. I do try to do it if I can do it or if the play that's up for major review isn't so important that it really deserves a whole column. If *Cats* gets a whole column it's because everybody wants to read about *Cats* and everybody wants to see *Cats* so far.

Root. Do you think the Colleen Dewhurst piece is one of your better pieces?

Kerr. It's very hard for me to tell. I usually don't look back. I find it very difficult to read myself on Sunday because I've gone over the piece several times, including the proofing. By that time I'm losing any objectivity anyway. Everything looks better in print than in a typewriter, as a rule. Sometimes you can't kid yourself. I do not like my piece on *A Doll's Life*. I didn't think the thing I was trying to say all through the opening came off; I didn't think my point was made quite clearly enough. I would love to have gone back afterward, I didn't realize it at the time, and redone the whole first page or at least two paragraphs. I think I could have cleaned it up, clarified it for you better. Mostly I go by what I hear from readers instead of trying to make a judgment for myself.

Root. You did a couple collections of reviews. What happens when you're preparing that kind of book and you have to go over your stuff? Do you tend to want to revise a lot? I think in *Journey to the Center of the Theater* you switched tenses somewhat.

Kerr. In all of them I change the tenses because I use the present tense almost always in reviews, and when you get into this kind of thing, by the time you can get the book out it's going to be another year after you finish it, and it would have to go into past tense. But I do more than that. Sometimes I blend two or three pieces into one . . . sometimes if I run across a whole paragraph I don't like, I get it out of there or rewrite it and make connections differently. All the routine credits go out, right away. I learned that on my first collected book with Jack Goodman of Simon and Schuster, which he sent right back to me and said, "Get the scene designers out of here." That is to say, you don't need to keep all of the journalistic credits which are just single lines anyway, unless the set or the lighting is a spectacular thing you want to write a whole piece about. You have to consider what the long distance reader can possibly find interesting.

Root. Do you end up feeling pretty good about most of them? Tom Wicker once said that, when he was doing a three-times-a-week column for the *Times*, he found that only about a third of them were really first-rate and he wasn't so crazy about the rest, but they sort of measured up to what his column ought to be. Since he's cut back to two a week, his percentage is somewhat higher. He says that meeting deadlines along the way and going the way you go, a certain percentage just aren't very good.

Kerr. I never tried to measure it. I have written more than three pieces a week; during the weeks at the *Tribune* it would average four and sometimes higher than that. The books are made up more of Sunday pieces than daily pieces, though there are a few dailies here and there. My guess would be something like this, that one in five is good enough to put in for a book, for this reason: I remember Bob Gottlieb, when he took over as editor at Simon and Schuster—and he's still my editor at Knopf—said, "Are you going to give us another annual collected book this year?" I said, "Oh, my God no, I just did one last year. I can't get enough good material out for that." He said, "When do you think you can?" I said, "Five years," and that's about what it has run. I get one year's worth of material every five years, as nearly as I can figure it. I was shocked. I started one of them, which one I don't remember for sure now, but it was while I was still on the *Tribune*. I started to go through the pieces, and I went through two years without finding even one that I wanted to reproduce, and I thought, Jesus, have I been this bad this long without realizing it and am I going to get a book here at all? Or do I send the advance back or what? Fortunately, in the next year, the third year, they started turning up useable again, but there was actually two years worth of material that I ended up throwing away. So it's discouraging sometimes.

Root. In "When Simple Essentials Are Overlooked," the piece on the *Hamlet* in Connecticut, I'm curious about how you decided on the things you emphasized there. When did you decide that it was going to be about the larger issue of productions not telling the story instead of being directly about the production?

Kerr. Well, by temperament I think I'm always looking to see if any broader thing can be said. I mean, that's the only reason you would, for instance, sit down to write a book of new material, because you're trying to say some broader thing, you're trying to relate things, connect them up. I think that's something that has always interested me.

When did I decide? I'll tell you one thing (this is just a bit cynical), when the production you're looking at isn't very good, you say to yourself, among other things, "Well, this particular production is really not worth doing a whole column about, so what does it have in it that would trigger a broader view to make it worth doing?" Something like that. If you're on daily, it's a news event; it must be covered and covered the next day, but on Sundays there's a choice and everybody knows you've got a choice, therefore what you say ought to seem important to you or at least semi-important or worth doing.

Root. The *Little Shop of Horrors* piece and the *Inserts* piece are both examples of your taking things which don't seem to have much redeeming merit and making them a spring board for going into larger issues.

Kerr. You certainly try for the spring board—I think I would try for it anyway—when you realize you're looking at something that is not of much intrinsic interest.

Root. When you said you're making connections, it seems as if you're drawing on your memory of other things, your experience with other things. Is that a lot different from when you started out as a critic?

Kerr. I don't think so.

Root. I'm curious about the kind of predisposition you bring to the writing. For example, obviously in the Colleen Dewhurst piece you've got a predisposition towards Colleen Dewhurst as a kind of actress who has a certain kind of presence on stage. The *Little Shop of Horrors* piece is essentially on the overemphasis on special effects and production rather than character, plot, story, theme. I'm trying to get at how you come on the genesis of an idea. Are you thinking about what you're likely to write on the way out of the theatre, driving home? Do you try to let it sit for a while?

Kerr. Well, in the old days when we were on daily you had to. During the first intermission you were trying out tentative leads in your mind. You weren't talking about it—you were probably talking to Dick Watts about six other things—but in the back of your head you were running over leads which you knew you would probably have to discard, because at the first intermission you don't even know enough about the show or even if you like it or not. But, yes, your head is working all the time on deadline reviewing because as soon as you get out of the theatre you've got to run to the office and do it in an hour. You don't have time to talk, think, anything. Roll up your sleeves and type.

Now working on a strictly Sunday basis I try to put it *out* of my mind for a day or two if I can do it. If I can see a show Tuesday that's opening Thursday, and I'm not going to write about it until Friday anyway, that's what I like, because it means I can put it away for a couple of days and let it gestate all by itself. Maybe it will throw up something I didn't count on or didn't realize. I like having a little more time to think about it, at least one day's grace.

Root. Sort of a period of incubation.

Kerr. Right.

Root. Do you ever have to do any research?

Kerr. Well, I'm using the books here in my library all the time, but mostly when I'm working on a book of my own.

Root. Not so much for your columns?

Kerr. No, not so much. It depends. I've certainly had *Old Possum's Book of Practical Cats* out on the desk while I was working on the *Cats* review because I didn't want to make any obvious bloopers if I was going to speak of the text. As it happens, I don't quote the text at all. It's years since you've read the book; you want to check things just so you don't make a mistake. Mistakes creep in.

Root. Do you find yourself being influenced by the column to look at the theatre in terms of the column, or even anything else in terms of the column? Is there a way in which doing this column gives you a certain mind-set or perspective on theatre or art or anything else?

Kerr. I think there are a couple of different mind-sets. One of them is, in my situation, if you've got a week in which there are *no* shows opening anywhere, you've got nothing at all to see, and therefore you've got nothing to write about, and you're going to a couple of social engagements in the course of the week, I would certainly go with a mind-set and listen, because many's the time I've picked up a phrase from a dinner party—you know, "as my dinner companion said"—and there's a whole piece rolling out of it. It just does suggest things that you had stored up in the back of your own head that you just didn't use yet.

Root. Is that kind of what happened on that piece about writing a review?

Kerr. I'll tell you where that came from. A year ago I did lecture at the New School. I was answering questions and again the question came up, and I realized how often it has down the years, about, "Don't critics just save up wise cracks and figure out how to get them in?" I said, "Listen, how many are there? How many can you quote?" and I threw them some and I said, "Can we add any to that really?" There're really very hard to do and all those are old ones and I realized afterwards there's an obvious piece in that but I hadn't done it. I wasn't sure I hadn't done it; I had to go back and look at last year's topics and make sure it didn't appear within about two months after that lecture, but it didn't. But I did it for that reason and because I had no other copy that week.

Root. So you had to recall that question-and-answer session?

Kerr. Yeah, that's one kind of mind-set. I keep a little file folder of hastily scribbled notes in the drawer that I don't know what to do with. Sometimes it's just a question I ask myself: When you shelve new books, do you throw away the jackets or do you keep them? I got what I thought was a good piece out of that; I go by the mail I got on it, one of the biggest volumes of mail ever, for me. That was all it was, just one sentence, which eventually I managed to figure out how to use for a piece.

There's another kind of mind-set in that you're half consciously waiting for something. About a year or so ago one of these dictionaries that send out questionnaires about new words, or new usages, or changing usages sent me a new one. One of the questions was the new term "gridlock," which is becoming part of standard usage, certainly in urban centers. And it's a good word, I think, it's descriptive, it gives you a picture, and you know exactly what's meant, and it does happen. But this same questionnaire said, "What do you think then of a variant that has been coined recently called 'pedlock,' meaning the same thing happens with feet?" And that seemed to be a really stupid coinage, because when does it happen with feet? Your feet never get that jammed up; you can step on someone else's feet and get out of the way. But I was going to the opening of *Little Johnny Jones,* and as I approached the theatre with one of my sons, I had been telling him about this dictionary thing and we ran into a very jammed crowd of sightseers outside. When I plowed my way through them to the ticket booth, I found myself plunging toward a barrier, a sawhorse, and caught in a mob of people. When we got up against the sawhorse, my son said "pedlock" and that clicked for me then, the mental set. That's it, I got the piece and the piece was simply a matter of having decided there was no such thing as a pedlock and then, oh boy, did I walk into a pedlock. That turned out to be a piece that drew mail. That was a half-prepared mental set waiting for the other half to fall in.

Root. Do you revise much for style, trying to get a certain rhythm to the words or . . . ?

Kerr. I try to get that from the beginning, but sometimes I will often revise to see if I can improve it any.

Root. Is there a certain kind of style that you're looking for? For example, is the style of the Sunday piece different from the style of the piece that you've written for daily?

Kerr. Yes, very. I was really kind of astonished. About two, three years ago the *Times* asked me to do daily again for a year and this time I said yes. I think I was getting bored or something. I needed freshening up and so I did do it for most of the year. Anyway, by this time I was so far away from daily reviewing, which I had not done in twelve years, that I thought I don't want to look back too much, I don't want to imitate something from *then,* but I did go back and look at the last review I did for the *Tribune.* I didn't recognize the person writing that review. I read that one review and said, "I don't know him." I closed it up. I don't say it was good, bad, or anything; it was just so different. It seems to me that for certain circumstances if you don't invent a personality you adapt whatever personality you have to the circumstances, a matter of what sounds right in this position or this job.

Root. What is the personality of the Sunday piece?

Kerr. Well, I'm still doing them, so that would be hard to answer. It's more easygoing; the daily pieces used to hit harder and faster at a thousand words. They were absolutely more definite, cockier, breezier; they went fast. I have one book that goes fast, *How Not to Write a Play,* the first book I did. I kept wanting to make qualifications everywhere, but I said, "Don't do it; you'll kill this book if you do it. You're doing something else here. This is not scholarly; this is argument," and so it moves very fast where some of the others take all kinds of time, rhythmic time, with qualifiers. If you're going to work in qualifying phrases, clauses, so on, as a regular thing, it'll make a different time sequence. I remember the first five or six years on the *Tribune,* I used to say to myself, "What kind of style do I have? Have I got a style?" I had no idea, I was just doing what I could do. Then eventually, I suppose, after you've done it a certain length of time, you begin to hear the same thing, the same metrical pattern.

Root. Let me point out one particular paragraph, from "When Simple Essentials are Overlooked," your piece on the Stratford, Connecticut, productions. "Catch you unawares as an idea? Very probably, since it's unlikely you've ever seen it that way. Shed new light," etcetera. It's quite a different kind of paragraph than you're usually writing. I'm wondering what you tried to accomplish with that.

Kerr. Conversational quality. Easy familiarity. Non-pontifical, I would say. I don't know, I can't still be doing it, but in the beginning, which is now thirty-two years ago, I had come from ten years of teaching at the graduate level in a university, and the one thing I was terrified of was sounding like an academic, going abstract, theoretical, and so forth, and so I used to force myself to deal with specifics rather than generalities, with precision, description, keeping away from the abstractions that you can easily, freely use in the classroom. If there are any theoretical or generalized statements, be sure they are illustrated, make it as graphic, as tangible as you can. I used to fight hard to do that. I'm probably still doing it. I was also trying to keep an easy conversational tone that would not suggest the academy or the teacher.

Root. Did that have to do with the reader that you perceived?

Kerr. Well, he is a different reader. If you're writing a serious book that might be used in a university classroom, you'll write in one way. When I sit down to do one of those books, *The Decline of Pleasure, Tragedy and Comedy,* something like that, I don't know how to change the tone altogether, but I always set myself a limitation, certain things I won't use. This is just a matter of toning yourself up. I'll go one whole book without a single parenthesis, no parenthetical structures. That is merely to constantly remind yourself that you are writing a more serious piece of work for a more serious reader and therefore let's not be chatty. Every once in a while you want a different rhythm. It gets very boring to repeat yourself all the time.

Root. Are there any people who have influenced your style? I mean any writers that you've read or any colleagues you've worked with, other critics that have had an effect on the way you write or used to write?

Kerr. I don't think so. I started writing, working on a newspaper, when I was a kid, and I had a movie column in the junior section of my hometown weekly. I got this notion, why can't there be a column of movie reviews by a kid for kids? What I really wanted was passes to all the movie theatres, which I got right away. I did this for eighth grade, first or second year of high school, and then I went over to the local daily paper and, although I was still only in high school, I was covering high school sports, even police court, playgrounds in the summer time, I kept a movie column going, which became reviews, not kid stuff necessarily. I was still a kid, but it was supposed to be straight reviewing. For influences I would have to go a hell of a way back. I did that one way or another for about ten years until I was out of college, then I stopped doing it altogether for the ten years I was teaching and did almost no writing other than playwriting, and so I was coming back to something I had done before but after a long gap.

Root. Where'd your sense of what a review was come from?

Kerr. The man I most liked to read among the reviewers at that time, in the formative period, would have been George Jean Nathan. Of course, he was the most celebrated of all those people at that time, but he used to kill me. I used to get out a book of his, like *Since Ibsen*, which is dated now, but I'd fall all over the library floor, reading it in my spare time, it was so funny. Then of course Nathan used language in a pyrotechnical way that I found interesting. I think the person who really had most influence on the rhythms I like and maybe some devices I like was G. K. Chesterton. He's not much read now, but I love his rhythms, his paradoxes, his ironies, and I suspect that every once in a while I copy some of them, even now. I'm sure I would have in the beginning.

Root. What's the difference between writing something like *Tragedy and Comedy* and writing the column? Is there a difference in the way you approach the problem of writing a full-length book?

Kerr. Yes. You need to have a long arch or span or whatever you want to call it that will sustain your book without having it crack into two or three pieces. While you don't know exactly how that's going to work out, you've got to have some generalized idea of where you're beginning and where you hope to end. You don't have to know all the bridge work that'll get you there but you must keep it in mind.

Root. Do you create a long outline of what you're going to do, a chapter-by-chapter model?

Kerr. No, but I usually have a lot of notes and the notes will be somewhat scattered, but if I had to put them together in sequence, I could play around with the notes on the desk and probably find it. I worked on a book called *The Silent Clowns* which is about silent film comedians, and I have notes this thick just from looking, and looking, and looking at the films. But as you look at them you also get ideas, I mean ideas about what happened, about how the audience viewed this thing, what effect it had on the films, what the audience was doing, and why the comedians themselves made some of the decisions they did and how did Chaplin arrive at this character who is really inexplicable in any rational terms or Harry Langdon, for that matter. If you get those ideas down, they interrelate after a while. You can see something that Chaplin did that was very similar to what Langdon did except it looks different. Then you try to do all that interweaving, which is the fun of it, and that's the part I like.

Root. I think that about covers it. I've got a good sense of how you go about doing this.

Kerr. I hope it's as honest as I can make it. It's not easy, you don't really know what you're doing, or a lot of time you think you're doing something and you're actually doing something else.

Can't They Do Better by Colleen Dewhurst?

Walter Kerr

The next time I see Colleen Dewhurst I want to see her with her hair combed.

I know perfectly well that this is going to be hard to arrange. Directors like to cast Miss Dewhurst in parts that call for her to look as though she'd just clawed her way through a rain forest—and while it was raining. In the current production of Ugo Betti's *The Queen and the Rebels*, director Waris Husein has even got her slathering cold cream all over her face and the creaming is supposed to constitute an improvement. While slathering, Miss Dewhurst is heard to murmur something about keeping up appearances. Actually, her appearance suggests she is about to swim the English Channel. Why are directors so fond of Dewhurst *en dishabille?* Obviously because the spectacle provides them with such wonderful contrasts.

You see, you can afford to dress the actress in a shapeless brown-and-plum mess of a dress—no matter what she weighs in at these days—because she is so splendidly proportioned. Sizable enough to look like a goddess, if there were any goddess parts going, but everywhere in scale, moving with grace whether shod or unshod (feet dirty or clean). And you can put up with that terrible tangle of bramble that encircles and half-conceals her face because the planes of her face are so beautiful.

In the Betti play, which is a Circle in the Square production housed at Broadway's Plymouth for a limited engagement, she is prodded into a ruthless shell of a building where captives who've been fleeing a revolution are being at least temporarily detained. Though there are three or four women among them, and though the brown-and-plum

Miss Dewhurst is for a time turned away from us, we identify her instantly and without trying. There's a flash of cheekbone beyond an impatiently poised shoulder, and there she is. These directorially created contrasts can be added to the contrasts Miss Dewhurst was born with—the jaw that seems to do her thinking for her, the rumble in her vocal cords that is also extremely musical—to arrive at a considerable, and most attractive, complexity.

We saw all that, magnificently, in O'Neill's *Moon for the Misbegotten;* we aren't ever likely to forget it. But does Miss Dewhurst have to go on *topping Moon for the Misbegotten* in the found-under-a-haystack sweepstakes? For awhile there, I thought there was going to be a change in the general direction of chic. When I finally saw her play a woman who wanted to be elected to Congress (*An Almost Perfect Person,* 1977, dir. Zoe Caldwell) and realized she'd spent nearly the entire evening looking socially presentable, I was prepared to do more than cheer her, I would readily have voted for her. Loving hands had been at work and she looked peachy-keen, to use a term of approval from my youth. But, all too clearly, the drift toward the salon didn't last. In *The Queen and the Rebels* she's back at the ranch.

I do understand that there's a possible plot reason for her backsliding in *The Queen and the Rebels.* The rebels who have halted the refugees at the border are searching, vindictively, for their onetime Queen. Their onetime Queen had been sentenced to death five years earlier but had miraculously survived the firing squad.

During the intervening years she may be supposed to have disguised herself, and I probably don't have to explain that the most obvious disguise a Queen could assume would be the stoop, shuffle and grime of a peasant woman. Thus any woman in this play has a semi-reasonable excuse for coming on disheveled, and I'm secretly wondering if that's why Miss Dewhurst picked it. Is she a gardener at heart, does she spend her days in the country tending to her bean-rows, does she prefer parts that permit her to come right into the theater nights without changing?

One thing, I think, is important here. If this splendid and innately majestic performer is going to continue to look like an eternal Trick'n'-Treater so that we shall only half-perceive the beauty that lurks behind the mask, then she is going to have to be very, very careful about the other qualities of the plays in which she chooses to appear. If I were she, for instance, I wouldn't consider for a moment appearing in any dramatic work whose time-and-place description on the program reads as follows: "The action of the play takes place in a large hall in the main public building of a hillside village. The time is the present."

Perhaps that doesn't sound so alarming to you. That's because you're not thinking. Notice, if you will, that we are being told absolutely nothing whatsoever. Neither are the actors. What village? In what country? What would the "main" public building of an unnamed community be? What was-is the "large hall" used for?

Nor is the "present time" of much help to us. The play was written in 1949. Was that the present or is this the present or does the present go on forever? (It was probably the author's intention to suggest that the present goes on forever, like the play.) And you can see all of this is unspecific, intangible, abstract. And it is exceedingly difficult for even the finest performers, combed or uncombed, to generate honest emotion when confronted with faceless backgrounds, faceless materials. General rule of thumb: if a play takes place in a void, avoid it.

Further caution: plays that pride themselves on being indefinite and impersonal tend, along the way, to turn into allegories. They will even tell you when this is happening. If one character says to another "This is a picture of the whole world, in a way," the play is now officially an allegory and no longer to be trusted. Allegories, in my view, do not belong on a stage. They belong squarely where Mrs. Malaprop put them, on the banks of the Nile.

Still further caution: watch the play's language for creeping images. As the evening increasingly detaches itself from reality in order to make its pontifically philosophical points, is the leading actress required to say things like "a rose has no other duty than to look as little as possible like an artichoke?" As an actress, do you feel the line swings? If that is one of the better lines, how much worse are the worse?

Final query: when the author at last remembers that beneath all of this chatty speculation on the nature of revolution he is supposed to be pursuing a dramatic plot, does he go all to pieces trying to wedge it in as hastily and as cursorily as possible? Indeed, in *The Queen and the Rebels* Mr. Betti seems to throw his hands into the air at the very thought that he must somehow do something about identifying the real Queen and arranging for her temporary escape, confessing his own ineptitude in the anything-goes dialogue he tosses Miss Dewhurst.

Toward the close of the first act, and while the men of the play are still talking themselves silly, Miss Dewhurst has come to the conclusion that a frail peasant woman, well played by Betty Miller, is the Queen. She is now given approximately eighty seconds in which to win the Queen's confidence and work out a highly improbable plan of escape. The Queen, no dummy, realizes that if she does manage to flee, Miss Dewhurst will be left in the hottest of hot water. "What will you do?" she asks, deeply worried.

"I don't know, but I'll think of something," Miss Dewhurst replies briskly, waving the line away before we can recognize it as one that is constantly turning up in broad farces. The actress is a whiz at whipping past her author's more unreasonable extravagances, and she almost makes an imposing moment out of Mr. Betti's ultimate conceit. The real Queen is now dead, though only Miss Dewhurst—more or less the village whore—knows that. Realizing that the world need someone "who will look up, and be looked up to" (realizing, in effect, that there must be a Queen), she allows herself to be identified as the revolutionists' prey, tried, convicted and shot. Listening to her try to lift the language to the level a climax demands, you long for a turn of phrase that will prove as persuasive as the tilt of her chin.

But the actress has squandered her enormous and wonderfully self-contradictory resources on writing that is merely pretentious. Lacking power of its own, the play can't use hers. In the end, it's just not worth Miss Dewhurst's getting all dressed down for.

A *Ghosts* That Grows
Evermore Lightweight

Walter Kerr

I will admit to considerable surprise the moment the curtain went up on the new revival of Ibsen's *Ghosts* at the Brooks Atkinson. I'm not accustomed to seeing the old warhorse, of which one can become foolishly fond, played in a setting that might do well enough for a stock company mounting of something by Philip Barry. I'm used to a *Ghosts* that's a bit more overstuffed: a lot of horsehair and heavy oak doors that rumble ponderously shut and big fat gaslamps perched next to handsomely tooled books, all that. Not that Ibsen's play is supposed to *look* eerie, as though poltergeists would begin banging away on the attic floor any minute. The ghosts in the play aren't, of course, ectoplasmic figures at all; they are echoes of the past, genetic hand-me-downs that tend to determine our present destinies ("We're all ghosts," ruminates Liv Ullmann as Mrs. Alving, "our mothers and fathers live on inside us"). But if a production of *Ghosts* has nothing whatsoever to do with *The Castle of Otranto* or even *The Turn of the Screw*, shouldn't it at least look substantial and, preferably, *serious?*

The slapdash touring set that seems to have been hastily pieced together by designer Kevin Rupnik has neither weight nor an invitation to solemnity about it. As Liv Ullmann walked into what purported to be her living room along the fjords at the preview I attended, I somehow didn't expect her to slip directly into conversation with John Neville as Pastor Manders but to take one look at the wallpaper and stop dead in her tracks. I could almost hear her wondering if this could possibly be the place where that husband had openly seduced the housemaid and carelessly sired a daughter, if this could be the place so patently degenerate in its atmosphere that she'd banished her own seven-year-old son from it before he could ask any more unanswerable questions.

The wallpaper was a very light lavender, it gave off a sunshiny glow that was positively blinding (in spite of the fact that it was reported to be raining outside and in spite of the further fact that there were no interior illumination except two spindly kerosene lamps, economically unlit), and the furniture it surrounded was not only characterless stuff but surprisingly spare. Mr. Neville, locking and unlocking his fingers, seemed acutely uncomfortable every time he was required to lean forward in a chair that was clearly never selected to accommodate his lanky frame. The room as a whole is a room without a past. It has no stain of living about it.

Surprisingly, neither does Miss Ullmann's performance. Miss Ullmann is playing a woman who has lived with drunkenness, seduction, disease, imposture, blackmail and lies beyond numbering—with incest and madness coming up. She has connived with none of this, except for a few face-saving fabrications. Instead, she has coped with the cesspool in which she's found herself, summoned up the strength to keep herself whole and sane while the universe was coming apart around her, and—through it all—she has so grown in intelligence that she is able to detect the flaws of logic by which the virtuous, as well as the profligate, live.

A very large order, but as her son Oswald says of her, she is a very strong woman. The part calls for enormous reserves: for cutting wisdom, for shrewd perception, for a keen sense of the right moment for candor, for anger and for understanding and for kindness when kindness is least expected. And humor, but a humor not unrelated to despair. No matter how you may regard Ibsen's clotted plotting, his transparent planting (the minute you hear that Pastor Manders is not going to insure the memorial just directed to Captain Alving, you know the whole thing will be cinders before another act is done), and his two-for-one coincidences, Mrs. Alving is a wonderful part. Call it a great one and you'll get no argument from me.

But Miss Ullmann comes to us—from the beginning, and her quality doesn't change a great deal—as though she'd spent her life gathering spring flowers and possibly playing volleyball. Healthy, pretty with her hair braided into a coronet, and utterly unmarked. No need to present the woman as ravaged, of course. She has *surmounted* her difficulties, swallowed hard and gone on growing. But she should, by all that's unholy, have acquired dimension along the way. Authority, force, a considerable arsenal of intellectual weaponry, a keen insight and an inner kindness. If she has not arrived at genuine stature, there is nothing to be shattered at the play's grisly conclusion.

Miss Ullmann, in what should be the commanding passages, is as watery as that wall paper. When the going is at its roughest, she is as insecure as Pastor Manders, a girl floundering in waters too deep for her, nothing like as sturdy or as self-knowing as Jane Murray's young housemaid Regina. There are, to be sure, effects Miss Ullmann can manage most readily, with swift asperity. When Mr. Neville, making a great to-do over the scandals he has been forced to digest in such a short time, anguishes "*How* am I going to deliver a sermon tonight?," the actress's quickly wry "Oh, you'll manage!" is just fine. So is her tart "Where did you hear that?" when Manders tells her that a local scalawag has reformed. And her impulsive, quickly retracted, urge to touch Manders lovingly when he confesses he has never lost his youthful feeling for her is nice indeed.

But too many gestures are aborted. Indeed, too few are ever begun at all. The actress tends to stand erect in a downstage position—often the same one—not really listening to the others, not reacting. Her hands are held in front of her, almost but not quite touching. They seem unused. And if she *can* deal with the occasional sarcasm, the mocking irony, of the role, she tends very strongly to make that the *only* tone of the role, of the play.

The result is that the play itself—or at least this production of it—grows evermore lightweight. Having established her skill with the knifelike riposte, Miss Ullman tends to bide her time, ride hurriedly past Mrs. Alving's sturdier diatribes, and then leap at any line that can be given a mild comic edge. Thus her discovery that the girl with whom son Oswald is trifling is really his sister, and her fury with herself for failing to tell them both the truth, goes by with much speed but little passion. A line is coming up that the actress is apparently waiting to pounce on, a line in which incest can be dismissed with a shrug: "Well, we're all descended from such a union." Tossed off, the line can most certainly command a snicker from out front. But the passage as a whole is a desperate, shaming, self-accusing, finally defiant one. If it contains a laugh it should contain a blunt laugh, a bitter one, a cards-on-the-table challenge. It is only a small part of something fiercer that a woman is trying to force herself to accept.

When it is made the dominant tone, though, the play itself becomes frivolous, cavalier, a matter of scoring debating points any which way. I do not know why Miss Ullmann has chosen to tangle with *Ghosts* at so light and uncommitted a level. Indeed, I confess to considerable puzzlement where the actress is concerned, to much mystification over the wild swings her career has lately taken. She has been brilliant in films, in many of them. On stage here, she was a provocative, even fascinating, Nora in *A Doll's House*. In O'Neill's *Anna Christie* she proved awkward and immature, in the musicalization of *I Remember Mama* merely bland. Why the curious shifts, the unexpected ups and downs? In the case of *Ghosts*, it's possible that Miss Ullmann is simply afraid of the play's creaking narrative bones, eager to insist that we not take them too seriously. And perhaps, overall, she is a kind of actress whose full powers surface only under the ministrations of certain directors (I am not thinking of Ingmar Bergman alone; the Lincoln Center production of *A Doll's House* was directed by Tormond Skagestad). Whatever reasons may be given for it, we are here confronted with a worrisome failure of imagination. A tremendously dimensional role has been allowed to lose weight before our eyes.

The balance of the company has at best the feel of a competent pickup unit for touring. Mr. Neville is of course a complete professional; he can't find a way to keep the burning of Captain Alving's monument from collapsing into outright comedy, though. Kevin Spacey focuses hard on the despairs of Oswald, honorably trying to make them reasonable; it's still hard to pump real anguish into "Mother, my spirit has been broken, ruined!" (Arthur Kopit adaptation). As Regina's presumed father, Edward Binns provides us with a box of makeup: incipent mutton chops, plenty of brown liner, conventionally groveling tugs at his hat. Only Jane Murray's Regina *insists* on being believed as well as heard. She's a girl who puts her foot down, and I commend her for it.

If the Play Is Bad, the Review Is Hard Work

Walter Kerr

I know I am never, never, never going to convince anyone that reviewers, as a breed, aren't a malicious lot whose primary occupation and principal delight is the shredding to pieces of bad plays. But I am, for the 65th time, going to give it a try—in spite of the fact that bad plays do indeed abound.

I was sitting there, just the other night, attending as dutifully as possible to yet another new play that grew worse by the moment, by the entrance, by the line, almost by the coffee costing no more than a dollar during intermission (please do not carry the cartons back to your seats, always supposing you plan to return to your seats). Some members of the slightly stunned audience—not reviewers, probably just nice ordinary people—were to be seen slipping away between acts into the early autumn night, and they were not to be scorned as slackers. There was nothing really to be hoped for up there on the stage.

Which promptly set me to musing again on the special ironies of my profession: on good reviews and bad ones, on reviewers' preferences and habits, on the popular impressions of reviewers that become lodged in readers' minds. And on the contradictions contained therein.

For instance, I imagine practically everyone agrees that reviewers would rather see a good play than a bad one. Reviewers may be ogres and they may be stupid, but they're not precisely insane. On the other hand, and in spite of the fact that they'd rather look at good than bad, there's an ineradicable general belief that reviewers much prefer to *write* about bad ones.

Rather than sit down to their typewriters to toss off ten paragraphs of praise, they'd rather—by far—be given the opportunity to bare their talons, trot out the fiendish phrases they've been saving up for months, and let the exhibit that's just opened have it straight in the teeth. That's more fun, isn't it? That's what makes reputations, isn't it? That's how all the memorable quips originate, isn't it? That's what the critic's been waiting for since the day he applied for a job, isn't it? I certainly knew that the young journalism student who was coming to talk to me the next day would expect me to answer "Yes" to questions one through four.

He came and he did. You see, he'd been reared on the great gag-lines of the past, the one-liners coined by reviewers who thereby and instantly became celebrated as wits, if they hadn't quite made that grade before. Eugene Field's "He played the king as though in fear that someone would play the ace." Dorothy Parker's "Miss Hepburn ran the gamut from A to B." And *"The House Beautiful* is the play lousy." Robert Benchley's "I always said I could laugh at Phil Baker till the cows came home; well, the cows came home on Saturday night." John Mason Brown's pronouncement that, as Cleopatra, Tallulah Bankhead "barged down the Nile and sank." Percy Hammond's wrap-up to the effect that "I seem to have knocked everything except the chorus girls' knees, and God anticipated me there." There are a few more that surely will come readily to mind.

But notice that. A *few* more. I'm sure everyone can add a couple, but can anyone add as many as eight or ten? I doubt it. The fingers of both hands will pretty much take care of the official count, and, to me, that says something. Reviewers haven't been slobbering gleefully over the bad plays set before them in order to rush into print with stored-up, or inspiration-of-the-moment, gems. The gems have been a limited crop, always, and they still are. We've all pretty much grown up on the same ones (everything quoted above was written before I got out of college, and, oh my friends, and oh my foes, that's quite a long time ago). We talk endlessly about how eager reviewers are to be wickedly witty. We then wind up swapping a mini-supply of quotable quips so limited as to suggest that the boys and girls have rarely tried at all. Mind you, I'm not saying the standard sallies aren't good ones. They are, most of them. I'm simply saying they're in such short supply that they must be enormously difficult to bring off. They're hard to do and twice as hard to do in a hurry.

No, reviewers don't leap with a wild enthusiasm at the worst plays to come their way, confident that so much badness will make them brilliant. Sure, they may dream nights, now and again, about giving birth to a beaut of a snapper that will instantly join the pantheon of greats. But when they wake up mornings, they wake up wistful; they know the score, know the odds against producing something memorable enough to be remembered beyond next Wednesday. And so they may, once in a while, try a darting little pun or two. Pun and run, you could call it. But most of the time most of the clan behave warily, and sensibly, not really caring to be caught not trying too hard.

But there's another, and much more important, reason why writing unfavorable notices is no gleeful exercise in easy triumph, and when I mentioned it to my student visitor I think he almost bought it. There was a glimmer of conviction in his eye, I swear.

It's this. Writing any review, whether in a hurry or at what is foolishly called leisure, takes energy. I think most people would agree to that. But it takes approximately ten times as much energy to write a bad notice as it does to write a good one.

Why? Because a good show creates energy. A bad one drains it steadily out of you. You come into the playhouse, it may be assumed, in a state of general physical fitness. And you are prepared, for at least the first twenty minutes of any enterprise, to sit up straight in your seat, to listen to the actors, to make a reasonable effort to follow the plot, to avoid coughing and program rattling and loud sighing. That's your contribution to getting the evening under way.

But pretty soon the play must begin to take over, to exert a sufficient power of commanding attention to keep you sitting upright and awake without conscious effort on your part, to make coughing or program rattling unthinkable for fear the noise might cause you to miss an eagerly awaited line, to bind you to the ongoing narrative with hoops of steel shaped by the playwright. Now suppose, in a poor play, this doesn't happen. You've done your bit to help sustain the first twenty minutes, but if the play isn't starting to do *its* bit—and is possibly beginning to look like an out-and-out dog—you're going to have to help carry it for the next twenty minutes as well. Maybe longer. You quickly begin looking for redeeming qualities, which really means you're looking for something to *write* about. Is there a perky ingenue with a touch of talent? Did a line of dialogue just fly by that had a whit of wit about it? Is there *one* good situation here that might be expanded into a nice, dirty quarrel? You keep alert, waiting for something, *anything*. And if, one by one, all possibilities vanish, you end up facing the fact that you're *going* to be nothing but a crosspatch in print again. In addition to which you're exhausted, spent.

You've tried to shore up the evening by offering your full concentration. And by the time the whole thing is done you're scraping bottom, energies depleted. The audience is at least free to go home. But it is precisely at this drained and dispirited point that the reviewer is called upon to do his work.

The reviewer, who clearly wasn't thinking when he applied for his peculiar job, is now expected to interest readers in something that didn't interest *him* in the least. Are lovely silken sallies, and a host of merry *mots*, going to rise from his typewriter like heavenly music in the circumstances? Well, you know the answer. It's true that, on certain rare occasions, a burst of anger, of real rage at what he's seen tonight, will overtake a reviewer and provide him with a temporary, possibly hysterical, energy. Most of the sorry time, though, bad plays make for slave labor.

Good plays, on the other and quite glorious hand, send energy pouring into the auditorium until you begin to feel that, at curtain-fall, you're finally going to see dancing in the streets (all that dancing in the streets that Alexander Woollcott kept promising us). It's a tangible thing, in the lobby at intermission. Everything's super-charged, and the lobby seems a huge bubble that is just about to break. It's an actual presence in the house, supporting the spectators almost physically and hooking them into a single crackling circuit. It's an uncontrollable animation on the sidewalks afterward, with nobody getting to finish a sentence ("Did you see what she did with that—?," "Listen, the line that killed me—," "I must tell Dick he's got to—," "My God I didn't know she could—"), as everyone explodes with his own personal review. Meantime, the reviewer strolls home or to the office with his head crammed with the stuff. He doesn't talk about it. Save that up for the typewriter later. Will the work be an absolute snap? Well, no, don't let me kid you. But the show's gift is a lift of the spirits, a drain of adrenaline, a pick-me-up born of pure passion. A good show makes a man *want* to review it whereas a bad one only makes him want to go home and lie down.

Well, I don't know if I've convinced my student or anyone else this time around, either. But I've convinced myself. Since it is obviously so much easier, I'm going to write nothing but favorable reviews this season.

Interview with David Denby

Root. To start things off, I'd like to know what your charge is from *New York* magazine—what are the conditions of your doing these reviews?

Denby. I'm to produce a piece forty-eight weeks a year; we publish fifty issues, so there's two weeks off right there, and I'm bumped from two other issues at the beginning of the summer and at the beginning of the fall—we do special issues that don't publish the critical columns. I may do a profile for the fall preview issue. But any rate I produce about forty-eight review columns, which are anywhere from four to six physical columns in the magazine. Sometimes when journalists say column they mean the whole piece and sometimes they mean the actual column line down the page, so there would be anywhere from twelve hundred to two thousand words. I choose the movies that are going to be reviewed. I let them know in advance what I'm doing. If the editor-in-chief of the magazine thinks that I'm avoiding something that the readers should know about, an important movie everyone's talking about or something like that, he may call me up and say, "I wish you would review this movie X and hold movie Y until next week," or, "Make your lead movie movie X and go long on that one and go a little shorter on Y." Sometimes we tussle back and forth over this issue, but in general I decide myself what I'm going to review and at what length and in what style.

That's a decision that's made on the basis of what I'm interested in and whether I have an edge on the movie, I have something I really want to say about it. The intensity of my feeling about a given movie is very important in determining how much I'm going to write about it, and also whether I think the *New York* magazine readers need to know about this movie. It's kind of a shifting back and forth between those two criteria: what I feel like writing about and what I feel the magazine reader wants to hear that week. Sometimes I think they should hear about a Hungarian movie that's opening in two weeks that they normally wouldn't bother with. The reader doesn't always know what he wants to hear, and you have to sort of take people by

175

the hand and draw them into a subject, particularly if it's unfamiliar or forbidding.

Root. What's your sense of who reads *New York* magazine?

Denby. I don't spend a lot of time thinking about that because if you particularize your reader too much you get into the danger of writing for that one sensibility and you cut off certain possibilities in yourself as a writer, but I assume that our readers are college-educated, working people, affluent or at least comfortable, with money to spend—because if they didn't have money to spend then the magazine would be a torment to read, because a large part of *New York* magazine is a service component that's telling you how to spend your money in the best way, everything from food to summer camp to clothing to movies and books as well. I assume probably a professionally-geared audience of people who are working in the professions in New York or in business who are college-educated, who are bright and have cash to spend, and beyond that I don't make any further assumptions. I don't believe a lot of black people read the magazine. Our readership is probably ninety per cent white, I would guess.

Root. Can you think of a film that you've not reviewed because you felt it wouldn't interest your readers?

Denby. Sure, I don't bother with schlock horror movies because I assume our readers aren't interested in them and I'm not interested in it. I don't even want to go to them; they just disturb my sleep and I don't have any particular feeling for horror as a genre, so I don't bring much to it. I'm not saying that it's impossible to write well about horror films. There are people who do it very well and who bring a lot to it, but I don't bring anything in particular to it so there's no point. It would just be an exercise. I don't see any point in just covering every movie that opens in order to put in my two cents. When Judith Crist was the film critic of the magazine, and she was here the first seven or eight years of the magazine's life, she more or less reviewed everything. I try to review one or two things a week, generally two things, and do at least one thing well. I'd rather do one thing well and one thing in a sort of summary way than to do three things in a kind of shallow, mediocre way.

Root. What's the normal procedure for doing a review? For example, what do you know before you go to the theatre?

Denby. Well, you've heard a lot about the movie because you've been getting press releases from the producing company for the last year and a half announcing that the project was under way, announcing who was going to be in it, who is directing it, who is writing it, and you might read stories in *Variety,* the weekly paper devoted to show business, about the production—whether it was running over budget, whether the actor got sick and disappeared or something like that—or you might have read something in a gossip column about two actors having an affair on the set. You hear rumbles from the industry through publicity people, or through people who work in the industry about whether or not the movie is any good or from friends who've seen it earlier, before you. So you almost never come into a movie completely cold.

I prefer coming in completely cold. The dramatic surprise of a completely fresh image on the screen is always wonderful. But in general one doesn't come in without some preconceptions, and every reviewer will tell you that his attitude towards a movie or play or a book can sometimes be set in opposition to what he's heard. In other words, if you've been sold already, if you've been built up a great deal by mainly other people who have seen the thing, you can say, "Well, this isn't so great," you can instinctively rebel against this consensus that's building or take it down a peg, or vice versa—if you hear that something is terrible and you see it and you suddenly see virtues in it. I don't like all of that conditioning but it seems to be inevitable. Any of us who talk on the phone to other people who work in journalism or the media are going to hear a lot about it. Also in New York there's so much talk whether or not a movie is any good. Among other things, it's a financial center so the stock prices of these companies rise up and down according to what they release so there's a lot of gossip.

Root. So you allow this stuff to bombard you?

Denby. You try to put it out of your head. Of course, you can't; but you try.

Root. Then you go to the theatre.

Denby. Generally, to a screening room; the companies like Paramount and Columbia and MGM have their own rooms in their corporate headquarters in large office buildings in midtown Manhattan. These are very comfortable, air-conditioned rooms, plush seats and so on, maybe 100 seats or 120. You see the movie two or three weeks in advance of the opening with other critics, other press people, editors, people from television, and a genre of person known as an opinion maker which is very important in New York—we have people who supposedly have influence—they might be from business or from some area—but they talk to a lot of people and could sway or move opinion. Sometimes college students are brought in. It's not all critics, I know that.

There are multiple screenings of every movie, depending upon how much the company wants critical approval. For something like Columbia's *Gandhi,* which was their big Christmas movie, a kind of serious attempt to make a political epic, they had literally dozens of screenings; by the time they're done, they may have had fifty to a hundred screenings. Another movie, if they just want to get it open fast, they may not have any screenings at all, or maybe one or two perfunctory screenings the week it opens, if they want to keep critics away from it as much as possible. So it varies, but normally there are say a half a dozen screenings available of a given movie and you pick and choose your time according to what's convenient to your schedule.

Root. Do you take notes during the screening?

Denby. I sit there with a steno notebook in my lap and I take notes in the dark which are then very hard to read the next day but I find there's no other way of doing it. There are people who actually have one of those little pens that have a little light in it and look down from the screen and write out a full sentence but I'm always afraid I'm going to miss something. I mean, the notes are simply little fragments, a little bit of dialogue or key word that will remind me of something that happened in the scene, something about the lighting, or something about the actor's expression. They're intended to stimulate your memory of the movie when you sit down and write about it maybe three or four days later or a week later. I may take a whole notebook full of notes with only a few lines on each page because I'm terrified in the dark of scribbling one note on top of the other. So I just write a few lines and turn the page and that is maybe on a Tuesday, and by Friday I'm ready to get going on my piece which is due the following Monday.

Root. Usually there's a four day layoff.

Denby. Yes, I might have seen the movie the week before also. But that would be very typical. I would see the movie Tuesday afternoon or Tuesday night, and say Friday afternoon at home I would sit down with this notepad in my lap and some paper on a clipboard and the cast and credits of the movie, which is just the publicity material that the company gives you when you see it; then I would try to replay the movie in my head using my notes as a memory aid, literally think it through, think what happens. In other words I might write down in my notes some reaction to a scene or something or just even a few elements or the visual components or even plot elements in a scene, and then I will try to reconstruct at home when I'm sitting there what it was that made me feel at that moment whatever it was I felt.

When you're sitting there in the movie, there are really two media: the medium of movie that's playing on the screen, and then there's yourself which is kind of a receiving medium, and you want to recreate what it was on the screen that produced those feelings in you that you had at that moment. Are you sitting there feeling bored or excited or upset or angry or aroused or horrified or something? Because the whole process of movie criticism is objectifying those feelings you have, those very subjective impressions, and any successful piece of criticism is going to have elements of both the gut reaction of "This is shit" or "This is great" and the very specific elements on the screen, something an actor did, something a director did. A review that consists entirely of description of a movie or entirely "I felt this, I felt that" would be inadequate. There's always this communication back and forth between those two reactions. So I'll sit there and replay the movie in my head and then make fresh notes on my paper on the clipboard under separate headings. It may be as simple as writing down the word "theme" and then writing everything under that that deals with thematic development in the movie, or writing the leading actor's, or actress's, name and describing the performance, or describing the elements of the director's work.

So then by the time I'm done with this process which, depending how complicated the movie is and also the intensity of my feeling about it, will take anywhere from forty minutes to five hours, I will then come out of that with four or five pages of notes of the kind I just described, with say, half a page on just the visual look of the movie. In other words the movie will have been broken down for purposes of analysis into separate topics in front of me, then I'll read over that and probably make an outline, generally if the piece is going to be a thousand words or more. My mind is not particularly well-organized, so I like to see where I'm going, and I like to see the whole piece in front of me on one page. It's just a good old solid high school outline; I'll try to write my lead to see where that's going to go and see the way the piece is going to develop, what points I'm going to develop.

My next idea about these pieces, particularly the ones that are more than just a couple of paragraphs, is that they really should read like essays. Certain notions in them should be developed through the piece rather than it just being a standard kind of review in which you give your opinion in the first paragraph, then you give a bit of the plot, and you run down a laundry list of acting, directing, lighting, camera movement. That sort of reviewing I think is boring, and it can be well-written or it can be poorly written, but I think that form of it is boring. What's more exciting is to organize whatever perceptions you have into some sort of essay that has a beginning, a middle, and an end, and you can do that even in three paragraphs. I'm not saying I pull this off all the time, but that's my ideal. With the other kind of review there's a lessening of reader interest when they get down to the different craft contributions in the movie, whereas this thing, if it's right, has a kind of dramatic logic that would hold you all the way through.

So that's part of the reason for making the outline because I don't have any form; there isn't any set form, there are no rules for movie criticism, there are a thousand ways you can organize a review. I'm always afraid of repeating myself. Sometimes I start by describing a scene and using that as the epitome of what the entire movie is doing; other times I will start with discussing the actors and use that as a lead-in; other times I'll begin in a summary way with an opinion of the whole movie. That third way is more conventional and I don't like doing it as much, but it's the standard way that most criticism is written—give a strong opinion pro or con right at the top. I like to draw people in and sort of create a little bit of a movie first before tipping my hand, and if you really describe the movie well the reader should be able to tell what you think right from the descriptive tone, the choice of language, the mood of your writing. You don't have to use all those trite critical words, like "it was well-acted" or "the lighting is beautiful" or something like that; you just describe what it is that's on the screen.

After the outline is made up, I don't necessarily stick to it, that's the next point. The point is that it's all there, that all the major points of the piece are there in front of me in one page and I can see them now; as I'm doing it I may reshuffle it or throw it out altogether, but at least I know what all the major points are and also what examples I'm going to use to illustrate them. Maybe it's a safety net or maybe it's a psychological thing, just for the security one wants to see all that in front of one in a longer piece before proceeding, but I know that several times when I've just started to write without an outline I sort of wander off down some lane and the piece winds up getting stuck in the sand, and then I have to sort of start over again and keep it on the main road, so it's better to know where you're going and what all the major points are.

Then comes the first draft which, let's say, is twelve hundred words, a major review, so it might be four and a half double-spaced typed pages. That will take probably half a day to write—six to seven hours, I would say. The first draft is very slow for me; I'm not a quick writer most of the time. Occasionally, it just flows out, but the stronger the response to a film obviously the easier it is to write the piece. It's those things that sort of feel gray that are agonizing and then you really have to pull it out of yourself.

Root. Are you going line by line carefully revising each sentence or choosing exactly the right sentences as you go through?

Denby. No, generally not because I know I'm going to do another draft. I try to get it down on paper in the right order and get it to say more or less what I want it to say and not be too fussy about specific wording. Also I spend a lot of time on the lead. Generally a lot of these pieces, if you get the first paragraph right, the rest of it sort of just flows from that. I may then write two or three versions of the first paragraph, easing into the piece because that sort of sets the tone of the piece and the strategy. I may do that two or three times, but the rest of it, I think, I generally write down once, although it's still slow and the first drafts are a mess physically and there're a lot of sentences crossed out or blacked out. I do it on the typewriter and make X's through sentences or try to reshuffle the clauses. When that's done I will probably do the same thing for the second movie that I'm going to review, which is generally the shorter review and it may not require an outline; maybe only five hundred words, say two pages, so it will be quicker—I'll then type the first draft of that too. This might be on a Saturday, then on Sunday I'll just rewrite the whole thing.

Root. Normally in the course of a week how many films will you have seen?

Denby. I'll normally have seen four or five perhaps and I'll be writing about two. I'll have this first draft and then I'll sleep on it, and the next day I'll read it through and make a lot of changes right on the copy, verbal changes and moving sentences around, crossing them out one place and writing them in another place in pen or pencil, right on the copy. Occasionally my wife will read the first draft, if it's readable, if it isn't such a mess that it's too hard to follow; she may criticize and say, "This is not organized well," and ask me to move a paragraph up or lead in a different way or something like that.

Root. Is this usually on Sunday?

Denby. Yes, on Sunday, but then for the second draft I'll set the margins of the typewriter for something approximate to the actual column width which would be, say, forty characters on the typewriter. I know at that point how many lines I have for the piece; if it's a four-column piece, it might be about 195 lines, if it's a five-column piece it will be more like 265 lines. I will have a line count the magazine will have given me by the end of the previous week. I will then set my typewriter at forty characters and type out roughly the right number of lines on my second draft. Now when I'm doing my first draft I know pretty much the length of it, how much I typed; that is, if I have normal margins on the typewriter I know that six pages at normal margins is roughly a five-column piece, six double-spaced pages, so I should have about the right amount of copy there anyway. When I set my margins more narrowly to forty characters I will get an exact line count by the time I'm done and try to come out to within five to ten lines of where I'm supposed to be on either side. You never can be exactly sure because when the thing is set sometimes it changes a little bit; it mysteriously grows or it mysteriously shrinks and then you can cut it or expand it.

The second draft goes much more quickly and I find it very plea- surable. I find the first draft agony; the second draft I think is a lot of fun when you actually have something there to work with, to play with. It's at that point your feelings of craftmanship take over and you start playing with sentences to make it flow better or take out repeating rhythm or take out rhymes, internal rhymes which often look terrible in prose, and to liven it up, maybe you put in a more metaphorical style or put in a simile to make something more powerful. That's where the polish comes, there in that transition from the first to second draft. That's the most pleasurable part of the whole operation. When that's done, which is often very late Sunday night or even Monday morning, say 3:00 A.M. Monday morning, I'll read the thing over and do more tuning of it with a pencil, crossing out words and writing in new ones, and then that goes to my editor on Monday.

Root. You bring it in or phone it in?

Denby. I come in the morning Monday and give it to my editor, Rhoda Koenig, who is also the literary editor of the magazine, and she'll read it and maybe spend half an hour reading it and then we'll talk it over and she'll make suggestions, generally of a very minor nature having to do with style and sentences, even individual words. In fact in three years I can't recall her saying, "This has to be rewritten." Once or twice, I believe, she said it, but that's all. It's an additional polishing . . .

Root. She's mostly looking for style or trying to make it fit into *New York* magazine?

Denby. Well, she has her own idiosyncratic, very sophisticated sense of style, I think, so she brings her taste to bear on mine. She's not dictating her opinions to me. She will make a check mark in the side of the column and say, "Did you really mean to put it this way?" or "I don't think this phrase works," and she'll explain why and we'll bicker back and forth and one or the other of us will win but I don't know who wins the majority of the time—probably she does, but she will never really force something on me unless she feels it's absolutely wrong, it's inaccurate, or it's so dreadful it's an offense against taste or usage. It's polishing really.

Root. When you're revising, particularly in the second draft, are you mostly looking for style? changes in style? You mention word choice, metaphors, which seems directed more at style.

Denby. I imagine that eighty percent of it is style. When you read the first draft over you may still see that there are holes in it; there are things you simply haven't said or are out of balance, that you've gone too far along in developing a point and left the other points out. I wouldn't say it's entirely style. I may compose fresh sentences in the beginning and when I'm doing the second draft and I try to sort of write them onto the copy, just peg them in the right place before sitting down to the second draft, because the more work you do on the first draft the easier it is to write the second draft obviously. But I think it's very important that you run it through the typewriter again because it just gets so much better. There are a lot of people, good journalists, who just do one draft and mark it up with a pencil and hand it in. I don't think I've ever done that in my life except for very, very short pieces. I find that as a piece of writing it just looks so much better; if I had time I might even do a third draft. I used to when I wrote for monthlies.

Root. Then, from Monday morning when does it go to press?

Denby. Then Monday morning we'll put it in the pouch to the typesetter at noon and it will come back by four and it will be set in columns on galley sheets and we'll be able to see the length of it. Generally I'm a little bit over so I'll have to cut, say, ten lines or fifteen lines, and I can make further changes at that point. Sometimes there are things you don't see until you read it in print; when you read it in print you read it so much faster because it's clean and you see that you've repeated words, that you have two contradictory notions, two nuances leaning in opposite directions fairly near each other, so you have to iron that out. It's just because you're reading it faster and you see things that you don't see on the typescript unless the typescript is absolutely clean, but mine never is because I'm always changing and marking it up until the time its grabbed out of my hands. So I do still more revisions in the galleys, and this is almost always just for style and rhythm, and then I cut or on those occasions when I'm short I add a few sentences to fill out the space. That generally happens Monday afternoon, sometimes Tuesday mornings which I prefer because I come in fresh with a full night's sleep. Then it's out on the newsstands the following Monday.

We were talking before about how revision is so important to the whole thing. It's often a psychological problem. Sometimes people are afraid that, if they pull the thing out of the typewriter and redo it, they'll get lost or it's too much work. You just have to get yourself over the hump and say to yourself, "Well, it's just work. It doesn't mean that I can't write if this still isn't good." You've got to get yourself up to that pitch of readiness to change it and do it over and do it over. One way of hearing what's wrong with a piece is to read it aloud, because if you read a piece aloud you hear failures of tone, your sentences that don't work, that are pompous or too long or too short. Or if you read it to someone else, if their attention begins to wander you know that something is not working, that the thought is not consecutive, clear. I sometimes read the pieces to my wife or just read them aloud to myself, and I'll hear just listening to my own words a sentence that's too stuffy or rhythm is wrong, too many polysyllabic, Latinate-derived words, and know that it should be written in Anglo-Saxon English. I find it very helpful if you have the time to put it in the drawer overnight and sleep on it, because when you read it the next day you're no longer involved in the compositional problems that a given sentence or given paragraph gave you—you're just reading it as a reader. It sometimes happens you can take a lot of pains on some paragraph and it still isn't any good, and if you look at it right away, as soon as you've finished all this labor, you don't feel like taking it out or redoing it because it's caused you as much effort already. But if you look at it the next day, you can sometimes see more clearly what's wrong. These are just little tricks, and of course it requires a long enough deadline so that you can do that.

Root. Tom Wicker said that he used to do three articles a week—now he does two—and that he thought about a third of this work was really good and the rest was professional but didn't quite measure up to the standards he'd set for himself when he started out. What kind of proportion would you say is true for you?

Denby. I think I'm between a third and a half according to my own standards. Of course, his standards might be higher for himself than mine are for me. You don't always know when you finish the piece whether it's good or not. You know whether it's professional or not, and of course you have an editor to help you, but you may not know until a month later when you pick it up and read it again. Sometimes you're shocked. There are things in there that should have been taken out, or it just doesn't come alive, which is a more frequent problem because for some reason or another it doesn't have a current of feeling, it doesn't have a temperamental vivacity that a piece of critical writing should have. It's just flat and dull and the only reason is that the movie hasn't stirred you in one way or another.

Root. Can you think of a review that you think is your best? or among your best?

Denby. No, I can't off the top of my head. I generally like the longer ones because I can work out a position in greater detail. I can also describe a lot more. Possibly one way in which my writing has improved since I've come here is that it's gotten a little bit richer descriptively, less thematic perhaps but more physical detail about actors or about how a movie looks or that sort of thing.

Root. One that comes to mind is the one on *Shoot the Moon.*

Denby. Yeah, I think that one was pretty good, *Shoot the Moon,* because I was very moved by that picture. There may be some warmth in the writing, even some power. That's a case of the movie getting you up and your sort of borrowing some of the energy from the movie. I do try to adapt my language and my style to the nature of the subject, what kind of film it is. If it's a very pop culture, thrown-together movie I try to write in a slangier way, and if it's more severe or classical or something like that I think I try to write it in a more chastened way. There is some leaning of the style in the direction of the movie, adapting the tone a little bit. Of course you don't want to lose your own voice either. I think generally the positive reviews are the better ones with a few exceptions.

Root. Have you ever changed your mind midway in the review or discovered anything in the course of writing it?

Denby. Yes, sometimes you realize that it's richer than you thought as you start describing it and you realize that there was more to it, just because you find you have a lot to say. But it also works the other way around, that you find yourself with not much to say or not much to describe, and you realize that your reaction was really very limited and dry and some part of your willpower was making you think this was a good movie. In that case you've got to retool the piece, pull it out of the typewriter, look over your notes, and make a new outline, and start over again. It's no disaster . . .

Root. Let me give you an example of something that you did recently, this favorable review of *My Favorite Year*. Do you remember anything of the circumstances of putting that piece together?

Denby. Well, Peter O'Toole was the thing that hit me the hardest, so I led with O'Toole. There's one, two, three paragraphs here at the beginning about O'Toole's performance and career and the character he plays in this movie, without really getting to the movie itself. I just gave the premise of it right at the beginning. That sort of throws the review out of balance a little bit, but you can do that when there is an outstanding performance of a star or someone who is well known. There's nothing eccentric about the way the piece was done. This one was actually a little bit late because I was behind; a lot of other critics had already written on it so I was conscious of trying not to repeat what other critics said. Now, that's an unusual circumstance; usually I come out at the same time as everyone else. I remember reading other critics to be sure I wasn't repeating any formulations of theirs.

Root. Do you remember with this whether it came out pretty easily?

Denby. This piece practically wrote itself. This, in fact, was one of the easiest-to-write pieces that I can recall. The first draft was written in about five hours, which is not very much for me; for another writer that might be a long time, but I'm just slow. I daydream a lot, fidget a lot. The reason was that Peter O'Toole was wonderful, and I realized at once that if I could just describe Peter O'Toole pretty well, just what he looks like and the character he played, that I would have half the piece already and the rest of it would fall into place. So this one was a case of, for me, unusual ease.

Root. Did you feel that there were certain things that you had to get in, if you were going to talk about the film that there were certain things about plot that have to be in?

Denby. Yes, those are all little craft things. It doesn't matter how you do it, you don't have to lay it out quite that explicitly, but you have to some way give the kind of movie it is, the genre, whether it's comedy or whether it's serious, and enough of the premise, the movie's thematic concerns as well as plot, to hold the reader's interest. Readers can be held by different things: they can be held by a purely thematic analysis of the movie or of the director's career, but that tends to be a little dry, and you've got to be a very good writer to pull it off. It's easier to hold people's attention and also to write well about the human material in the movie, the acting, the performance, the character, the fate of a character. It's a narrative medium and that's what finally people respond to in movies.

Look at the success of *An Officer and a Gentleman.* It's really a remake of a movie that was made in 1942; it's very old-fashioned in its assumptions except for the degree of frankness about sex, and the reason it's a huge hit is one thing happens after another and you're involved with those characters and you care about them. Despite all the experiments and everything, unless there's some narrative base, you're not held to a movie emotionally, and that's something I try not to forget. Occasionally in my pieces I will try and tell the story of the movie myself but mixed in with a lot of critical ideas besides. How much you're going to tell is another issue—you don't want to give away the plot altogether so that there are no surprises.

But one way of holding the reader is to involve them in the fate of a given character. I did a piece recently that a number of people seemed to like, a review of the movie *Fast Times at Ridgemont High,* and I talk about this girl losing her virginity and she was fifteen and she was lying on a bench in the San Fernando Valley in a baseball dugout and she read what was on the ceiling and how the director, who was a woman, put the camera up on the ceiling which is something a male director probably wouldn't have thought of doing since men generally, when they're losing their virginity, are not on the bottom. I think I caught people's interest because here was a girl losing her virginity at fifteen, then I sort of digressed and went around to discuss other things and about the movie being set in California in the San Fernando Valley in a shopping mall and what that meant. But that got people hooked, the human factor.

Also I thought it was an interesting notion of what it said on the ceiling of the dugout. In fact, on my first draft of the piece the first words of the piece were "Surfer Nazis," which is now on line eight, where I say where she reads what was written in graffiti. So I was really starting with the detail and then the next sentence was, "That's what it says on the roof of the dugout in which Stacy Hamilton was losing her virginity at the age of fifteen!" There was nothing wrong with it, it was just a little convoluted in terms of the sentence structure. I read it aloud to my wife and she said, "It doesn't work." There was nothing wrong with it as an idea; I just didn't execute it, so instead I started, "In *Fast Times at Ridgemont High* Stacy Hamilton is busy losing her virginity and she looks up and this is what she sees." In other words I did it in a straightforward way, but I still started with a given image from a movie.

I was saying before how boring it is to have that formula of first the judgment about the movie, then the genre, then a little bit of the plot, then the laundry checkoff list of acting, directing, writing. Walter Kerr is the master of this. He starts with one thing that somebody did on stage, one scene, one way a certain line of dialogue was inflected, and uses that as a way of getting into the whole play or performance, as an epitome of what's going on. That takes a certain amount of skill and you have to think about doing it in advance and outline it if you're inexperienced. Otherwise you're not going to know how to get from point A to point B, from the specific to the general. All criticism, in any case, is a weaving together of the specific to the general, of very specific notations and the way people look and talk and move or thematic ideas in movies and larger general notions of what's going on. So here you're talking about a whole movement of a piece going from specific instance to that being the way into what the whole movie's about. If anything, that became a cliché. There was a period when I was doing piece after piece starting with a little line of dialogue or one image from a movie.

Root. Here you're saying that this works in at least two ways. One is that it sets off thematically talking about the movie but that it's also something very catchy to get all the readers into the piece.

Denby. I drew readers into this piece, *Fast Times at Ridgemont High*, with a discussion of these kids and I have here one, two, three, three whole paragraphs of plot and about how the movie is seen "from a sympathetic but skeptical feminine eye." I don't get to judgment of whether the movie is good or not until the fourth paragraph, where it says, "From the ads you might get the impression that *Fast Time at Ridgemont High* is another raucously blue beer party celebration of raunchy teens like the repulsive big success *Porky's* but it's actually very sweet, a fresh funny exploration of adolescent anxieties and confusion." That paragraph could have run right at the beginning and most critics would have put it at the beginning, I think. Instead I thought it would be more interesting to draw people in by discussing the characters and what they're going through. I think that's something that takes a little bit of experience, because at first you're nervous and afraid you're not going to be able to sustain interest that way. But I do it as often as I can, and also it should be clear just from the seriousness of which I'm describing this that I like this movie to some extent or at least take it seriously without giving the judgment right away. You've got to reassure the reader with your tone that you know what you're doing.

Root. Which of these two reviews do you think is the better, the one you were more satisfied with?

Denby. I think *Fast Times at Ridgemont High* is probably more interesting because I sort of come out of parts in the movie, this whole shopping mall world, and that was fun to do that even though it's only a paragraph and a half. Also I felt happy about it because it was a popular movie and still is, but it was not taken seriously by other critics, and so I felt I was breaking a little ground or maybe helping the director a little bit. It was a first film by a woman director, Amy Heckerling, and must have had a difficult time breaking through. Whereas this one, as I say, I was late and so I felt as if I was riding on other people's coattails on it, although it still hasn't become a hit yet so maybe my review will help a little bit. That one gave me more pleasure when I saw it in print. It's fun when you can help a movie that either has not been praised or does not have a big ad campaign behind it. *Diner* was a case in point earlier this year, a film that a couple of critics really saved because the studio really didn't have any faith in it. In fact they were going to dump it.

Root. Have you ever been unable to write a review?

Denby. Not in recent years. Earlier when I was starting, yes, ten years ago and not for *New York* magazine. I was writing for the *Atlantic Monthly* in the early seventies. I remember scrapping a few pieces that I couldn't seem to pull together, and they were longish reviews. That was merely inexperience and I felt defeated that day or even that week. I don't think it did me any real harm and probably if I had tried again, put it aside for a week and tried again, I would have might have been able to pull it together. It was just a case of it reading in such a turgid way, I thought, "Oh God, no one else is going to want to read this." But I can't recall recently being unable to write a review. I'm sure there are some that aren't terribly good or that the writing is crotchety or dull or something, maybe because I was fighting it or I didn't have anything particular to say. When you're very excited about a movie or angry about a movie, they're a lot easier. It's just a question of organizing your responses. It's when you have to pull it out of yourself that you don't feel much of anything, like a religious person undergoing a period of spiritual dryness, having nothing in your soul. Critics have periods of dryness too. It just sometimes can be a physical thing, or your life is just not going very well, or other times it's just the movie itself, but you just don't feel very responsive at all. It happens in film festivals when you see two movies or three or four movies a day for two weeks, which is why I stay away from as many festivals as I can.

Root. Does part of your ability to turn these out or to succeed in getting them done as opposed to giving up on them come about by the rhythms of your work?

Denby. Absolutely, regular rhythm to the work. Now I want to insist that my life is not a model for anyone. I mean, I go to bed at four o'clock in the morning and get up at noon about half the days through the year. So does my wife. It happens that neither of us have nine to five jobs, but it's not good. We're out of sync with the rest of the world. People call us in the morning when we're still asleep or we take the phone off the hook. But the fact is that it's a regular rhythm that works for the production of this column and also for the other work that I do, because I write a monthly column for *House and Garden*, and I occasionally write pieces for the *New Republic*, longer pieces, in my spare time.

So I seem to be getting a fair amount of work done, but I find the weekly schedule is heaven. I mean I wasn't really happy as a movie critic until I started at the *Boston Phoenix* exactly six years and one month ago. There's enough time to say what you want to say and to write and rewrite which I keep stressing is so important, and yet it's every week. You don't get slack and rusty because writing is really like hitting in baseball. If you get three weeks off, you're going to be rusty when you get back. Your timing is off, you have trouble formulating sentences. It's amazing. On the other hand, if you write every day you get stale, not rusty; you start to write the same way, use the same formulations. So I feel very lucky to have this weekly job. I think it's a nice rhythm.

Root. What's the difference in the way that you compose the longer pieces that you do and the regular column?

Denby. Well, it's hell because I have to work on it in my spare time. I have been working on one now that's almost thirty double-spaced pages, and I've been working on it for months one or two days a week.

Root. Is this commissioned work?

Denby. Yeah, it's something I talked over with an editor. There's no deadline. It's nothing to do with movies. It's very hard because I have to get myself back into it each week, I just don't sit down and start working on it. It takes three or four hours to go over all the notes and get into it again, get going.

Root. If he had given you a six month deadline—something like that— would it have gone faster?

Denby. Well, I need some kind of urgency to get myself moving, since I'm basically lazy. There was a deadline that was really set for the end of July and I went over that, and I thought I wasn't going to do the piece after all, and now I'm doing it again and it's so late that it doesn't matter. It's going to be just as awful in a month as this week, so the pressure is off, but even if it's a three month deadline I probably would benefit by having it.

Let's face it, writing is very hard, what I've been describing is very hard; even though I can do it and I can do it every week, its still as hard as anything I can think of doing. It's a lot easier working in an office. I've done some teaching and teaching is hard too, but I think writing is harder. It's harder than driving a truck. It's not as physically demanding, but it takes a lot out of you psychologically, particularly when it doesn't go well. You have to get yourself up and keep up the pressure or else you're just going to settle for second best.

Root. In that longer piece, are you doing the same technique of sitting down and writing your thoughts, then doing an outline and then drafting?

Denby. Yes, I had a great many pages of notes, then an outline, then I'm actually going to do three drafts. It was just an extension of the normal procedure, only a lot bigger. In fact, the bigger the piece, the more necessary it is for me to make an outline. It's as simple as that. But, even when I write these very little pieces at the end of the regular column, I almost never just put the page in the typewriter and sit down and write. I usually have to think about the order of the ideas or the order of the sentences, and I may scribble a few of them out in longhand and then do it. That's just the way I am. I like to know where I'm going when I start writing the piece. Maybe eventually I won't need that. There are people who just start writing without much thinking and it comes out fine. They just seem to pull it out of themselves.

Root. Do you do a lot of rehearsing, playing the lines over in your head before you write?

Denby. Yes, I do. Someday if I have any money I'll buy one of those computers where you just compose a line and immediately recompose it if it doesn't work, because that's one of the things that is annoying when you're trying to get the things right, pulling the page out of the typewriter and redoing it over and over. Yeah, I usually run the thing through my head a couple of times. Also as you're writing you don't want all the sentences to have the same rhythm, you don't want them all to have the verb form "to be," which is a weakness of mine that I don't use active verbs. I like beginning with dependent clauses but, for instance, here it says, in my review of *Tex*, "Smart, a good athlete, Mason, eighteen, has to pay the bills and play daddy for Tex and it burns him up," so the subject of the sentence is Mason but it begins with a dependent clause and it's a nice way of picking up speed and also changing rhythm. But you can't do it twice in a row because it has a sort of sing-song rhythm then. So that's the kind of thing you think about when you're writing, although sometimes I don't notice that until I'm revising.

Root. We were talking about the difference between your writing now and your writing when you were younger. Is there any way in which you're drawing on certain things that you've worked on in the past and have knowledge on from working at this ten to twelve years?

Denby. Sure, the information you're using and also interpretations or your basic notion of the director's abilities, his career, you may have worked out once before, and you may be drawing on it or playing off it but at least it's there. I happen to be badly organized, so I don't have easy access to things that I wrote a dozen years ago. I have to start clipping these things or else it will be chaos. So I usually go by my memory of what I said and what I felt. You try to use it without repeating it; you may draw on it, but it's more fun if you vary it or turn it inside out. I don't think anyone who reads *New York* knows what I wrote in the *Atlantic* in 1971; I doubt it very much. It gets easier up to a point; it's easier because you're just more facile, the sentences come faster.

Also a number of things have changed in my writing. One thing that's notable is that most young critics are not very good at writing about acting; they're better at writing about the thematic material in the films, and the reason I think is very simple: when you're writing about how a theme is developed, it's not all that different from a college paper, but when you're writing about performance, you're writing about people, and young critics tend not to have that much experience of either performance or of life and so your prose is drier. As you get older, you're less afraid about writing about sex, you're less afraid about writing about physical things, and as a result the prose not only gets warmer but probably, not funnier, but wittier or has a kind of a basic humor about the notions that I develop that probably was not there when I was twenty-six. That's just a question of experience and living a bit.

Root. When you started writing reviews, how did you know how to write a review?

Denby. Well, I always read a lot of criticism, and I fell under the influence of Pauline Kael when I was in college. In fact I reviewed her first collection, *I Lost It at the Movies*, for my college paper, and then when I went to film school I used to read her and some of the best critics of the past like James Agee and Robert Warshaw and Manny Farber, whose work had been collected. There's that and the standards that those people set, and side by side with that the feeling that you can do it as well or better than most of the critics who are actually working at that time. I was in fact a graduate student at Stanford making films, but I had gone to journalism school at Columbia, then I decided that maybe I wanted to make documentaries, so I went out to Stanford and did that. I took a summer off, and started to write criticism and got some of it sold to a film magazine, and from there got the job at the *Atlantic*. But I guess I had always written reviews, even in high school; I had written them about music or something or in college I wrote them when I went to the Metropolitan Opera. I love reading criticism; I read a lot of literary criticism when I was an undergraduate at Columbia; friends and I would spend a lot of time discussing things we had seen and giving our opinions and sort of arguing with each other.

Root. Do you have a feeling of ever doing a piece and saying this is rather Pauline Kael-ish?

Denby. Well, I did when I was younger, and other people noticed it in my writing, and a lot of people have fallen under her influence because she was a great critic and her language and her self-assurance is intoxicating. About a half a dozen years ago I made a very conscious effort to take that sort of stuff out. I think I'm still closer to her than to any other critic, but I think it doesn't sound like her writing anymore, and people have told me in recent years that it hasn't sounded like her at all. But it was an issue for me, and in a certain point of my career it did not do me any good that I was her protégé, both in a career sense and in the sense of my own morale; on the other hand she opened up a lot of paths not only for me but for a lot of people, so I think on the whole she's been a whole positive power in the whole scene.

Root. Is there any other writer who influenced your style?

Denby. Oh, some of my teachers at Columbia like Lionel Trilling, who was a great literary critic, and Stephen Marcus and maybe a little bit Dwight McDonald and a little bit James Agee. I'm not sure if there's anyone else. George Orwell, maybe. These are the nonfiction writers and critics, most of them that I read over and over again, for partly style and partly point of view. With Orwell particularly, it's a certain attitude toward life that's partly political as much as anything. They're all very good writers. I can't read writing that has some profound theoretical base but that is written in jargon. I simply cannot read it, and as a result, a lot of European film criticism that's very heavily theoretical doesn't interest me. I feel insulted that a writer hasn't taken more care. When it comes to movies I like something that has a very descriptive and tactile and specific surface rather than theoretical surface. Manny Farber, who's not very well known, is kind of a critic's critic, and has a book called *Negative Space*, is just a wonderful influence.

Growing Up Absurd

David Denby

In *Fast Times at Ridgemont High*, Stacy Hamilton (Jennifer Jason Leigh) is busy losing her virginity in a baseball dugout somewhere in the San Fernando Valley when she notices what's above her—a naked light bulb and some graffiti in black (SURFER NAZIS, it says). The director, Amy Heckerling, has done something that most male directors wouldn't think of: She's pointed the camera at the ceiling during Stacy's willing but less than joyous initiation. The shot is brief, but it makes its point about the dead, alienating thing that's happening to Stacy as she lies on the dugout bench. A high-school freshman, Stacy, fifteen, finds herself in this ungrateful position because she's been listening to her friend and mentor, Linda Barrett (Phoebe Cates), who is beautiful, older (a senior), and apparently very sophisticated. Linda, who works with Stacy at a shopping-mall pizza parlor, is shocked at Stacy's lack of experience ("God, Stace, you're fifteen!"), so Stacy finds herself a boy right away. The sex is more painful than anything else, but she feels she's a mature woman now.

Jennifer Jason Leigh hasn't quite shed her baby fat yet. With her long blond hair and adorable smile, she's pretty in a slightly dumpy way, but she becomes positively beautiful as she wills herself into a trancelike seductiveness, luring boys from school into her house. First there's Mark "Rat" Ratner (Brian Backer), a timid lump with a sheepish Woody Allen smile who dons a tux every night for his job as a ticket taker at the movie theater on the other side of the mall. When Rat panics at her bedside and flees, she puts the moves on his slick and showy friend, Mike Damone (Robert Romanus), who thinks of himself as the campus Mr. Cool. Mike has a prancing rhythm to his walk and an obnoxious smirk, but he turns out to be rather skittish, too.

The boys are seen with a sympathetic but skeptical feminine eye, and perhaps only a woman could bring out the sick, puzzled expression on Stacy's face when Mike runs away from her. Stacy knows she's supposed to be responding to the grandeur of her new situation, but so far she hasn't had an instant's pleasure. All of this is ruefully comical: Stacy is a nice girl who wants only to be accepted, and everything goes wrong for her.

From the ads, you might get the impression that *Fast Times at Ridgemont High* is another raucously blue, beer-party celebration of raunchy teens, like the repulsive big success *Porky's,* but it's actually very sweet—a fresh, funny exploration of adolescent anxieties and confusions. Set in the school-and-shopping-mall teen world north of Los Angeles, the movie is an adaptation of Cameron Crowe's book about his under-cover "return" to high school (he was twenty-one) in the fall of 1979. Perhaps Crowe, who wrote the screenplay himself, provided such quintessentially male moments of humiliation as Rat's shameful retreat from Stacy's house, but the overall tenderness of the movie—the curiosity combined with delicacy, the emotionally specific responses to sex—comes out of Heckerling's direction. It's her first feature—an auspicious debut.

Fast Times at Ridgemont High is composed of short comic vignettes about kids bluffing and faking and competing for sexual status among their friends; the bluffs lead to a quick collapse and terrible embarrassment, which the movie defines as the basic emotion of teenage sex. Stacy and her friends are shucking off their clothes before they've explored friendship or the pleasures of courtship or romance—a theme that is developed satirically, not as a moral judgment. Amy Heckerling is the right person to direct sex farce: She brings real heat to these hasty encounters, and yet she never falls into a trance herself—we always know what the characters are feeling and why.

The young actors are fresh—rounded up from TV, theater, modeling—and the settings are fresh, too. At the beginning of the summer, on vacation in California, I dropped into a shopping mall in the northern part of the Valley (not the one in the movie, which is in Sherman Oaks). The mall had over a hundred shops—not just the usual clothing stores and movie six-plex, but also an Italian-shoe store, a Belgian-waffle parlor, two taco stands, a bratwurst house, a French bistro with red-checked tablecloths. Each store had its distinctive decor (the wood on the walls was variously aged, gnarled, pockmarked, or natural), and each decor made reference to something genuine that existed somewhere in the world (in Paris, in Florence, in New York). Since there was no place else to go (the town was an instant condo nightmare, with rows of tan-and-brown houses), this collection of cultural images really was the entire world for the kids who lived there. Leaving the mall, I got myself all worked up wondering how the kids in that town could possibly know what a real neighborhood felt like, a place that had some flavor and culture of its own . . . wouldn't they be stunted forever?

Of course, it's easy for New Yorkers on holiday in California to flip out, receiving intimations of the Apocalypse on the freeways or under the palm trees. The filmmakers, on the other hand, don't see the mall as the end of civilization, only as the latest in teen scenes—a place for kids to work, hang out, and flirt. Nothing much is made of it, but nearly all of them have jobs there (presumably, in hard times, allowances have been cut off) serving pizza or flipping hamburgers. The only one who doesn't is Jeff Spicoli (Sean Penn), a stoned surfer so utterly wasted by drugs that he can barely utter an intelligible sentence. Penn, who has stringy hair and a mean little mouth, is marvelously swinish; he's the biggest laugh getter in the movie, but his Jeff is also the least important of the kids. No one wants to have anything to do with him (he's too far out of it), except for the fiercely professional history teacher, Mr. Hand (Ray Walston, in a serious, steely performance), who is so appalled by Jeff that he makes reclaiming him a special project.

Ridgemont High is a comedy about the normal crises of growing up in America. The filmmaker's point about the mall is that the kids have taken it over and turned it into a high-school cafeteria; they'll survive the mall and bad sex and maybe even get something out of school. The movie is part of the new conservative spirit in the country: No one rebels, no one is even restless or dissatisfied. Amy Heckerling keeps the material vignettish and small, and she and Cameron Crowe resolve the characters' stories by rewarding the good-hearted and punishing the smug. The movie is slightly goody-goody, yet it's charming. If Heckerling had given it a distinctive rhythm and a formal style—something comparable to George Lucas's neon-on-black design for *American Graffiti*—she might have made a classic. At this point, she doesn't have much interest in the sensuous or kinetic elements in filmmaking, but she's got something else that often eludes more exciting directors—an instinctive intimacy with her characters that brings you close to the screen.

Show of Shows

David Denby

As Alan Swann, the drunken, swash buckling movie star who dominates *My Favorite Year,* Peter O'Toole is magisterially funny—flamboyant yet controlled, egotistical yet enchantingly attentive to his fellow actors. The time is 1954, and Swann, a matinee idol for decades, has agreed to do a guest shot on the hit TV show *Comedy Cavalcade,* which stars the great Stan "King" Kaiser (i.e., Sid Caesar). O'Toole's Swann is patterned after Errol Flynn, with traits from John Barrymore, the poetry-quoting Richard Burton, and no doubt a fair amount of O'Toole himself thrown in. Fantastically disorganized, a man indulged by everyone, most grievously by himself, Swann is a lush, a scoundrel, a spendthrift of his own talent. His looks are going. Yet the magnificence is still there. At the Stork Club, trying to pick up a luscious Abbe Lane type, he gets sidetracked into dancing with an elderly woman— an adoring fan. He wants the bimbo, but at that moment he performs for the fan, giving her everything he has in a slow, courtly waltz that is so graciously accommodating it goes way beyond noblesse oblige and becomes quite moving.

This would seem to be the role Peter O'Toole was born to play— though he's been a while coming into his birthright. As the action hero of *Lawrence of Arabia* and *Lord Jim* he trembled and stared with more neurotic intensity than could be comfortably fitted into those relatively bland big-budget spectacles; as the man-about-town whom every woman wanted in *What's New Pussycat?* he was charming but also easily distracted, vaguely put-upon, and almost superfluously classy. But a few years ago, after many indifferent parts, he was on top of his game in *The Stunt Man* as the viciously manipulative big-time director.

My Favorite Year is the one that will make O'Toole a Hollywood favorite. Skinny and pale, with pageboy bangs and a thin mustache that would have been an anachronism even in 1954, he looks a little hollow, a little played-out. Women may mourn the O'Toole who was a startling golden beauty in *Lawrence*, but much has been gained too. His Swann is a drunken Englishman with style, a man superbly prepared for disgrace. Swacked, O'Toole waves his arms wildly and lets his eyes wander with alarming freedom as he sinks deeper and deeper into enjoyment of the scandal he's creating on all sides. But then, like Proteus surfacing from the depths, he rouses himself from his stupor and makes a devastating remark. In the end, he always pulls himself together; his obligation to the public demands no less.

When O'Toole is onscreen, the movie is spellbinding; when he is absent, it is merely funny, good-hearted, and entertaining—a commercial comedy with a tender feeling for its New York live-TV milieu. The story is told from the point of view of Benjy Stone (ne Benjamin Steinberg), a very young hotshot gag writer for *The Comedy Cavalcade* who has been given the unenviable—indeed unperformable—task of keeping Swann sober and shipshape the week of his appearance. The screenwriters, Dennis Palumbo and Norman Steinberg, are both graduates of TV comedy, but from a later era than the fifties. Since the film was produced by Mel Brook's company, it's likely that the character of Benjy was based partly on Brooks, who worked for Sid Caesar on *Your Show of Shows.*

I wish the screenwriters had made Benjy as tough as Brooks. He is bright but he's also an Alan Swann idolater who has to be disabused of his faith only to find it again, and some of this stuff is second-rate. When Benjy makes big speeches at Swann, telling him he's got to live up to his legend or he, Benjy, will be crushed, we're in the sermonizing world of a bad Broadway play. As Benjy, Mark Linn-Baker, a Joe Papp alumnus, shows both the strengths and weaknesses of his theatrical background. Short, with rounded, pillowy cheeks, a needle nose, and a Kewpie mouth, Baker looks like a Hirschfeld cartoon of himself— you could read his expression from the last row of the theater. He delivers his lines decisively, but he's a glib, busy actor with frantic hands and a fretful walk—he looks like he's trying to act everyone off the stage.

Benjy is part of a writing team that has to come up with bigger and bigger laughs every week, a task that is turning them all into wrecks. The chief writer, Sy Benson (Bill Macy, in an acidly funny performance), has become a jealous, embittered screamer—he must toady to King or lose his job, and he's got the taste of bile in his mouth.

Richard Benjamin, who directed (it's his first film), loves this milieu enough to show us how the rivalries and hysteria—the tantrums, flip-outs, accidents—were not merely the by-products of live TV but part of what made it possible, the pressure that produced the laughs. Benjamin keeps his actors shouting, with bananas in their ears, but for this subject the noise and abrupt rhythms work.

As King, Joseph Bologna has Sid Caesar's heft, his bullying force (though not his giggly high voices and accents). He plays him as a young brawler, a functioning paranoid who rewards a favorite with a gift (some steaks, or maybe whitewall tires), stomps on anyone who crosses him. What makes King lovable and even heroic is his fearless pursuit of laughs. When he and Swann join each other before the cameras in the movie's rousing finish, it is the meeting of two champions.

More explicitly than any show-business movie that I can recall, *My Favorite Year* divides the world into the funny and the unfunny, the show people and the civilians. There is even a scene in which the girl Benjy pursues (Jessica Harper) tries very hard to tell a joke that Benjy has taught her and fails. The filmmakers mean to be generous— they mean to say that she is wonderful anyway, even though she's not a performer. But they can't show us how she's wonderful. In this failure they only betray their real feelings. This movie is an insider's view of the way show-business people entertain us by entertaining one another (almost everyone else bores them). Watching *My Favorite Year*, you may not feel you're part of that world, but Benjamin has made its bizarre workings credible and funny, and O'Toole is there to touch it with greatness.

Interview with Neal Gabler

Root. I would like to know something about your background in writing—how you got into doing film criticism.

Gabler. When I was in high school, I did a lot of writing for my school. I was fortunate enough to be in a school—Lane Technical High School in Chicago—that had a daily high school newspaper. I started working there when I was a freshman; by the time I was a junior I was sports editor, and, by the time I was a senior, I was editor-in-chief. So that gave me a lot of writing experience right there and, then, when I went to the University of Michigan, I felt very much out of the mainstream and wanted to be connected with the University in some way. Somebody told me they were looking for a film critic on the *Michigan Daily*.

There were two major interests I had always had in mind—one was sports, particularly baseball, and the other was movies. From the time I was very young, six or seven years old, I saw everything, every important film whether it was for children or not. It was just something I grew up with. My mother liked film, my brother was interested in film, and I guess I picked it up that way. I had been in one of the film societies in Michigan as well, so I wrote some reviews and got the job. Eventually I was doing two or three pieces a week and they were getting longer and longer, and just as my interest in film evolved, so my writing ability evolved. From there, I started thinking seriously about making writing a career for the rest of my life. By the time I graduated, I had applied for my first job, which I ultimately didn't get, at the *Chicago Daily News*. They were looking for a critic and thought I was too young but were very encouraging. I got jobs writing for other places and I went to law school.

I didn't like law school from the minute I stepped into it. In 1975 I started a film program at the University of Michigan. I became a teaching fellow pursuing a master's in film and loved teaching almost instantly. I kept writing; my criticism was getting slightly more academic and scholarly and that's the direction I wanted it to take it. I got a job teaching film at Penn State, got the idea for *An Empire of Their Own*, a book on Jews in Hollywood, and sold that to a publisher. All this time I'd been writing for *Monthly Detroit*—in 1978 I just submitted some pieces to them and they'd liked them—and that sort of brings me up to the whole *Sneak Previews* thing.

Root. What does *Monthly Detroit* ask of you?

Gabler. I think every place I've ever worked I've seen myself as making incursions into the magazine. When I first wrote for *Monthly Detroit* they wanted ten short two-sentence-long blurbs on current films. I did that for about two months and then, through both my desire and theirs to have something more substantive, we moved into a brief review of something like 750 words, and blurbs of 750 words, somewhere between 1300 and 1500 words total. Then that initial piece got longer, month by month, with the blurbs staying pretty much the same, until finally I reached the point where I wanted to write longer pieces. So we dropped the blurbs and I was writing about 2000 words a month. Now, because of planning for the magazine's space, I generally write about 1600 words.

Root. Do you have a set procedure that you follow?

Gabler. In terms of subject matter, I know when my deadline is, and I try to do one of two things.

First, I see if there's a film that interests me so deeply that I feel the compulsion to write about it. For me, criticism is a way of giving something back to the movie. If a film impresses me enormously, criticism is my kind of valentine to it, not just praising it but analyzing it, showing what it's doing and why.

The second thing is if a film is important enough to write on. There may a film that's some sort of cultural phenomenon, and you feel compelled to write about it. Usually I'll take a broader view and I'll sit down and ask myself, "What's gotten my goat?" or "What interests me?" or "What do I feel I have to write about?" or "What do I want to share with my readers that's happened this last year or this last month or whatever?" And based on that I'll select my subject.

In terms of format, in terms of how I go about writing something, when I was doing only *Monthly Detroit* and writing my books, I'd generally give myself a long lead time on it and I'd have several subjects sort of floating around in my mind. I'd always keep cards and pads all over the place. I'm always scribbling things down, whenever anything occurs to me that I think I might someday write about, even if I think it's not going to happen until a year from now.

Root. Do you file those systematically?

Gabler. No, I just sort of stick them in books and things like that. They're just sort of scattered all over the place, and I pick them up and they'll inspire me and I'll sit down and generally outline the piece very carefully before I write.

The pieces are very, very carefully organized. One of the things you will find in all of my pieces, whether you like the criticism or not, is organization. There's always a logical development in every argument, and that's exactly what I see the piece as, an argument. Maybe that's my law school training, but they're briefs for my feelings about the movie or about the trend or whatever.

Essentially, I'll sit down with that outline and then I'll start writing, generally in about three sessions. I'll sit down for a few hours and write part of it, then go back and read it. I always reread, almost everytime I add a sentence. I read everything in the piece to polish it, to hone it, because I don't have that much time. The best way of doing it, obviously, is to put it away for a month, come back to it, and repolish the whole piece, but I don't have time to do that, so I'll sit down, I'll work for a few hours, I'll write as much as I can, I'll take a break, I'll come back to it. Sometimes it'll take me a couple of days to write one piece of criticism, if the ideas are complex and I really feel this need to simplify them and make them more accessible for the reader.

Root. Do you then come back to them and redo them in longhand?

Gabler. I do everything in longhand. There was a period when I composed at the typewriter, but I found something when I started writing for *Monthly Detroit* and my pieces were getting longer. When you're writing longhand, there's more of a struggle with prose. You're much more likely to sit and think, to feel the tension of writing. At the typewriter I found something facile creeping into my prose, and I think that's one of the reasons I had a crisis of confidence at that time. The machine almost was creating this kind of glib voice that wasn't mine. When I sat down and actually struggled through the prose and started doing what I always do, making little arrows and crossing out, I think the prose got tough—it got smarter. When I compose at the typewriter, I get the feeling of instant gratification, because I see the piece in a kind of pristine state; when you write the way I write, typing the final draft is the reward—it's the culmination of a long and grueling process of getting your ideas down.

Root. Do you revise from typed draft and then retype a final draft?

Gabler. I don't have time to revise from my typed draft for *Monthly Detroit*. I will revise it on the draft, but I'll do more revision for *Sneak Previews*, which is more like writing haiku. Your every word counts, because you have so little time. Your critical opinions have to be distilled to something so tight that every word you use has to be functional, and so I revise several times, because I'm striving for a complete distillation of thought which I don't have to do writing for print.

Root. What kind of format do you have for *Sneak Previews?*

Gabler. The format is very, very rigid. You're always writing about a minute and fifteen seconds of copy for the film reviews.

The whole run-down of the program is this: They show a clip called a tease. One of us reacts off the tease in two or three sentences, very, very brief.

Whoever doesn't react off the tease then sets up the program, telling the films that we're going to review. He introduces the other critic, the one who reacted off the tease, and then he goes into this minute fifteen seconds.

There are almost always two clips. The way the process works now is we try to get into that first clip as quickly as possible.

Root. You're writing with the clips in mind and you know what they're going to be before you start writing.

Gabler. So almost every piece takes this format. "Our next film is such and such"—I will then give an apposition that describes at least the type of movie, so the audience knows what we're talking about in a generic way. "It's about . . ."—we tell the story of the movie in a sentence or two generally. "In this scene . . .," which always begins that last line, "so and so and so and so"—we turn and there's the clip. Then, what's known as coming off the clip, you turn away from the screen and you say, "Later," or whatever—you advance the plot, very briefly, I'd say ten or fifteen seconds, then back to the screen. You come off the second clip with what is known as a comment.

Again, the comment is brief. I've shortened my top copies so that I can lengthen my bottom copies, so we'll be into clip in, let's say, twenty seconds for the first clip and ten seconds for the second, so that will leave me about forty-five seconds or so to do the comment. I'll generally ad lib off the clip, saying something that you can gather from it about the film, and then go into the commentary.

That commentary is not formatted—then we're just writing criticism. And it ends with some punch line that will tell the audience exactly how we feel about the film in no uncertain terms. That is the format of the minute fifteen seconds. The crosstalks, which is what they're called, are not rehearsed.

Root. So that when you finish with that punch line, you sort of turn or draw back a little bit and then Jeffrey's response is not scripted.

Gabler. No. Jeffrey and I will talk about his response and my response in the conference room when we're going over our scripts and he'll say, "Well, I felt this way," and I'll argue back. This is just so we get the lay of the land.

When we go on the air, we generally tape the show in about four segments. We break after every second clip, so we tape the show up to the second clip of every film and then the producer will come out after that, and refresh our memories about what we said in the conference room. Then we just do it. Occasionally we'll redo a cross-talk when it's going very badly, just for presentational purposes, so it plays better on the air.

Root. Do you feel you have to change your voice, the persona you project, between the two media of print and television?

Gabler. There's a difference between changing your voice and changing your style. I come in and write the copy the way I want the copy to be, and I'll find that when the producer goes over it, which they do scrupulously, we spend more time on copy than we do in the studio. They'll change words because they feel the words are just too vague, generally, because they feel that nobody will know this word, or because it's not a good TV word because it sounds like another word. But read my copy on *Sneak Previews* and then watch the show. There is a world of difference between reading it, in cold, hard print, and hearing it spoken on the show. The voice in the *Sneak Previews* comments and the voice in my criticism is unmistakably the same— the rhythms, the way I use language, the way I turn a phrase, the metaphors I use—unmistakably the same person.

Root. How do you respond to that experience coming off of writing sixteen hundred word essays?

Gabler. It's a very, very different experience. The two experiences exist in different realms. In an article I wrote for *Variety* [8 Dec. 1982] I made the point that what I do in print is radically different from what I do on television. What I do on *Sneak Previews* is simply convey to the audience what the movie's about and whether it's any good. I don't do any of the things that I consider the higher calling of film criticism. So I was shifting not only into a different medium but I was also shifting into a whole different kind of criticism. More accurately, I was shifting from criticism to something that's not criticism.

Root. You make the distinction in *Variety* that it's reviewing.

Gabler. Right, because I think reviewing literally means to "re-view," to look at it once again for your audience. Now that's different than to criticize it; that word connotes a whole different kind of examination. *Sneak Previews* is close to reviewing, although it's not exactly reviewing. What I do in *Monthly Detroit* is criticism. I think that very, very *few* people in this country are practicing criticism. I hold that criticism on television is a consumer's guide.

Root. Here's a fairly recent piece, "Beach Blanket Cinema." Do you think this is a fairly typical article of yours?

Gabler. Not quite as good as my other stuff. This is a little weaker.

Root. What makes it weaker?

Gabler. Time. I don't think it's a bad piece, but I think it could have used a little bit more focus and it begs for a little more depth, particularly near the end.

Root. What were you trying to accomplish here?

Gabler. I was trying to look at what I think is a trend in film since last year and that is, a different way of looking at adolescence. I felt that if you look at some of the most popular films of the year, like *Porky's,* which is probably going to be one of the top ten highest grossing pictures of the year, that this is a year in which there were a fair number of films that dealt with adolescence in ways that were different than films in the past. I wanted the article to examine those differences and to possibly explain why they are different and what these differences say about adolescent culture in 1982.

Root. Do you recall when it dawned on you that there was this crop that was different?

Gabler. I think when I saw *Fast Times at Ridgemont High,* which I detest. I'm amazed actually, parenthetically, that it got good reviews. Maybe it's because it was a woman who directed it. I think there's been only one woman director who has gotten attacked in this country, Joan Darling for *First Love,* and since then women can make any-thing—she can make *The Toy* and they'll say it's great. I think this got good reviews because it was directed by Amy Heckerling. She's not only a woman but a first time director, and the film was certainly competently made. But the film offends me because it's trash, it's junk, and it's a certain kind of trash, it's smarmy trash, and it's smarmy sanctimonious trash on top of it.

Watching the film, I said, "This film *is* different." The characters are all out of the barrel of hackneyed, clichéd characters of the past. The sweet guy, the dorky guy, all that kind of stuff. The characters you've seen a thousand times, but the whole movie's attitude toward the characters is very, very different. Every year there are five films that I detest so vehemently that I have to ask myself, "What is it about this that I really detest?" That sort of triggered me thinking about it.

When you put it up against *Porky's*, which is a film I don't detest at all but which is just a kind of dopey movie . . .

Root. What's the time frame on this? How long was this between seeing the two films?

Gabler. I saw *Porky's* pretty much when it opened. I saw *Fast Times* two weeks before it opened, at a screening, so it had been from March to August, I guess, between the times I saw the two films, and in between there it had been *Diner*, which is very much a film about my kind of adolescence, and I'm trying to think of others that I mention in here.

Root. Could you have written that article simply on the basis of *Fast Times* or would you not have bothered?

Gabler. No, I wouldn't have bothered because that would be a piece on *Fast Times at Ridgemont High* and it would have seemed like a kind of overkill. Here I'm taking this absolutely inconsequential movie and using a blunderbuss on it and acting as if this film was somehow representative of all teenage culture, which would have been wrong. But when you put it in the context of a film like *Porky's*, which was an immensely popular film, grossing over one hundred million dollars, these films reverberating off of one another sort of struck something in me, and then when I thought of *Diner*—which I think is one of the best films of the year—and what that says about adolescence, I saw a piece beginning to form in my mind. But it was the popularity of *Porky's* that I think clicked this into place. If *Porky's* had been as moderately successful as *Fast Times at Ridgemont High*, I probably wouldn't have written the piece, but I think when you put the combination of things together and see the audience look forward to these films, how large the total audience was, then I think you got a piece. And when you see how different filmmakers and different studios are obviously pitching their movies to a certain aspect of youth culture, that makes a piece.

Root. Did you make notes on *Fast Times* when you saw it?

Gabler. Yes, I make notes on everything. This pad has notes on *Honky Tonk Man*. I don't write on lines because I write in the dark, but I write on every film that I've seen.

Anyway, the genesis of the piece was thinking about those two films and I thought that issue was significant. I always go back and try to create as large a context as possible. That's always the starting point for any of my pieces, again because I think the value of criticism is not just talking about one single element or one single film but to try to create the broadest sense of context, trying to write criticism for the ages essentially—you can't really do that in a magazine like *Monthly Detroit* but that's the goal. So I went back and reviewed other teenage movies, trying to factor out the traditions of teenage movies which I said were true. You know, the kind of *A Date With Judy* teenage film and the *Dead End* kind of film—those two approaches to adolescence signified a tradition of thinking about adolescence. With those two things in mind, then the beginning of the piece shaped itself.

Obviously I knew how the piece was going to be shaped. It was going to talk in the broadest possible context about adolescence; that's why I begin with, "Since the late 19th century, when American novelists began recognizing youth not simply as the legatees of the past but as the torchbearers of the future," blah blah blah. I wanted to set this up: What did adolescence mean in the context of American life? Well, it didn't mean much in the early and mid-nineteenth century, but by the late nineteenth century and certainly by the early twentieth century, adolescence meant a great deal, because, as I say here, more and more adolescence was being seen as a kind of preparation and a kind of promise—America's promise lay here. So there was the context and that was why adolescence has become important to us dating from that in the late nineteenth century.

Okay, I knew that idea was going to start the piece because, as I said, it provided the broadest possible context. I moved from that into the notion of these two traditions. Because I've started from the broadest possible context, now I'm moving into film—you'll notice that most of my pieces will do that unless they start from the broadest possible context in film itself. But here I've started even one step higher than that and tapered it in. So now we're moving to these two traditions. I have to explain briefly the traditions; although that's not the thrust of the piece, I have to spend two or three paragraphs discussing what they are because I'm going to play off of that idea. A better, longer piece would have played off of these two traditions much more fully than I did here, which is one of the weaknesses of the piece.

So I talk about the first and I talk about the second and then I try to factor out, are there any similarities here? Since the whole thesis of the piece is going to be that there is a brand new tradition or trend being created, I then have to distinguish that tradition from these other two. This is exactly my thought process, because in reading the piece you get a sense of not only the way I wrote the piece but the process I went through thinking about the piece, which is why I'm going over it now. You can read the piece and get everything I'm saying, but the process in which I organized and thought about the piece, the protocol you were talking about, is the piece itself.

Root. Except that you start with those films and see that sort of dissonance.

Gabler. I start with the films—that's sort of out there—and I know that that dissonance is going to create the piece. Then, once that decision is made and once I've drawn notes and things like that about possible approaches to the piece, once I've sat and thought about what I want to say and all of that going before, I actually sit down and do it. I mean, what is it I want to say about these movies? Once I've set that in my mind, namely that there's a difference, namely that the difference clearly has to do with sex, but thirdly, that that's not enough, Gabler, sex is simply a kind of metaphor for a sense of freedom, irresponsibility, and an attitude toward adolescence, that it has nothing to teach us, that nothing has anything to teach us anymore—now that's all before I start writing the piece. Then I start going through this process that I'm talking about now, which is essentially to follow the piece, and I hit that point where I say, "Okay, now, I've got these two traditions and this third one that's a kind of nascent tradition, what do I do with them?" I try and factor out what's similar in these other two traditions in terms of our attitudes toward adolescence, and the thing is that it's a passage to maturity. These other films don't ever regard maturity at all. In a film like *Fast Times at Ridgemont High* or *Porky's,* maturity is meaningless. It's not, "This is the only time you can have sex"; that kind of context doesn't surround these movies as it does a *Beach Blanket Bingo.* In terms of outlining the piece and putting down these kinds of ideas in a rough outline, I come to that conclusion: that this really is a significant thing, and obviously I'm always looking for the most significant, the most telling, the most important thing to my readers. That, I think, is the difference between adolescence as a bridge between childhood and maturity and adolescence being no bridge whatsoever.

Root. Did you do any research or are you simply drawing from memory? Did you say, "Now that I'm looking for the context here, maybe I'd better take a look at my collection of film books and see what I can find"?

Gabler. That I didn't do too much. I do that for a lot of pieces. For example, I wrote a piece on Steven Spielberg and another on Richard Pryor, one of my better pieces this year. I sat down and read everything on Pryor and everything on Spielberg. I wanted to know whether I was repeating somebody. If somebody's already written a piece on something, I don't want to do it. By the same token, when people say things that are significant, I have no problem with quoting other critics, and I do it frequently because if they put something in a beautiful way, then I might as well use that and give them credit for it. This piece I did because nobody had ever written exactly on this. Vincent Canby had written a piece about a week later, in fact, on youth films, but that didn't have anything to do with what I was doing. So I was relying on memory and not only that—as one of my friends once said, "It's not whether what you write is true or not, it's whether it's provocative." I've always thought that for journalism, truth is the highest priority, but for criticism it's thought provocation.

Root. Does writing a monthly piece mean that you feel you can't do what someone does in a weekly article? A weekly critic like David Denby can walk into the theatre, see the thing, go home and write it, and next week it will be published.

Gabler. Right, that's *Sneak Previews* essentially, which is even more instant. I'll see a movie and there are times when I'll write that night on a movie that I'm going to fly into Chicago and review, which is not good for criticism. I trust myself an awful lot—I trust my instincts and impressions and seldom, for better or worse (this may say something about my lack of maturity), see my opinions changing. When I see the same film two years later, I say I was right on the button the first time I saw it.

But yes, I think what I'm doing here is very different from something that Vincent Canby can do because I can savor something and I can sit down and think about it for as long as I like and write without making any concessions whatsoever, because the magazine doesn't tell me to and because I'm writing for a monthly. You don't want to open up *Monthly Detroit* and read a review of *48 Hours* unless I'm going to analyze the film in detail. When I do take a single film, which I do about a fourth or a third of the time, you'll notice that my reviews are very analytical. I'll talk about how the camera's used, how the film is structured, and almost always the aim of the piece is nonjudgmental. It's not, "I don't like this movie" or, "I do like this movie, you ought to go see it," because by that point it's almost immaterial. The real thrust of the piece is, "This is what this movie is doing, this is how it's doing it, this is my experience of the movie." Maybe that's why I like Robert Warshaw so much, because the whole idea of his book is the immediate experience, discussing his experience of the film in a way that I think is detailed, analytical, and informative, but will not tell you whether to go to see the movie or not.

Root. Do you find yourself trying to change things from month to month, do a single film, a single person, try not to do two genres in a row?

Gabler. Right, I do, I'm conscious of that.

Root. You said the Steven Spielberg piece was one of your best pieces?

Gabler. Yeah, one of the better pieces.

Root. Can you think of one that's an example of your best work, one that really stands out?

Gabler. I think "Why Movies Are Bad" is one of the most well-written pieces. A nice thing when you write for magazines, as opposed to television, is that you can go back and look at it a year from now, a month from now, and it has an independent existence. It's as if you never even wrote it. The language, the ideas, are something that you have no feel for whatsoever. This piece—and I'll say it immodestly— is a damn well-written piece. It flows, it's well argued, it's interesting. I'm very proud of this one.

Root. Can you think how that evolved?

Gabler. I'll tell you why it's a better piece: because it evolved over a longer period of time. These ideas were sort of sitting around in my head and I thought, this is a piece I'm going to write when I don't have anything to say one month. I really wanted to sort of let it all out, so the piece was sort of steaming in my mind for months. Every time an impressive movie would come out that I loved and every time it failed at the box office or every time I talked to one of my friends and he said, "Ah, geez, that movie was so boring," my own interest in this piece went up a notch. There's an evangelical flavor to the piece and, by the time I sat down to write it, that's exactly the mood I wrote it in. It had a lot of thought behind it that had been developing over a long period of time and it had a sense of evangelical fervor behind it, and I think that for both of those reasons it was a good piece, one of my better ones.

Root. Is there anything in there that you think was difficult to write?

Gabler. Everything I write is difficult for me. Writing is hard for me. I see flaws in everything that I write. That's what I never forget. I say these things get an independent existence, but the one thing that never gets independent is the mistakes. I can tell you now the mistakes I made when I was writing for the University of Michigan paper ten years ago. Writing is difficult for me and I try and make it as painstaking as possible. I *want* it to be as painstaking as possible. When things go easily it's almost a sign that when I look at the piece three months from now I won't like it.

Root. I was wondering whether there was anything in the article where maybe a transition gave you a lot of trouble or an example or a point of structure gave you difficulty.

Gabler. This was a piece that I didn't have any trouble with structurally. I'd taken those notes from the cards I told you about, and somehow when I pulled out those cards I could just sort of put them in order and they fell together beautifully. The shape of this piece almost created itself, and I think you sense that when you read the piece. There's a real logic to this piece and the transitions in this piece were not particularly difficult. Sometimes I have real difficulty, and when I do I generally take a step back and say, "I'm not writing something well, I haven't organized the piece well." If the transition comes with great difficulty, then I've made a mistake. I've also learned something else in the time that I've been writing. I was always so conscious of transitions in my early writing that I realized hardly anyone else, certainly no reader, is that conscious, and you can get away with almost anything, and when you read it later, you'll find that the flow was pretty good.

I can think of one problem in this piece structurally—I don't think it's a problem when you read it. When I move into the television stuff I remember one thing that was difficult is that I wanted to talk about television but I didn't want to give the sense that I was somehow being definitive. I think another one of the problems with the "Beach Blanket" thing is that it gives the sense that I *think* I'm being definitive, even though any reader and I myself know that I'm *not* being definitive. That's not good and so how do you talk about television and all the things televison has inculcated in us without being definitive and without seeming to be definitive, and yet lay all these things on the line? I think I did it fairly well. I call television "symbol and symptom," which immediately takes me off the hook in a way because that means I don't have to discuss *that* so much as I have to discuss its effects because it's symptomatic. There's one way I think I really get out of this. Take a line like this: "One can enumerate some of them." See how I'm cutting so I'm not going to rob my argument of its force because this is exactly the point of the piece where I'm going to lose the reader, yet it's also the point of the piece where I'm hitting the major point that I want to make. Now this is the thing I didn't do as well in that piece on beach blanket movies, but I do much better here because I say—and I knew this very self-consciously when I was writing the piece—"I can enumerate some of them without in so small a space examining." One of the things I have to do is talk about the habits of mind that television creates. I do it without giving a sense of definitiveness and then I move on to do this. That's the only difficult structural part of the piece. If you carry off that, the rest of the piece works.

Root. Do you think there's a turning point like that in all of these articles?

Gabler. Yes, I think there is. I generally write this at the top of the page: "What's the thesis of this?" That does two things for me. One, it tells me the piece is worth writing, because I have to know right off the bat; if what I'm saying doesn't have sufficient magnitude, then it shouldn't be written. I've found myself beginning a piece and thinking, "No, really, that shouldn't be written."

Root. Can you describe what ones didn't work?

Gabler. I'd say of the recent ones that "Beach Blanket Cinema" works less well that any other piece I've done recently.

Root. Can you think of one that you started and threw out because you realized it wasn't pulling together?

Gabler. Yes, this happens, not that frequently, but it happens a few times every year, generally because I either haven't thought it through enough or what I really have is a shard of an idea and not a full idea.

Root. Do you ever discover what you're about, what you think, as you write?

Gabler. No, never.

Root. Because you work it out too much?

Gabler. Right. I would never discover while I write because to me that would be too frightening. It means that I've missed something in the initial process and then I'd start having all sorts of second thoughts about what I was doing, because I like to think, when I start, that I have command of the material. When I say I've tossed away pieces that don't work, I don't mean that I've ever started writing pieces that don't work. I would never get to that point. What I mean is that in this initial process of organizing my ideas and taking these cards out and trying to see what's happening, I find there that I don't have anything to say. But if that happened when I'm writing, I would be absolutely terrified; I don't want to discover while I'm writing. I want to know by the time I write exactly where I'm going, so that kind of process is out.

Root. Do you find yourself creating or rehearsing lines almost aloud, in your head, before writing them?

Gabler. Oh, yes, and that's another reason for the cards, because I'll come up with things that I know are very well put, that I'm afraid I won't be able to do. There are lines that I'll say when I'm thinking of the genesis of the whole piece. Generally when this happens, that's when I'll start writing things out on cards. It's not simply a word or phrase, it's generally more like paragraphs that don't run into one whole piece. But portions of those paragraphs do run because I like the way I put it and I just have that inspiration at that moment and the words seem right to me and it comes out in a very intense kind of verse. I have these little intense verses all over the place that become kind of studs for the longer tapestry of the piece. If I've done my job the piece will have a kind of thoughtful quality with these kinds of little studs in them that were written out of much greater heat than I ever write my pieces. I almost never write my pieces out of heat.

Root. Does writing criticism influence the way you look at the world?

Gabler. I think the way you view the world affects your criticism more than being a critic affects the way you view the world. Stanley Kauffmann once said, "I could no sooner teach somebody to be a film critic than I could teach you to be a human being." Criticism is a matter of temperament. It's not always the best temperament to have and a lot of my friends assume it's a kind of idiosyncrasy of mine, but that's the way I am and I've never been any different.

John Simon once said, "To have a critical temperament is a kind of privilege." The Kauffmann quote and the Simon quote together are really on point in terms of criticism. I began as a critic and then I became a film critic. I've been critical of myself—I almost never am satisfied with anything I do, whether it's on *Sneak Previews* or my own work. I'm not easily satisfied, but then I think that's one of the things that can make me a good critic.

I'm always looking for connections. I guess the reason I probably became a film critic, the way some people become novelists, is that I find that I can express a good deal of how I feel about the world through film criticism. It organizes, it focuses, and it provides an opportunity for me to talk about politics, as I often do in my pieces. If you read my pieces, then you know who I voted for, how I feel about romance, morality, virtually everything.

Root. Who influences your writing?

Gabler. As I mentioned earlier, I reached a point once where I had a crisis of confidence in my work, wondering, What kind of critic do you want to be? and, What kind of criticism should you be writing? What's your voice? All these years I'd been this one person and now suddenly I was saying, it's not really commercial criticism and Pauline Kael is the only really commercial critic.

The influence in film criticism is so heavily Pauline Kael. I think it's incredibly detrimental to the development of American film criticism. Not that she's a bad critic; she was probably the best. But if a kid wants to be a baseball player, he looks up to a thousand people— if he wants to be a film critic, he either looks up to Pauline Kael or to nobody. If you look up to Pauline Kael, you destroy yourself, because her style is so idiosyncratic. What are you going to do—be idiosyncratic too? It's a contradiction in terms.

In any case I knew my criticism was getting less commercial and I didn't know whether I wanted to write a very academic kind of criticism or whether I wanted to write a very impressionistic kind of criticism; for the first time in my entire life, my voice had seemed to fail me. When I was in that crisis, one of the ways I got out of it was that I made a certain decision. I said, "I don't want to be a Pauline Kael." That's disposable criticism. Kael is a good enough mind and a good enough writer that her criticism has had some staying power, but it doesn't have the highest value that I think criticism can have. It has an idiosyncratic kind of value, that's all. It doesn't have the staying power of a Lionel Trilling or of any great literary criticism. Film criticism has had only one of those and that's Robert Warshaw.

Root. What about James Agee?

Gabler. Maybe the most overrated film critic of all. Agee came along at a time when film was so disreputable that the fact that someone of his credentials would ever dabble in it immediately gave him a kind of legitimacy that no other film critic had had. He wasn't even the best film critic of his day, much less of history.

Now I look at Robert Warshaw for the excellence of his criticism and for the intention of his criticism, but not for his style. It's too dangerous. I think I have my own style and it's uniquely mine, sort of a bridge from a very academic criticism on the one hand to a very colloquial criticism on the other. I didn't do it intentionally, but it wound up that way.

My idols of criticism are the people who set the highest possible standards for themselves—the Lionel Trillings—regardless of what I feel about the content of the criticism. I don't always agree with Robert Warshaw, but the quality of his criticism is first-rate. Among film critics he is nonpareil.

Root. If you're writing for *Monthly Detroit*, do you have a different sense of who the audience is than if you wrote for *Time*, let's say?

Gabler. I wouldn't write with that sense in mind because I think that's dangerous. I write for me. I always have done this since the time I started writing. I write to please me. If I do that, I know several things: I'll never be condescending or patronizing to an audience; my reviews will always have a sense of integrity and intelligence; and I'll always be interested in what I'm doing.

So I'd write the same way for *Time* magazine, but of course they would never hire me to write this way. They wouldn't want me—I'm not their kind of critic.

Root. You were interviewed for a television critic spot on a New York television station. Would you have to change your style of delivery for that job?

Gabler. Yes, but that's different. If the agent had said to me, "They love your camera presence but don't like the way you write, want you to change it," I would have said, "I don't want the job." But what he said to me was, "They love the way you write, think your copy is great, but they want you to give a more energetic delivery." Now that's nothing. That one is style, the other is substance. Start changing substance, you're wrong. This is what I do for a living, this is what I'm going to be remembered for, if I'm going to be remembered for anything. To compromise this is to compromise my whole life.

Beach Blanket Cinema

Neal Gabler

Since the late nineteenth century, when American novelists began recognizing youth not simply as legatees of the past but as the torch-bearers for the future and individuals in their own right, adolescence has been a staple of the national literature. Writers seized that sublime transition from youth to maturity—that period when one suddenly realized one had begun learning the lessons of life, whatever they might be. In this country especially, we have learned to cherish adolescence, to recall it nostalgically as the time when everything before was promise, everything behind, prologue. But for the movies, adolescence has held an attraction much deeper, even than this metaphorical one. The movies seemed to realize that they themselves were like adolescence—bursting with dreams—and the theater was a place where one could check one's responsibilities at the door and be transported back to the blissful condition of youth.

If this made teenagers an irresistible subject for movies, it was the same glorious sense of irresponsibility that made the movies so irresistible to teenagers. The medium was theirs, a redoubt from the assaults of school-taught culture. But I don't think this has ever been truer than in the last year, when the teenagers and the movies formed an unholy alliance so sturdy that almost nothing but teenage movies penetrated the marketplace. (Even *E.T.* is essentially a pubescent/adolescent film.) What is most striking about this, I think, is not that teenagers have triumphed, since this has been evident for years. What's striking is that the movies' attitude toward adolescence has undergone one of those profound changes that occurs once every decade or so and that usually signals some profound change in how we view youth and, even more importantly, in how youth views itself.

Reprinted with the permission of *Monthly Detroit,* Crain Communications, Inc.

Styles of adolescence develop like styles of clothes: From them arise certain traditions which are then exploited by businessmen, novelists and filmmakers. In the movies, perhaps the most powerful and enduring tradition began with William Wyler's urban melodrama, *Dead End*. In *Dead End*, which is set in a New York slum where criminals are bred the way some neighborhoods breed athletes, a band of teenagers takes its inspiration from one of the slum's more esteemed graduates—a snarling convict on the lam. They're little tough guys— threats to civic order—but they have the film's sympathy because they are also victims. Shaped by society, they were, paradoxically, alienated from it; and in *Dead End*, as well as in the films of tortured adolescents that descended from it, adolescence was not a rite of passage or a state of grace so much as an awful hell in which one was sentenced never to feel connected, never to plug one's wild, restless electricity into something productive. By the late Fifties, and in the Sixties and Seventies, if there were any larger message in this—if adolescence functioned as a metaphor for the meaning of maturity—it was that America (read "parents") had failed to provide a coherent, legitimate set of values for its future (read "children"). Awash in materialism, it had loosened the moorings between generations, between past and future.

Set against this message—which was best embodied by James Dean's quivering, sensitive filament of a soul—was another tradition. This one reached back at least as far back as *Our Dancing Daughters* in the 1920s through *A Date With Judy* and on through *Gidget* and *Beach Blanket Bingo:* the comic counterparts to the tragic vision of adolescence. No longer angst-ridden sufferers, teenagers were privileged ones, granted the wonderful dispensations of beach parties and puppy loves and hot rods and sock hops. America's materialism, which had in the first tradition opened a crevasse of misunderstanding, was now bounty for youth to share.

James Dean on one side; Frankie Avalon on the other. They represented the adolescent dialectic; but both of their traditions, different as they were, did hold one common premise: that adolescence was a discrete period, a stage of life one outgrew. At some point, both the anguish and the giddiness yielded to maturity. (The films themselves seldom chronicled that transition, which was left to another genre— coming-of-age—and another time.) The idea was that the transition to adulthood, while personally significant, was the same for everyone and every generation. Adolescents, however much they might cavil over their parents' injustices, would eventually grow into their parents. Values would eventually be shared, even if the aesthetics of youth and adulthood were not.

Of course, by the late 1960s, it was clear that the aesthetics of adolescence expressed not simply youthful vigor and iconoclasm, but a new set of *values*. Youth somehow saw itself as truer, purer, less compromised, and if the values of youth later converged with those of the parents, it was a defeat ("selling-out," we called it then). Offhand, I can think of a half-dozen movies about blitzed, beatific hippies and their befuddled parents, but the film that captured this conflict best was one that ostensibly eschewed any mention of politics, one that was set not in 1969 or 1970 but in 1962, and one that was made by George Lucas who, more than any other figure, may be responsible for the conquest of our arts by the pubescent/adolescent sensibility.

Lucas' *American Graffiti* makes no explicit reference to Vietnam (until the epilogue) or to our national torment and waywardness, but these are implicit in the overpowering sense of wistfulness for what the teenagers believe they are leaving behind: their innocence and happiness. In the past, teenagers awaited adulthood as the next stage after getting a driver's license; it was something they had been denied. In *Graffiti*, one senses that adulthood is like Dante's portal, where one enters only to sacrifice the pleasures one had. *Graffiti* was essentially a modern rendition of *A Midsummer Night's Dream*, a compression into one magical evening of the threshold of adulthood where everyone has to make his decision to cross, to look magic in the eye and recognize it as a feature of the past. It's a film of recognition, then, but also of concession. In *American Graffiti*, adolescence is better—a judgment that has enormous national implications if you read it that way.

In the same way, *Diner*, which is one of the best films of the year, is about our reluctance to relinquish adolescence, even though the five buddies in the film, like Fellini's *vitelloni*, are past the age for high school gambols. They know that conceding to maturity means dim futures, unfulfilling jobs, loveless marriages and no more nights hanging out at the diner. That last may be the most important to director/ writer Barry Levinson, because the diner is the film's living metaphor for the very marrow of adolescence: camaraderie. Some women I know accuse the film of being misogynistic, and the characters, though not the film itself, may be. For one of them, marriage seems like a futile attempt at turning his wife into one of the guys. For another, on the verge of marriage, there is the realization that matrimony is the termination, the end of fun and the beginning of real responsibility.

All of this is rather touchingly condensed in *Diner*'s last scene—Eddie's wedding—where the bridal bouquet is tipped like a volleyball from one timid hand to another until it lands on the table at which the friends sit—a *memento mori* for their palling around.

Diner, however, is the product of an older sensibility (Levinson is in his forties) and is made *for* older sensibilities, which is no doubt one reason why it didn't take off at the box office. Teenagers, the movies' major constituency, don't have to be wistful or nostalgic, and they don't understand people who are. Their movies are *Porky's* or *Fast Times at Ridgemont High*, two unadulterated pieces of garbage, but nonetheless significant for what they tell us about adolescence.

Porky's is about a dim group of Florida high schoolers who pay a visit to a notorious cathouse outside the country and then are stung by the roly-poly proprietor after giving him their payment in advance. Of course, they seek revenge, but before they do so, they engage in one sexual escapade after another. Watching the film is rather like reading graffiti on the walls of a john—it positively revels in its smarminess. *Fast Times* has gotten a better critical reception because it was directed by Amy Heckerling (women get critical *carte blanche* these days), but it is worse than *Porky's* because, after its heroine engages in her series of sexual escapades, the film has the audacity to get sanctimonious and has her spout that hoariest of bromides: Romance is better than sex.

It doesn't take a genius to see this is an afterthought. In these movies—and we're promised a spate more next year—sex is better than romance . . . or intelligence or adventure or just about anything. Sex is the new dispensation of youth, and where, in older, more cautious films, one tentative sexual encounter marked the transit to adulthood, now quantity prevails. Films like *American Graffiti* and *Diner* report how traumatic it is to grow up because the future condemns us. Hedonistic films like *Porky's* and *Fast Times* report how wonderful adolescence is because there are no moral restraints anymore.

Teenagers obviously respond to this image; it's the image they want to have of themselves. And maybe it would be merely a less euphemistic way of citing the ecstasies of youth if it weren't for a kind of gloating in the reduction of all activity to the sexual—a pride that there is nothing else they must learn to equip them for life. In these films, teenagers have it all: the sex, the money, the glory, the movies. Without any lessons to learn, they are the frightening, oversexed symbols of today.

Bad Films? We Have Ourselves to Blame

Neal Gabler

Over the last two years, going to the movies has become awfully dispiriting, which is one reason, I imagine, why fewer people have been rousing themselves and why the film industry's gross receipts, when adjusted for inflation, have been steadily declining. I am always hearing the plaint that there is nothing worth seeing anymore, while most of the films that have been turning profits hardly constitute a commercial or artistic beachhead. Given this state of affairs, it is tempting to blame the Neanderthals who run the film industry because, after all, they set the agenda. But one mustn't forget either that Hollywood operates very much like a political system. It serves a constituency (the audience) and it has very few principles save the paramount one of trying to read its constituency and pander to its taste.

It is not and never has been a system given to bold ventures. Nor is it, at least at the present time, a pluralistic system, targeting certain films for certain audiences and scaling budgets accordingly; *Jaws, Star Wars*, and *Raiders of the Lost Ark* have taught film executives, who are thick-hided cynics anyway, that a studio can survive twenty-five disastrous films if it releases one with colossally broad appeal. Of course the film constituency is fluid. The system must adjust. In the film companies' corporate offices one often hears the word "demographics," as if it were some sacred incantation. Does film have the right demographic appeal? Since the preponderance of moviegoers until very recently has been under twenty-five, the demographics have dictated that the preponderance of films aims at this teenage denominator. It is no knock on adolescence that if Dostoyevski, Joyce and Hemingway had deliberately tailored their work to the adolescent intellect, they too might have turned out a *Taps* or a *Superman II*.

Reprinted with the permission of *Monthly Detroit*, Crain Communications, Inc.

Obviously, teenagers didn't seize films, though they were an ideal audience with plenty of time and spending money, and executives' mouths must have watered torrents at the prospect of that time and money being spent fruitfully in movie theaters rather than recklessly on record albums. No, teenagers won the movies partly by default and largely with the complicity of the film industry. Now, however, the system no longer functions smoothly. Adults stay away from all but a few films, and teenagers, whose discretionary income has shrunk, are fickle and unpredictable; this year's *Neighbors* isn't always last year's *Stir Crazy*. Everyone is dissatisfied. Meanwhile, films seem to get worse.

When a political system malfunctions, as ours is now under Reagan, we usually blame it for offering inadequate choices rather than taking the blame ourselves for letting mediocrities command the apparatus. In truth, though there are thirty absolutely rotten movies for every good one (a ratio that is probably no worse than that of any art), the film industry has provided a somewhat better choice than the political system. There are still a few magnificent films being made and there are more interesting ones, but the problem—and it is a serious one—is that most of us are not going to see these films. We prefer the tripe and the treacle. Who do we blame then?

If we even care any longer, I submit that we ought to begin blaming ourselves. These days, I know I find myself hesitating when asked to recommend a film not because there are so few good ones, but because I am almost certain that the films I would recommend, warts and all (*Prince of the City, Reds, Four Friends, Shoot the Moon,* to name a few), would probably bore and disappoint my inquisitor.

Something has not only happened to our films. Something terrible has happened to us, something that has made us less receptive to the excitement and electricity of real films. No matter how much you may like the commercially successful films of the last year—*Raiders, Superman II, Stripes, Taps, Absence of Malice, On Golden Pond*—they never provide the good, heady rush of having been challenged, of having to traverse an emotional distance, of having to reach outside oneself, of having been changed—in short, of having had an experience. All of these films play it safe, reminding us not so much of life, but of other films we've seen. They risk nothing lest they offend.

The best in art has almost never appealed to the majority at the time it appears—now we all play catch-up. In American film, though, which is lashed by its cost to commerce, the best has usually operated within fairly well-defined conventions we could all appreciate. Even the best films of the last decade abided these configurations so that they were always accessible at some basic narrative level. Though a film like *The Godfather* or *The Deer Hunter* was doing much more than telling a story, so long as it "was" telling a story, the rest was cargo.

There is nothing startling or blameworthy in any of this. Most of us choose the easiest course in watching our films, reading our books, listening to our music. We regard these as something like intellectual dessert; and it is, I think, because so many of our best films now do not make these concessions that audiences either ignore them or complain when they do see them. The best of our new films exhibit a kind of bravado. Neither *Prince of the City* nor *Reds* nor *Four Friends* nor *Shoot the Moon* is particularly strong on narrative. None operate within strict conventional limits; in fact, they test these limits, shrugging them off, and in doing so they test us, test our own emotional and intellectual range—for brave, unconventional films can only be sustained by brave audiences.

Since all of these films engage us intellectually, it is easy to speculate that audiences aren't going to see them because they don't want to think, as if going to the movies were primarily a self-improvement course and not a pleasure that rarely and at best may also lead to self-improvement. It is a particularly easy speculation for film critics, none of whom, to my knowledge, spend their days slaving over a conveyor belt or leaning behind a counter or hunching over a desk. I cannot imagine anyone with the capacity for pleasure crusading against entertainment, and I certainly wouldn't tout *Prince of the City* or *Reds* if I didn't find them infinitely more entertaining and engrossing than a *Taps* or *On Golden Pond*. Yet all worthwhile art—and most worthwhile entertainment, too—is also heuristic, which is to say that it leads the way for us, prompting us with questions about our lives and our society; indeed, this prompting is inextricably bound into the aesthetic experience I mentioned earlier. It provides a pleasure on a different order.

I think that most of us are willing to accept this intellectual element in our films, but we want it confined. It is not so much thinking per se as "degree" of effort a *Prince of the City* requires that daunts us and keeps us away. Simply put, it is difficult. *Prince of the City* questions the very basis of civic virtue and personal honor and examines the conflict between them. *Reds* demonstrates the process of idealism into actuation and the sacrifices one makes in the process. *Shoot the Moon* dissects the condition of loneliness both within and outside the modern family. These films are not equally good and certainly none is flawless, but on the other hand, our popular films are raising such burning questions as: Does the press ever distort the truth? (*Absence of Malice*); Will military school without compulsory Freudian analysis lead to militarism? (*Taps*); Can a daughter accept her curmudgeonly father? (*On Golden Pond*). Here is the pretense of brow-furrowing thought without its substance, and the questions, in any case, are hardly heuristic: The answers are givens.

Still, as I have said, one cannot really scold an audience for not wanting to think. What is more perplexing and depressing is an audience not wanting to feel or, more accurately, wanting to feel so narrow a stripe of emotions that one begins to suspect an emotional immunity. Our best films have always made us feel and feel authentically; one need only recall such extraordinarily rich and popular films as *Bonnie and Clyde, 2001, The Godfather,* or *The Deer Hunter.*

Our popular films now do something else. They seem synthetic, confected. In *Raiders of the Lost Ark*, which is a perfectly wonderful silly film, everything is calculated (calibrated) for effect, and when we react it is not because we sympathize with the characters and share their adventure (Indiana Jones is practically a cipher), but because director Steven Spielberg knows how to punch the right buttons. Though it entertains, it has as much to do with an aesthetic experience as a roller-coaster ride.

A better example is *On Golden Pond*, a film that shamelessly exploits the imminent mortality of its principals, though not so shamelessly as it exploits us with its steady barrage of domestic crisis rhetoric. From its fakey geriatric relationship that doesn't even permit its coots the chink of a little bickering (they're like two cuddly animals) to its fakey subplot of a daughter who is shoved through the door at the beginning solely so she can reappear at the conclusion and suddenly (daughter ex machina) make amends with her father, to its fakey upbeat ending sans deaths, there is not a moment, not a second in it that isn't fraudulent and goopy. The emotions are simply posited, laid out on the table like so many ingredients without ever getting whipped up into a recipe. These days, it seems, the ingredients are enough, so long as we can go through the motions of feeling.

To have genuine aesthetic experiences one must possess the proper emotional equipment and the willingness to use it. This is particularly true for the best of our recent films since most of them operate experientially: *Reds* catching us in the sweep of John Reed's idealism so that even hard-liners find themselves cheering Lenin; *Prince of the City* tossing us into the protagonist's own whirlpool of confusion and letting us experience the same sort of ambivalence he feels toward his deeds; *Shoot the Moon* creating and sustaining a plaintive, tentative rhythm that is the perfect objective correlative for loneliness. These are feelings the depth and magnitude of which we recognize from our lives and from our art, and the films that elicit them demand that we respect the complexity of emotions—above all our own.

Somehow we have come to lose that respect, grumbling whenever a film makes the slightest intellectual, emotional or even physical demand upon us. (I know people who cannot sit through *Reds* because it is too long.) In so doing, we have gradually redefined the nature of the moviegoing experience and, I think, cheapened it. Of course the vices of the moviegoing audience are no different from the vices of the culture generally; one can enumerate some of them without, in so small a space, examining them: There is passivity. With so many incursions being made upon us by work, family and friends, we have become increasingly inert and callous in defense. There is solipsism and the need for instant gratification that are concomitants of the liberation of self. There is the diminution of excellence in society where the pursuit of excellence is neither encouraged nor rewarded. There is creeping functionalism in which we perceive our lives as instrumental with art and ideas unnecessary frills.

Televison is the symbol and symptom of all of this, and the television aesthetic, more than any other single source, is the infection of the movies that are successful, as the major conditioning agent of the audiences that go to see them. Films like *Superman, Taps, Absence of Malice* and *On Golden Pond* so clearly resemble TV programs that one can hardly tell the difference. Televison creates certain habits of mind. It is a careless medium, spitting out programs to fill the schedule, and it has engendered a general carelessness. Our popular films now often look as if they were made in someone's basement, and the scripts are so shoddily cobbled that in *Superman* and again in *Superman II*, our Man of Steel does what he explicitly is told he cannot do (turn back time in the first; regain his forfeited powers in the second). These are no plot lacunae; they are plot canyons. But then we demand so much less of our films that one seems almost churlish for demanding craftsmanship, much less sense.

Television also trivializes our emotions. We realize that nothing on it is very serious or very good to begin with, and it diminishes our expectations so that we not only settle for less but are actually disgruntled when we aren't pampered and pandered to. I am fairly certain, as a friend of mine speculated, that the success of a nonentity like Timothy Hutton (who is precisely the sort of amateurish TV actor a studio would have sent packing to drama school even ten years ago) is because he is a TV generation's idea of Holden Caulfield, a generation who mistakes his twitchiness for sensitivity and wouldn't know any better because it doesn't read. TV flyweights like Kate Jackson make films now, and we don't complain that in the past we went to movies to get away from such flyweights. New stars shine faintly. *Superman*'s Christopher Reeve, who may make a charming TV game-show host some day, makes George Reeves seem like Brando by comparison. With these as the lures, it is no wonder more and more people are gabbing during movies as if they were ensconced in their own living rooms; the movies make it seem that way.

Most important and most damaging for film, television nourishes a complacency that is the very antithesis of aesthetic exploration. On TV, regardless of what disruptions occur in the first fifteen minutes of program, they will all be magically resolved in the last fifteen. Nothing will linger to make us think or feel. We can satisfy ourselves that even the thorniest problems are tractable and, moreover, we do not like to be told otherwise. Television removes the struggle, the healthy engagement with a work that ensnares us; it removes it because there can be no ensnaring when strict limits are placed on our feelings and when the outcome is a foregone conclusion. This kind of entertainment cannot bite very deeply, and that's why *On Golden Pond* doesn't even dare upset us. It only teases us with old Hank Fonda's attack, teases us to pilot us home once again to our complacency.

TV has contributed to all this, yet TV is not a lone culprit upon whom we can heap the entire responsibility. Television engenders habits; it does not hold an antenna to our heads. We are the ones who have become less feeling. We demand simple answers. We encourage the worst films, those most like TV, and discourage the best. And we are the ones who are slowly destroying the movies by not patronizing the best of them. We must look not to the stars but to ourselves.

5

Being and Becoming a Writer

There are limits to how much we can assume from the evidence about composing the working writers provide in this book. Because this study was an attempt to look at the composition of regularly produced nonreportorial published nonfiction, the kinds of writing they talk about in the interviews and exemplify in the texts have been limited in terms of genre and circumstances of composing. Nonetheless, the composing processes these writers reveal are not unique; they are replicated by other writers as well, not only in nonfiction, professional, and academic fields but also in "creative" forms of writing as well. Moreover, as we have noted throughout, the ways these writers compose corroborate the evidence of current composition research and reinforce the reliability of certain academic models of composing.

In the opening chapter some emphasis was given to the importance of the paradigms underlying the composing of working writers. The evidence accumulated in the interviews and texts suggests that being a writer is made possible by certain fundamental attitudes, approaches, and activities that working writers share. Becoming a writer may depend upon understanding these fundamental elements essential to working at writing. In this final chapter we will rehearse these elements.

To begin with, working writers need a personal commitment to their writing. Again and again the writers in these interviews spoke of selecting topics according to what interested and excited them, of trying to find what they wanted to say about a given topic, and of writing to please themselves. Such commitment was an element of both the most expressive writing, such as the essay columnists produce, and the most argumentative writing, such as the political columnists produce. On the one hand, the essays that Kathleen Stocking had the most trouble with were the ones that she had the least commitment to because the subject either generated no strong feelings on her part or generated strong feelings that the circumstances of her column prevented her from expressing—she found herself with little to react to in the article on reservation gambling and little of interest to Detroit readers in the article on a small town coffee club. On the other hand, the critics reported making notes and deciding topics for reviews on a basis of what they responded or reacted to in performances, in spite of the fact that their task was strongly informative as well as critical. The professional commitment has to be fueled by a personal commitment or else the composing is impeded.

The idea of personal commitment is echoed in much current composition theory, particularly in expressions of the need for "ownership" in writing. The aspiring writer needs to have some sense of commitment to the writing project he or she is engaged in, whether it is expressive writing about one's own life experiences or transactional writing about academic or workplace subjects. In all areas of student academic writing the single greatest cause of trite or inept writing is probably lack of commitment or outright indifference. The other major problems, inexperience and ignorance, can be overcome by experience and knowledge, but without personal commitment, the aspiring (or perhaps in this case the nonaspiring) writer is unlikely to even address those other problems.

The working writer also needs certain kinds of knowledge. One is a knowledge of the topic, not only of the immediate subject of the composition in progress but also of the context of that subject. Being a writer demands a deeper and broader knowledge of the topic than the specific writing task may focus on, in part because that greater knowledge allows for greater flexibility in language and in part because it allows the writer to make the connections that generate the writing in the first place. A limited topic knowledge, even among writers who may have considerable skills of expression, can inhibit composing even at the level of sentence construction and word choice. It also prevents development of a promising idea. Several writers mentioned the ways certain material lay dormant until new information was added to it, suddenly creating connections that made it relevant or significant or worth writing about. To a certain extent, being a writer is not possible unless you are a writer about something, unless you have a field of expertise upon which to draw regardless of whether you use it explicitly in your writing.

To the knowledge of topic must be added a knowledge of the rhetorical situation. Different kinds of writing make different demands upon the writer. For example, writing arts criticism is not the same as writing political opinion. Not only do they draw upon different kinds of knowing (one analyzes a play or film in a different way than one analyzes current events or political statements), but they also draw upon different techniques of presentation. The working writer's familiarity with a genre keeps him from wrestling consciously with its intricacies at the expension of developing his subject. Being a writer usually allows for a consistent task environment where the writer's sense of audience (who will read the piece), general purpose (whether it is a review or a reflection or a political analysis), and design (how long, how formal or informal, how specific, how structured, and the like) will all remain the same from composition to composition. Even when working writers shift from one genre to another they need to acquire a sufficient knowledge of the rhetorical situation before they can proceed as readily as they could in a genre with which they are more familiar. Some of the writers in this book work in more than one form—Richard Reeves not only writes his column but also documentary screenplays; Tom Wicker writes both political columns and novels. At the very opening of the book, discussing the model of writing Reeves had to modify in order to write successfully, we saw an example of someone shifting forms (from reportage to "real writing") and having difficulty making the transition.

Aspiring writers often have difficulty with the knowledges necessary for working at writing. Their knowledge of a topic may be cursory and undeveloped, and their experience with a rhetorical situation may be limited. The problem is amplified for student academic writers; they routinely have to work in totally different genres from one assignment to the next, thus having no opportunity to accumulate expertise in a specific form, and they are often confronted with half a dozen different topic fields about which they are expected to write with only the most superficial knowledge and very little understanding of broader context. Over time, academic writers working continually in a single discipline generally acquire the knowledge of topic and genre sufficient to succeed in writing for that discipline; in this they replicate the experience of the working writer. But aspiring writers without that exposure to a specific area or a specific form are less likely to have the advantage of going through the repetition that creates a predictable task environment.

Working writers need a familiar and flexible understanding of the composing process. Being a writer demands familiarity because a writer familiar with the composing process is able to recognize possibilities and probabilities in the subprocesses he engages in. For example, David Denby doesn't worry about careful crafting or choosing exactly the right sentences in the first draft. Instead, he says, "because I know I'm going to do another draft, I try to get it down on paper in the right order and get it to say more or less what I want it to say and not be too fussy about specific wording." He can do that because he has confidence in his revision: "The second draft goes much more quickly . . . I find the first draft agony; the second draft I think is a lot of fun when you actually have something there to work with, to play with." On the other hand, Jim Fitzgerald realizes that, if he establishes certain ideas in his opening or lead, the course of following through on those ideas will provide the text. The differences in these two approaches may be accounted for by the differences in work demands, purpose, and genre between these two writers.

The composing process of every writer may indeed involve planning and prewriting, drafting and transcribing, reviewing and revising, but the ways the writer engages in these activities may vary greatly with the individual task or the personality of the writer. Some writers may be highly recursive, leaping back and forth from one activity to another, now planning, now revising, now planning again, now transcribing, now planning further, now revising text, now revising plans, in no predictable order; the act of writing, particularly with complex, complicated, long sections of text may demand for some writers such exploratory reflexive uses of the process. Some writers may be highly linear, working one section through to completion before moving to the next, engaging in one activity to satisfaction before moving on to a successive activity, following through the process in clear stages. The evidence here is that the recursive behavior takes place mentally and largely in the prewriting stage in such a process, and that it works more often for smaller, simpler projects and for repetitive, highly similar projects. Some writers may be largely recursive in one project, largely linear in another.

Familiarity with the process may also mean an awareness of work habits that help or impede the composing. Most of these writers have regular work habits, partly because of the need to meet regular deadlines, but also because short, frequent writing sessions are more productive for them than long, infrequent ones. As in the example that opened the book, the attempt to write a composition in a single sitting reveals a lack of understanding of the writer's own energy curve, the need to be recursive, and the advantages of working from a text in progress. Most of these writers planned one day, drafted another day, revised on yet another day, using the time in between to recharge and to reflect, if only subconsciously, on what they had achieved. Only in the case of a writer working from previously rehearsed material is there any evidence in this book for one-draft composition. When Richard Reeves wrote an article on the plane and phoned it in to his editor upon landing, he was in part condensing and refocusing for a different audience and genre material that had already been part of a longer article in another market; in fact, he even boilerplated part of that earlier article onto his column. Even the piece that Kathleen Stocking speaks of as having come through her was one she had rehearsed mentally many times in the process of waiting for the incident that would serve as the centerpiece of the essay. Most often for these writers, the composing takes place over a period of days, incrementally.

Being a writer demands flexibility within the composing process because changes in the nature of a task and in the topic knowledge or genre knowledge needed for the task may require adjustments in strategies and expression that inflexible assumptions about the process could not accommodate. The writer's recognition that each composition is unique and demands reexamination of the composing process frees him to solve the problems inherent in shifting rhetorical situations.

Obviously, in the act of becoming a writer an aspiring writer has to acquire familiarity and flexibility in regard to the composing process. Student academic writers are often constrained by the limitations of an assignment; if all assigned pieces of writing are five-paragraph themes, with one paragraph of introduction, three of development, and one of conclusion, the student may master that form at a cost to his flexibility within the composing process, his familiarity with the options available to him, and his adaptability to the demands of his subject.

The working writer needs to have stored resources in knowledge, strategies, and skills in order to use them with some degree of unconsciousness at the same time that he gives conscious attention to a particular knowledge or strategy. As discussed earlier, the various skills required of the competent writer, if demanding of conscious attention, would place too many constraints upon composing for the writer to attend to any of them satisfactorily. Carl Bereiter refers to this as "automaticity," which he defines as "proficiency such that the behavior in question requires little or no conscious attention" (89). This concept is perhaps a given of lower-level skills like punctuation, spelling, and standard usage, but it is also necessary of higher-level rhetorical elements, such as awareness of audience or generic elements. Whatever is stored in long-term memory frees the writer from the need to attend to it as if it were new information. The writing project that demands of the writer manipulation of unfamiliar knowledge in an unfamiliar format for an unfamiliar audience would be particularly daunting for any writer, but the experienced writer would at least have stored rhetorical strategies and a knowledge of his own composing practices as resources to draw upon. The aspiring writer needs to acquire those resources.

So far we have been discussing what the working writer needs to have (and what the aspiring writer needs to acquire). The individual work habits and techniques of the working writers in this book have been explored in earlier chapters and need not be specifically repeated here, but one essential element of composing that is a means of maintaining and acquiring facility in writing needs to be reviewed here— habitual and constant engagement through writing. One aspect of this engagement we have identified as "assiduous string-saving." Working writers routinely record the observations of themselves and others about the ideas and issues that may surface in their writing. In some cases the writing has been specifically about the topic the writer intends to express himself about, as Walter Kerr, for example, takes notes on a dramatic performance he intends to review. In other cases similar writing is used to accumulate information for potential future use, as when Jim Fitzgerald adds randomly to his folder in expectation of making later connections or as when Neal Gabler makes notes on every film he sees, whether he intends to review it or not.

Such informal writing assists the writer in several ways. In the cases we have noted, the writer uses string-saving as a way of making connections with other materials, but it also assists in storing knowledge for future reference, not only in the journal or folder where the words have been written but also in the memory of the writer who has reinforced his ability to recall those materials by attending to them in writing. Moreover, the engagement with writing improves facility with language. In specific cases, informal writing rehearses the language the writer will later use in composition, sometimes by finding early and appropriate language, sometimes by auditioning possible language that will later be abandoned or revised. In a more general way, the regular use of writing as a means of expression facilitates the development of expression in writing. As Hazlitt observed, "The more a man writes, the more a man can write."

Furthermore, the working writer uses writing as a means of discovery. Writing is not merely the recording of preconceived thoughts but the conceiving of them, because the writing surfaces ideas and insights that would not otherwise appear. Some of this discovery takes place in the drafting of the text, and some takes place in the preliminary activities such as note taking or planning. The working writer develops the expectation that some discovery will take place along the way, as it does in the writing of Jim Fitzgerald, who is adept at using the text produced so far to generate the text to come, or uses the discovery in the connections made in the informal writing to design and restructure the piece to be written.

Some part of the working writer's ability to use informal writing and discovery through writing is related to realistic expectations about writing itself. Being a writer demands an understanding of the limitations of one's ability as well as of its potential. Most of the writers interviewed suggested that while all of their published writing was acceptable, not all of it was their best. Each was aware that in the course of their writing not everything they produced would measure up to their highest standards, although all could point to particular pieces they were proud of. They were aware of the limitations of format and audience and occasion and opportunity, recognized that some material might do the job in one circumstance and fail in another, and expected to produce a body of work in which perhaps a third or less of what they produced was of the quality they hoped to achieve.

Aspiring writers are sometimes frustrated by their ideas of acceptable writing. Student academic writers are often frustrated by their teachers' ideas of acceptable writing. The testimony of these working writers—and the evidence of virtually any writer's collected works—is that not all writing by any author is of a uniform quality. In part that is because the writer learns through the writing of one piece the things that make the next piece better, or the later piece falters because the writer cannot bring to it the same things he brought to the earlier piece. Working writers accept this, aspiring writers need to accept it, and so do academic writers and teachers.

These elements, so essential for being a writer, so necessary to acquire for becoming a writer, come about for the working writer and the aspiring writer in the same way. Again and again in these interviews, and especially in the places where writers have had to learn their trade, we see that working at writing is made possible by immersion in context and experience in expression. The more a writer is part of a specific discipline or task environment, is engaged with subject matter and genre through writing, and writes specific kinds of compositions on specific kinds of topics, the more he or she is able to write. The aspiring writer gains these abilities by being immersed in a context and writing; the working writer maintains these abilities the same way.

References

Anderson, Chris. Introduction. *Literary Nonfiction: Theory, Criticism, Pedagogy.* Ed. Chris Anderson. Carbondale, IL: Southern Illinois UP, 1989. ix–xxvi.

Beach, Richard. "Self-Evaluation Strategies of Extensive Revisers and Non-Revisers." *College Composition and Communication* 27.2 (1976): 160–64.

Bereiter, Carl. "Development in Writing." *Cognitive Processes in Writing.* Ed. Lee W. Gregg and Erwin R. Steinberg. Hillsdale, NJ: Lawrence Erlbaum, 1980. 73–93.

Berkenkotter, Carol. "Decision and Revisions: Planning Strategies of a Publishing Writer." *College Composition and Communication* 34 (1983): 156–69.

Berlin, James A. *Rhetoric and Reality: Writing Instruction in American Colleges, 1900–1985.* Carbondale, IL: Southern Illinois UP, 1987.

———. *Writing Instruction in Nineteenth-Century American Colleges.* Carbondale, IL: Southern Illinois UP, 1984.

Berlin, James A., and Robert P. Inkster. "Current-Traditional Rhetoric: Paradigm and Practice." *Freshman English News* 8 (Winter 1980): 1–4, 13–14.

Bizzell, Patricia. "Thomas Kuhn, Scientism, and English Studies." *College English* 40.7 (1979): 764–71.

Braddock, Richard, Richard Lloyd-Jones, and Lowell Schoer. *Research in Written Composition.* Champaign, IL: NCTE, 1963.

Britton, James, et al. *The Development of Writing Abilities, 11–18.* London: MacMillan, 1975.

Denby, David. "Growing Up Absurd." *New York* 27 Sept. 1982:50–51.

———. "Show of Shows." *New York* 18 Oct. 1982: 72–73.

Dowst, Kenneth. "The Epistemic Approach." *Eight Approaches to Teaching Composition.* Ed. Timothy R. Donovan and Ben W. McClelland. Urbana, IL: NCTE, 1980. 65–86.

Emig, Janet. *The Composing Processes of Twelfth-Graders.* Urbana, IL: NCTE, 1971.

Faigley, Lester, Roger D. Cherry, David A. Jolliffe, and Anna M. Skinner.

Assessing Writers' Knowledge and Processess of Composing. Norwood, NJ: Ablex, 1985.

Fitzgerald, Jim. "Crime Coverage Has Been Touchy Topic for Ten Years." *Detroit Free Press* 16 June 1986: 12D.

——. *If It Fitz.* Detroit: Detroit Free Press, 1985.

——. "When It Comes to Taxes, This Chrysler Uses a Dodge." *Detroit Free Press* 4 June 1986: 18D.

——. "Yeah, but Could Roger Help Ann with Banking?" *Detroit Free Press* 6 June 1986: 14F.

Flower, Linda. "Rhetorical Problem Solving: Cognition and Professional Writing." *Writing in the Business Professions.* Ed. Myra Kogen. Urbana, IL: NCTE, 1989. 3–36.

——. "Writer-Based Prose: A Cognitive Basis for Problems in Writing." *College English* 41 (1979): 19–37.

Flower, Linda, and John R. Hayes. "A Cognitive Process Theory of Writing," *College Composition and Communication* 32 (1981): 365–87.

Gabler, Neal. "Bad Films? We Have Ourselves to Blame." *Monthly Detroit* 5.12 (1982): 52, 54, 56.

——. "Beach Blanket Cinema." *Monthly Detroit* Dec. 1982: 31–32, 34, 36.

Gere, Anne Ruggles. "Insights from the Blind: Composing Without Revising." *Revising: New Essays for Teachers of Writing.* Ed. Ronald A. Sudol. Urbana, IL: ERIC/NCTE, 1982. 52–70.

Graves, Donald H. "An Examination of the Writing Processes of Seven-Year-Old Children." *Research in the Teaching of English* 9 (Winter 1975): 227–41.

Hairston, Maxine. "The Winds of Change: Thomas Kuhn and the Revolution in the Teaching of Writing." *College Composition and Communication* 33.1 (1982): 76–88.

Hardwick, Elizabeth, ed. *The Best Essays of 1986.* Boston: Ticknor & Fields, 1986.

Hayes, John, and Linda S. Flower. "Identifying the Organization of Writing Processes." *Cognitive Processes in Writing.* Ed. Lee W. Gregg and Erwin R. Steinberg. Hillsdale, NJ: Lawrence Erlbaum, 1980. 3–30.

Hillocks, George, Jr. *Research on Written Composition: New Directions for Teaching.* Urbana, IL: National Conference on Research in English/ ERIC Clearinghouse on Reading and Composition Skills, 1986.

Hodges, Karen. "A History of Revision: Theory versus Practice." *Revising: New Essays for Teachers of Writing.* Ed. Ronald A. Sudol. Urbana, IL: ERIC Clearinghouse on Reading and Communication Skills/NCTE, 1982. 24–42.

References

Howarth, William L. Introduction. *The John McPhee Reader*. New York: Farrar, 1976. vii–xxiii.

Kerr, Walter. "Stage View: Can't They Do Better by Colleen Dewhurst?" *New York Times* 10 Oct. 1982: H3.

———. "Stage View: *Ghosts* That Grows Evermore Lightweight." *New York Times* 5 Sept. 1982: H3, 12.

———. "Stage View: If the Play Is Bad, the Review Is Hard Work." *New York Times* 26 Sept. 1982: H3, 22.

Kinneavy, James L. *A Theory of Discourse: The Aims of Discourse*. 1971. Reprint. New York: Norton, 1980.

Lloyd-Jones, Richard. "Primary Trait Scoring." *Evaluating Writing: Describing, Measuring, Judging*. Ed. Charles R. Cooper and Lee Odell. Urbana, IL: NCTE, 1977. 33–68.

Matsuhashi, Ann. "Pausing and Planning: The Tempo of Written Discourse Production." *Research in the Teaching of English* 15 (1981): 113–34.

Murray, Donald M. "One Writer's Secrets." *College Composition and Communication* 37 (1986): 146–53.

———. "Responses of a Laboratory Rat—or, Being Protocoled." *College Composition and Communication* 34 (1983): 169–72.

———. *A Writer Teaches Writing*. Boston: Houghton, 1968.

———. "Writing as Process: How Writing Finds Its Own Meaning." *Eight Approaches to Teaching Composition*. Ed. Timothy R. Donovan and Ben W. McClelland. Urbana, IL: NCTE, 1980. 3–20.

North, Stephen M. *The Making of Knowledge in Composition: Portrait of an Emerging Field*. Portsmouth, NH: Boynton/Cook, 1987.

Odell, Lee, and Dixie Goswami. "Writing in a Non-Academic Setting." *Research in the Teaching of English* 16.3 (1982): 201–25.

Olson, Sigurd. *Songs of the North*. Ed. Howard Frank Mosher. New York: Penguin, 1987.

Perl, Sondra. "The Composing Processes of Unskilled College Writers." *Research in the Teaching of English* 13 (1979): 317–36.

Pianko, Sharon. "A Description of the Composing Processes of College Freshman Writers." *Research in the Teaching of English* 13 (1979): 5–22.

Polanyi, Michael. *Personal Knowledge: Towards a Post-Critical Philosophy*. Chicago: U of Chicago P, 1968.

Reeves, Richard. "Fixing the Broken Senate." UPS 16 Dec. 1984.

———. *Jet Lag: The Running Commentary of a Bicoastal Reporter*. Kansas City: Andrews & McMeel, 1981.

———. "What Is Ted Kennedy Running For?" UPS 4 Nov. 1984.

References

———. "Why We Are in Afghanistan." UPS 2 Dec. 1984.

Root, Robert L., Jr. "'Assiduous String-Savers': The Idea-Generating Strategies of Professional Expository Writers." *Minnesota English Journal* 18.2 (1988): 17–24.

———. "Humpty, Alice, and the Composition Prism." *Reinventing the Rhetorical Tradition.* Ed. Ian Pringle and Aviva Freedman. Conway, AR: Canadian Council of Teachers of English/L & S Books, 1981. 105–12.

———. "Marketplace & Classroom: The Writing Processes of Professionals and Students." *Language Arts Journal of Michigan* 1.2 (1985): 10–15.

———. "Style and Self: The Emergence of Voice." *Journal of Teaching Writing* 4.1 (1985): 77–85.

———. "Writing in the Dark: Composing Criticism." *Journal of Teaching Writing* 6.2 (1987): 203–10.

Roundy, Nancy, and David Mair. "The Composing Process of Technical Writers: A Preliminary Study." *Journal of Advanced Composition* 3.1–2 (1982): 89–101.

Schuster, Charles I. "Richard Selzer and John McPhee: A Contrastive Analysis of the Composing Process." Paper. Annual Conference of NCTE. San Antonio, TX, 22 Nov. 1986.

Selzer, Jack. "The Composing Processess of an Engineer." *College Composition and Communication* 34 (1973): 178–87.

Sommers, Nancy. "Revision Strategies of Student Writers and Experienced Adult Writers." *College Composition and Communication* 31.4 (1980): 378–88.

Sowers, Susan. "A Six-Year-Old's Writing Process: The First Half of First Grade." *Language Arts* 56 (1979): 829–35.

Stocking, Kathleen. *Letters from the Leelanau.* Ann Arbor: U of Michigan P, 1990.

———. "Up North: Dreaming Detroit." *Detroit Monthly* Mar. 1986: 28, 170.

———. "Up North: Mozart and Ace." *Detroit Monthly* July 1986: 23–24.

———. "Up North: Piecing the Ribbon Together." *Metropolitan Detroit* Aug. 1985: 88–90.

Walker, Scott, ed. *The Graywolf Annual Three: Essays, Memoirs, & Reflections.* Saint Paul: Graywolf, 1986.

Wicker, Tom. "In the Nation: Enough Is Enough." *New York Times* 10 Oct. 1982: H3.

———. "In the Nation: Jerusalem and Saigon." *New York Times* 24 Sept. 1982: A27.

———. "In the Nation: Reagan's Apple Pie." *New York Times* 10 Sept. 1982: A23.

————. "In the Nation: Recycling an Idea." *New York Times* 19 Sept. 1982: D19.

————. "In the Nation: There He Goes Again." *New York Times* 12 Sept. 1982: D21.

————. *On Press.* New York: Viking, 1978.

Witte, Stephen P. "Revising, Composing Theory, and Research Design." *The Acquisition of Written Language.* Ed. Sarah W. Freedman. Norwood, NJ: Ablex, 1985. 250–84.

Writers at Work: The Paris Review *Interviews.* Ed. Malcolm Cowley. New York: Viking, 1958.

Young, Richard. "Paradigms and Problems: Needed Research in Rhetorical Invention." *Research in Composing.* Ed. Charles R. Cooper and Lee Odell. Urbana, IL: NCTE, 1978. 29–48.

Zwinger, Ann, and Edwin Way Teale. *A Conscious Stillness: Two Naturalists on Thoreau's Rivers.* New York: Harper, 1982.

ROBERT L. ROOT, Jr., professor of English at Central Michigan University, teaches courses in composition, the teaching of writing, literature, and media; he is a consultant on writing and coeditor of *LAJM, The Language Arts Journal of Michigan*. In addition to articles and convention papers on composition, literacy, writing across the curriculum, and popular culture, he has written two books, *Thomas Southerne* (Twayne, 1981) and *The Rhetorics of Popular Culture: Advertising, Advocacy, Entertainment* (Greenwood Press, 1987). He is currently working on a critical study on E. B. White and the essay, and also on a guide to writing.